FULL
SPECTRUM
DOMINANCE

TOTALITARIAN DEMOCRACY IN THE NEW WORLD ORDER

F. William Engdahl

Cover art by David Dees
www.deesillustration.com

Published by: edition.engdahl
                 Wiesbaden

ISBN: 978-3-9813263-0-7
Library of Congress Control Number: 2009927425

Printed in USA

To Margot, whose support and incisive suggestions helped make this book a reality.

Introduction

Less than two decades have passed since the collapse of the Soviet Union and the end of a decades-long polarized world of two opposing military superpowers. In late 1989 Communist East Germany, the German Democratic Republic as it was known, began to break the barriers of Soviet control and by November of that year the much-hated Berlin Wall was being pulled down stone-by-stone. People danced on the wall in celebration of what they believed would be a new freedom, a paradise of the 'American Way of Life.'

The collapse of the Soviet Union was inevitable by the end of the 1980's. The economy had been literally bled to the bone in order to feed an endless arms race with its arch rival and Cold War opponent, the United States. By late 1989 the Soviet leadership was pragmatic enough to scrap the last vestiges of Marxist ideology and raise the white flag of surrender. 'Free market capitalism' had won over 'state-run socialism.'

The collapse of the Soviet Union brought jubilation everywhere, with the exception of the White House where, initially, President George H. W. Bush reacted with panic. Perhaps he was unsure how the United States would continue to justify its huge arms spending and its massive intelligence apparatus — ranging from the CIA to the NSA to the Defense Intelligence Agency and beyond — without a Soviet foe. George H.W. Bush was a product and a shaper of the Cold War National Security State. His world was one of 'enemy image,' espionage, and secrecy, where people often sidestepped the US Constitution when 'national security' was involved. In its own peculiar way it was a state within the state, a world every bit as centrally run and controlled as the Soviet Union had been, only with private multinational defense and energy conglomerates and their organizations of coordination in place of the Soviet Politburo. Its military contracts linked every part of the economy of the United States to the future of that permanent war machine.

For those segments of the US establishment whose power had grown exponentially through the expansion of the post World War II national security state, the end of the Cold War meant the loss of their reason for existing.

As the sole hegemonic power remaining after the collapse of the Soviet Union, the United States was faced with two possible ways of dealing with the new Russian geopolitical reality.

It could have cautiously but clearly signaled the opening of a new era of political and economic cooperation with its shattered and economically devastated former Cold War foe.

The West, led by the United States, might have encouraged mutual de-escalation of the Cold War nuclear balance of terror and the conversion of industry—West as well as East—into civilian enterprises to rebuild civilian infrastructure and repair impoverished cities.

The United States had the option of gradually dismantling NATO just as Russia had dissolved the Warsaw Pact, and furthering a climate of mutual economic cooperation that could turn Eurasia into one of the world's most prosperous and thriving economic zones.

Yet Washington chose another path to deal with the end of the Cold War. The path could be understood only from the inner logic of its global agenda—a geopolitical agenda. The sole remaining Superpower chose stealth, deception, lies and wars to attempt to control the Eurasian Heartland—its only potential rival as an economic region—by military force.

Kept secret from most Americans, by George H.W. Bush, and by his friend and de facto protégé, Democratic President Bill Clinton, was the reality that for the faction that controlled the Pentagon—the military defense industry, its many sub-contractors, and the giant oil and oil services companies such as Halliburton—the Cold War never ended.

The 'new' Cold War assumed various disguises and deceptive tactics until September 11, 2001. Those events empowered an American President to declare permanent war against an enemy who was everywhere and nowhere, who allegedly threatened the American way of life, justifying laws that destroyed that way of life in the name of the new worldwide War on Terror. To put it crassly, Osama bin Laden was the answer to a Pentagon prayer in September 2001.

What few were aware of, largely because their responsible national media refused to tell them, was that since the fall of the Berlin Wall in November 1989, the Pentagon had been pursuing, step-by-careful-step, a military strategy for domination of the entire planet, a goal no earlier great power had ever achieved, though many had tried. It was called by the Pentagon, 'Full Spectrum Dominance' and as its name implied, its agenda was to control everything everywhere including the high seas, land, air, space and even outer space and cyberspace.

That agenda had been pursued over decades on a much lower scale with CIA-backed coups in strategic countries such as Iran, Guatemala, Brazil, Vietnam, Ghana, the Belgian Congo. Now the end of a counter-vailing Superpower, the Soviet Union, meant the goal could be pursued effectively unopposed.

As far back as 1939 a small elite circle of specialists had been convened under highest secrecy by a private foreign policy organization, the New York Council on Foreign Relations. With generous funding from the Rockefeller Foundation, the group set out to map the details of a postwar world. In their view, a new world war was imminent and out of its ashes only one country would emerge victorious—the United States.

Their task, as some of the members later described, was to lay the foundations of a postwar American Empire — but without calling it that. It was a shrewd bit of deception that initially led much of the world to believe the American claims of support for 'freedom and democracy' around the world. By 2003 and the Bush Administration's invasion of Iraq on the false and legally irrelevant assertion that Saddam Hussein possessed weapons of mass destruction, that deception was wearing thin.

What was the real agenda of the relentless Pentagon wars? Was it, as some suggested, a strategy to control major world oil reserves in an era of future oil scarcity? Or was there a far different, more grandiose, agenda behind the US strategy since the end of the Cold War?

The litmus test as to whether the aggressive military agenda of the two Bush administrations was an extreme aberration of core American foreign military policy, or on the contrary, at the very heart of its long-term agenda, was the Presidency of Barack Obama.

The initial indications were not optimistic for those hoping for the much-touted change. As President, Obama selected a long-time Bush family intimate, former CIA Director and Bush Secretary of Defense, Robert Gates, to run the Pentagon. He choose senior career military people as head of the National Security Council and Director of National Intelligence, and his first act as President was to announce an increased troop commitment to Afghanistan.

The purpose of the present book is to place events of the past two decades and more into a larger historical or geopolitical context, to illuminate the dark corners of Pentagon strategy and actions and the extreme dangers to the future — not only of the United States but of the entire world — that their Full Spectrum Dominance represents. This is no ordinary book on military policy, rather it is a geopolitical analysis of a power establishment that over the course of the Cold War had spun out of control and now threatens not only the fundamental institutions of democracy, but even of life on the planet through the growing risk of nuclear war by miscalculation.

— F. William Engdahl, April 2009

Contents

CHAPTER ONE

A War in Georgia—Putin Drops a Bomb

We have about 50% of the world's wealth but only 6.3% of its population...In this situation, we cannot fail to be the object of envy and resentment. Our real task in the coming period is to devise a pattern of relationships which will permit us to maintain this position of disparity without positive detriment to our national security. To do so, we will have to dispense with all sentimentality and day-dreaming; and our attention will have to be concentrated everywhere on our immediate national objectives. We need not deceive ourselves that we can afford today the luxury of altruism and world-benefaction.
*   – George F. Kennan, US State Department Policy Memorandum, February 1948[1]*

Guns Of August And One Of Those Funny Numbers

"Eight eight eight" is one of those funny numbers, like 666 or 911. Some people attach great mysterious significance to it. So it was more ominous than otherwise that on the eighth day of the eighth month of the eighth year of the new century, a small land in the remote Caucasus mountains of the former Soviet Union decided to order its rag-tag army to march into a territory as tiny as Luxemburg to reclaim it in the name of a greater Republic of Georgia.

On that day much of the world was looking elsewhere, to Beijing, as China launched the dramatic beginning of the 2008 Summer Olympics. Many world leaders were in Beijing for the event, including the President of the United States, George W. Bush, and the new Prime Minister of Russia, Vladimir Putin.

The surprising news that the Georgian Army had invaded the breakaway province of South Ossetia at first drew little interest. Few people in

1

the West had ever heard of South Ossetia. The region was remote and believed to be of little political significance.

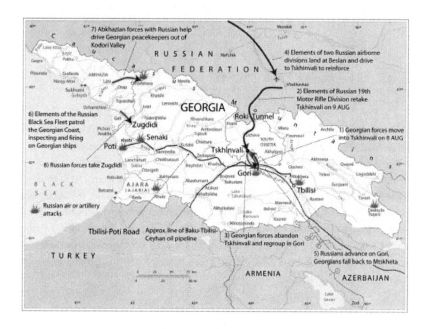

A US-backed attack by Georgia in August 2008 surprised
the West when Russia responded so swiftly to defend Ossetians

As it turned out, the small Republic of Georgia and its invasion of South Ossetia would mark the onset of the most dangerous phase in world affairs since the Cuban Missile Crisis of October 1962 when the two Cold War adversaries, the Soviet Union and the United States, stood 'eyeball to eyeball' and came a hair's breadth from nuclear war.

Some began to fear a 21st Century rerun of the Guns of August, when an equally remote event —- the assassination in August 1914 of the heir to the throne of the Austro-Hungarian monarchy by a Serb assassin in Sarajevo – triggered the outbreak of the Great War in Europe.

Others spoke of a New Cold War, a reference to the mutual balance of terror that dominated world affairs from roughly 1946 until the fall of the Berlin Wall and the collapse of the Soviet Union in 1989-1990.

That 1962 Cuban crisis, as some recalled, was triggered by US reconnaissance photos showing construction of a Soviet missile base in Cuba, some 90 miles from Florida. Such a missile base would give Russia the ability to launch a nuclear strike on the US homeland within minutes, not allowing US nuclear bombers sufficient time to respond.

What few in the West—outside the Pentagon and highest US and NATO circles—were told was that the Soviet missile installation in Cuba was not a provocation out of the blue. It was Russia's response, however ineffective and however reckless, to the earlier US decision to place its Thor and Jupiter nuclear missiles in Turkey, a NATO member dangerously close to Soviet strategic nuclear sites.

As with Cuba in 1962, so with Georgia in 2008, the crisis was the direct consequence of an aggressive provocation initiated by military and political circles in Washington.[2]

End Of A Cold War, Seeds Of A New One

The Cold War ostensibly ended with Mikhail Gorbachev's decision in November 1989 not to order Soviet tanks into East Germany to block the growing nonviolent anti-government candlelight protest movement and to let the Berlin Wall, the symbol of the 'Iron Curtain' dividing Eastern from Western Europe, fall down. The USSR was bankrupt, economically, militarily and politically.

The Cold War was over. The West, above all the United States of America — the symbol of liberty, freedom, democracy and economic prosperity for much of the world, above all for the peoples of the former communist countries of Eastern Europe — had won.

With the end of the Cold War, Washington proclaimed its aim was the spread of democracy to those parts of the world that had been rigidly confined within the Soviet socialist system since at least the end of the Second World War and in many cases since the 1917 Russian Revolution.

Democracy was Washington's most effective weapon to increase its control over the emerging nations of the former Communist bloc in Europe. The word 'democracy,' however, as the ancient Greek oligarchic families well knew, was a double-edged weapon; it could be manipulated into an enraged mob and hurled with directed fury against one's political opponents.

All that was needed was to control the techniques for shaping public opinion and the levers of economic change. In these, Washington was well equipped; it dominated global media through instruments such as CNN, and orchestrated economic transformation through its control of institutions such as the International Monetary Fund and the World Bank.

Washington would spread democracy after the collapse of the Soviet Union. But it was to be a special kind of democracy, if you will, a 'totalitarian democracy,' welding American economic, political and cultural hegemony together under the military control of NATO.

Most of the world was jubilant at the offer of American-style democracy. In Berlin the Germans, from both east and west, played Beethoven's *Ode to Joy* and danced on the Wall. In Poland, Czechoslovakia, Hungary, and across the nations or regions which had been locked into the Soviet side of the 'Iron Curtain' since 1948, the citizens were euphoric in celebration of what they believed would be the beginning of a better life, a life of freedom and prosperity, the 'American Way of Life.' They believed the propaganda that had been beamed at them over the years by Radio Free Europe and other US and Western government media. Paradise on earth was about to arrive, or so they thought.

The euphoria was short-lived. Almost immediately, Washington and its Western allies imposed a form of economic 'shock therapy' on the former socialist, centrally planned, state economies. The International Monetary Fund (IMF) demanded immediate 'market reforms.' This was code for the complete transformation of entire economies.

The IMF staff had in no way been prepared for the complexity of transforming the inter-connected economic space of six former Warsaw Pact nations (Bulgaria, Czechoslovakia, East Germany, Hungary, Poland, Romania) and fifteen former Soviet Republics. The IMF technocrats, under orders from US Treasury Secretary and former Wall Street banker, Robert Rubin, demanded immediate privatization of all state-owned industries, devaluation of the Russian ruble, and devaluation of each of the other six national currencies.[3]

IMF 'shock therapy' (Structural Adjustment Policies) flung open the doors of the former Soviet bloc to dollar-holding Western speculators. Among those in the stampede were the American hedge fund billionaire George Soros, the fugitive metals trader Marc Rich, and aggressive banks such as Credit Suisse and Chase. The IMF policies allowed them literally to loot the 'Crown Jewels' of Russia for pennies. The loot included everything from oil to nickel, and from aluminum to platinum.

A tiny handful of Russian businessmen -- mostly former Communist party or KGB functionaries -- seized invaluable state-owned raw material assets during the corrupt Yeltsin era and became billionaires overnight. They were accurately referred to in the media as Russian 'oligarchs' — men whose wealth would allow them to become the new masters of post-communist Russia — the money masters. But, there was a catch: their new wealth was denominated in dollars. Russia's new oligarchs were tied, so Washington believed, to the West and, specifically to the United States. Washington's strategy had been to take control of post-Soviet Russia by taking control of its new billionaire oligarchs.

As a logical consequence of draconian IMF policies imposed on Russia during the 1990's, unemployment exploded and living standards plummeted. Most shocking, life expectancy for Russian men fell to 56 years during this period. The elderly were left without pensions or adequate medical care in many cases. Schools were closed; housing fell into disrepair; alcoholism, drug addiction and AIDS spread among Russian youth.

IMF demands included savage reduction in state subsidies in an economy where all necessary social services from daycare to medical care had been provided free or at nominal cost by the state. The Russian population was again being put through hell, half a century after they had given more than twenty three million of their finest young citizens in battle so that the United States and Britain could dominate the postwar world. As many Russians saw it, economic shock therapy was a strange way for the West to show gratitude for the end of the Warsaw Pact.

The last Soviet leader, Mikhail Gorbachev, had tried to revitalize the Soviet state from within with *Glasnost* and *Perestroika;* these had failed. Now, in return for Gorbachev allowing the West, via the controversial

IMF, to dictate the terms of economic transformation into the 'capitalist paradise,' the administration of US President George H.W. Bush had offered Gorbachev a promise. Specifically, the official promise was that the United States would not extend NATO eastward to envelop the newly liberated countries of the former Warsaw Pact.[4]

Gorbachev trusted this pledge from the Bush administration in good faith, as official policy. And so it seemed. In the chaos of the moment, however, Gorbachev apparently forgot to get Bush's promise in writing. Memories in Washington were good, but conveniently short when it suited them, as subsequent events would show.

In response to that solemn US pledge, the formerly mighty Soviet Union, now a vastly reduced Russia, had promised Washington and NATO that it would systematically dismantle its formidable nuclear arsenal. Toward that end, the Russian Duma had ratified a Start II Treaty that provided a schedule for reduction of actively deployed nuclear weapons. They made the ratification contingent on both the US and Russia adhering to the 1972 Anti-Ballistic Missile Treaty which prohibited deployment of an active missile defense shield by either side.[5]

On December 13, 2001, George W. Bush gave Russia notice of the United States' withdrawal from the ABM treaty. That was the first time in recent history the United States had withdrawn from a major international arms treaty. It was done in order to open the door to the creation of the US Missile Defense Agency.[6]

An exhausted Russia had dissolved the Warsaw Pact, its counterpart to NATO. It had withdrawn its troops from Eastern Europe and other regions of the former Soviet Union. The satellite states of the Soviet Union and even the former Soviet Republics were encouraged to declare themselves independent countries—albeit usually with Western promises and enticements of possible membership in the new European Union.

The Republic of Georgia was one such new country, even though Georgia had been an integral part of a Russian empire extending back to the days of the Czars well before the Revolution of 1917.

'We Won!'

Despite the solemn pledges and apparently official agreements of Washington not to extend NATO eastward, George H.W. Bush and later, President Bill Clinton, went back on their promises. They enticed the countries of the former Warsaw Pact, one by one, into what was to become a newly enlarged, eastward expanding NATO.

George Herbert Walker Bush was the scion of a wealthy New England family that had made its fortune over decades, first with investments in Hitler's Reich and continuing through powerful alignments with Rockefeller oil and armaments industries. "We won," he proclaimed now, as if hailing an NFL Super Bowl victory and not the cessation of a military and political contest that often held the fate of the entire planet in the balance.

As one observer described the new American arrogance in Washington in the beginning of the 1990's and George H.W. Bush's administration: "Presidential travels abroad assumed the trappings of imperial expeditions, overshadowing in scale and security demands the circumstances of any other statesman...America's anointment as the world's leader [was] in some respects reminiscent of Napoleon's self-coronation."[7]

The author of these critical comments was no outsider or opponent of American power. He was Zbigniew Brzezinski, former National Security Adviser to President Jimmy Carter and senior foreign policy strategist for several presidents and advisor to many, including presidential candidate Barack Obama.

Brzezinski was a careful student of the master of Anglo-American geopolitics, Sir Halford Mackinder. He knew well the dangers of imperial arrogance at the peak of empire. Such arrogance had in his view caused the collapse of the British Empire apparently at its peak between the end of the 19th Century and the outbreak of the First World War.

Brzezinski warned that such domineering arrogance on the part of Washington a century later could lead to a similar crisis of American hegemony. America, he warned, could lose its status as 'Sole Superpower' or as 'the American Empire'—the term favored by neo-conservative hawks such as William Kristol, editor of the Weekly Standard and Robert Kagan, Senior Associate at the Carnegie Endowment for International Peace.

Zbigniew Brzezinski had been one of the architects of the war in Afghanistan against the Soviet Union in the late 1970s. By provoking and then masterminding that war, in which the US Government had trained Osama bin Laden and other radical Islamists with advanced techniques of irregular warfare and sabotage, Brzezinski had done more than perhaps any other postwar strategist, with the possible exception of Henry Kissinger, to extend American dominance through military force.

Brzezinski was no softy. He was an ardent American imperialist, what in Washington was called a 'realist.' He knew that American imperial domination, even when it masqueraded under the name of democracy, needed careful attention to its allies in order to maintain global power and to control what he called the chessboard — Eurasia. Other powers were to be managed and maneuvered to prevent the emergence of rivals to US dominance. In this context, in his widely debated 1997 book, *The Grand Chessboard,* Brzezinski referred repeatedly to US allies, even including Germany and Japan, as America's "vassals."[8]

Brzezinski had no quarrel with the apparent end goal of the Bush-Cheney foreign policy — namely, a global American Century, an Americanized version of imperial rule. Rather, Brzezinski differed only in his vision of the means with which to reach that goal.

"Symptomatic of the first decade and a half of America's supremacy," Brzezinski had noted, "were the worldwide presence of US military forces and the increased frequency of their engagement in combat or coercive operations. Deployed on every continent and dominating every ocean, the United States had no political or military peer."[9]

One area where US military forces were being deployed was in the tiny Central Asian former Soviet republic of Georgia, where since at least September 2003, the Bush Administration had been providing direct US military assistance and advisors to the tiny but strategic country that had declared its independence from the Soviet Union in 1990.[10]

The events in Georgia of August 2008 could not be understood without going back to the 1990s and the history of US NATO expansion to the doors of Moscow. The Administration of George Bush, Sr. had broken its promise to Russia not to expand NATO to the east. Now, in 2008, another Bush Administration was putting enormous pressure on a reluctant European Union and European governments to admit two former Soviet Republics, Georgia and Ukraine, into NATO.

That new NATO expansion came in the wake of a bold announcement in early 2007 by the United States Government that it planned to install advanced missile bases and radar stations in two former Warsaw Pact countries, now NATO members: Poland and the Czech Republic.[11]

The Bush Administration claimed that the decision to place its deceptively-named Ballistic Missile 'Defense' infrastructure in Poland and the Czech Republic was allegedly to defend against 'rogue states like Iran.'[12] This assertion produced the strongest response from the Kremlin. In actual military fact it was not defensive at all, but a major offensive gain for Washington in any future military showdown with Moscow.

In February 2007, Russia's President Vladimir Putin addressed the annual Munich, Germany International Conference on Security, formerly the Wehrkunde Conference. Delivering a keynote speech that was extraordinary by any standards, Putin's remarks caught many in the West by surprise:

> NATO has put its frontline forces on our borders...[I]t is obvious that NATO expansion does not have any relation with the modernisation of the Alliance itself or with ensuring security in Europe. On the contrary, it represents a serious provocation that reduces the level of mutual trust. And we have the right to ask: against whom is this expansion intended? And what happened to the assurances our western partners made after the dissolution of the Warsaw Pact?[13]

These frank words from Russia's President unleashed a storm of protest from Western media and politicians. Vladimir Putin, a former KGB career officer who had briefly headed the FSB (the KGB's successor organization for foreign intelligence), could be accused of many things. He had clearly climbed to the top of Russia's power pyramid not by being a 'nice guy.' One thing Vladimir Putin could not be accused of, however, was being stupid, especially when Russian vital interests were threatened.

For the first time since the end of the Soviet Union in 1991 Western media spoke of a New Cold War between the West and Russia. In fact, however, the speech of the Russian President only made open and public a process that had never ended, even with the fall of the Berlin Wall in November 1989.

Origins Of The Iron Curtain

The Cold War began in the late 1940s with, among other events, the formal creation of the North Atlantic Treaty Organization, but even with the collapse of the Soviet Union in 1989-90, it had never really ended. That was what was so uncomfortable about Putin's speech and so difficult for Western listeners to digest.

Putin had, in effect, exposed the dangerous implications of Washington's entire post-Cold War NATO expansion strategy as one of encirclement of Russia and not one of guaranteeing peaceful transition to Western-style democracy for the nations of the former Soviet Union.

Washington, the de facto commanding head of NATO, had been steadily advancing its military superiority over Russia since the collapse of the Soviet Union. With the projected deployments to Poland and the Czech Republic, this had reached the point where Russia felt compelled to react openly and bluntly.

What was unfolding clearly in the first years of the new millennium was aggressive military expansion by the United States. Underneath layers of calculated misinformation and effective propaganda campaigns about spreading US-style democracy to the former Soviet Republics and Eastern bloc countries, the United States was steadily building towards a military confrontation unlike any the world had seen since the Cold War.

The principal architect of the original Cold War policy of 'containment' was George F. Kennan, US State Department Director of Policy Planning. In 1948, in an internal policy memorandum classified Top Secret, he outlined the foreign policy objectives of the United States as it was creating the post-war empire to be known as the American Century.

Kennan's thesis, eventually declassified, was stunningly clear:

We have about 50% of the world's wealth but only 6.3% of its population....In this situation, we cannot fail to be the object of envy and resentment. Our real task in the coming period is to devise a pattern of relationships, which will permit us to maintain this position of disparity without positive detriment to our national security. To do so, we will have to dispense with all sentimentality and day-dreaming; and our attention will have to be concentrated everywhere on our immediate national objectives. We need not deceive ourselves that we can afford today the luxury of altruism and world-benefaction.[14]

America's leading post-war planners had been involved in the 1939 War & Peace Studies Project of the New York Council on Foreign Relations. Their strategy had been to create a kind of informal empire, one in which America would emerge as the unchallenged hegemonic power in a new world order to be administered through the newly-created United Nations Organization.[15]

The architects of the post-war US-dominated global order explicitly chose not to call it an 'empire.' Instead, the United States would project its imperial power under the guise of colonial 'liberation,' support for 'democracy' and 'free markets.' It was one of the most effective and diabolical propaganda coups of modern times.

So long as the United States was the world's largest economy and American dollars were in demand as de facto world reserve currency, this charade worked. As long as Western Europe, Japan and Asia depended on US military protection, the *de facto* American Empire could effectively portray itself as the beacon of liberty for newly independent nations of Africa and Asia.[16]

A genuinely fearsome East-West barricade arose as tanks, bombers and weapons of mass destruction were rolled into position around the socialist economies of the Warsaw Pact after 1948, as well as the new Peoples' Republic of China and Tito's Yugoslavia, separating them from a US-dominated 'free world.'

It was during this period–between Churchill's famous 'Iron Curtain' speech in Fulton, Missouri in 1946, and the formal creation of the US-dominated North Atlantic Treaty Organization in April 1949 — that

Eurasia was effectively placed beyond the reach of US economic policies. Eurasia — the vast geopolitical treasure stretching from the River Elbe in Germany down to the Adriatic, through Sofia, Bulgaria, across the Black Sea, the Caspian Sea, through Central Asia and China -- was henceforth sealed off from the direct influence of US investment capital and, for the most part, beyond the reach of US economic policies.

The 'Geographical Pivot' Of History

Unknown to most of the world, it had always been the goal of US foreign policy to secure total economic and military control over Russia. Throughout its numerous established institutions — its military-industrial sectors, multinational energy corporations, and the US National Security State consisting of the Pentagon, CIA, National Security Agency, Defense Intelligence Agency, and numerous specialized intelligence agencies — the US foreign policy establishment worked towards the goal of securing total control over Russia above all other goals.

Even while the United States and the Soviet Union were still formal allies in the war to defeat Germany, the United States started to prepare for war with the Soviet Union. In the summer of 1945, at the time of the Conference in Potsdam concluding World War II, and within days of the first successful test of the atom bomb in the New Mexico desert, the US Pentagon was secretly developing a new American policy of 'striking the first blow' in a nuclear war. The first plan for all out conventional war against the Soviet Union, called TOTALITY, was drafted by General Dwight Eisenhower on the order of President Truman in 1945.[17]

The first plan for a nuclear war against the Soviet Union, including a pre-emptive strike, was completed soon afterwards by the Joint Intelligence Committee within the Joint Chiefs of Staff, just two months after Hiroshima and Nagasaki.[18]

There was no sentimentality in Washington about wartime exigencies. It was strictly business—the business of establishing unchallenged American supremacy—benignly called the 'American Century.' According to the British father of geopolitics, Sir Halford Mackinder,

Russia represented the "geographical pivot of history."[19] In a seminal policy paper in 1904 before the Royal Geographic Society in London, Mackinder had unequivocally asserted that control over Russia would determine who would or could control the vast expanses of Eurasia, and by extension the entire world. The British Foreign Office clearly agreed with him.

Already more than a century ago, Mackinder was convinced that while Europe expanded overseas to India, Africa and other colonial lands, the Russian state, based in Eastern Europe and Central Asia, would expand south and east, organizing a vast expanse of human and natural resources. That enormous space, he predicted, would soon be covered with a network of railways, thereby greatly enhancing the mobility and strategic reach of land power for the first time in history.

Against that geo-historical backdrop, Mackinder identified the northern-central core of Eurasia as the 'pivot state' or 'heartland' of world politics. He placed Germany, Austria, Turkey, India and China — lands immediately adjacent to the pivot region — in an 'inner crescent' around the Heartland or pivot state.

He warned that, "The oversetting of the balance of power in favour of the pivot state, resulting in its expansion over the marginal lands of Euro-Asia, would permit the use of vast continental resources for fleet-building, and the empire of the world would then be in sight.[20]

As Mackinder saw it, either a Russo-German alliance, or a Sino-Japanese empire that conquered Russia, would be able to contend for world hegemony. In either case, "oceanic frontage would be added to the resources of the great continent," creating the geopolitical conditions necessary for producing a great power that was supreme both on land and at sea.

British foreign policy, from the Russo-Japanese War of 1904-05 until the creation of NATO in 1949, had been obviously premised on Mackinder's analysis. It was dedicated to preventing, at all costs, the emergence of a cohesive Eurasian pivot power centered on Russia and capable of challenging British global hegemony.

America's Manifest Destiny: Control Of Eurasia

Meanwhile, however, Mackinder's counterparts across the Atlantic in the United States, were developing their own ideas of what they called America's Manifest Destiny — an American global imperium. America had conquered its western lands to the Pacific Ocean, achieved victory in its unevenly-matched contest with Spain in 1898. Conquering the Philippines, far from America's shores, in its first openly imperial war had given America's political and financial establishment its first taste of what global imperial power might be like.

Around the same time as Mackinder's landmark 1904 essay on Eurasian geopolitics, Brooks Adams, an influential American propagandist, envisioned the advent of an American world empire and the conquest by the United States of the entire Eurasian geopolitical space.[21] Scion of one of the country's most respected elite families dating back to the founding fathers, Adams deeply influenced American leaders of his day, including his close friends, Presidents Theodore Roosevelt and Woodrow Wilson.

During the Cold War in the early 1950's the ideas of Brooks Adams, particularly his justification of an American global empire conquering the Eurasian continent, were revived as a policy guide for US Cold War planning.[22]

Adams had promoted a policy of aggressive expansionism aimed at transforming Asia into an American colony, giving the United States a vast new frontier in Asia. The US conquest of the Philippines in 1898 in the Spanish-American War had been envisioned as the first step in that process. That expansionism, a kind of global American 'Manifest Destiny,' remained a conscious if unspoken goal of leading foreign policy strategists all the way through the Cold War and beyond.

The American architects of post-War power -- centered in and around the powerful Council on Foreign Relations, the Rockefeller Foundation and, above all, the Rockefeller faction in US politics and economics — had adopted Mackinder's geopolitical view as their own. The leading strategists within Rockefeller's faction, including Henry

Kissinger and, later, Zbigniew Brzezinski, both men part of the powerful Rockefeller faction in US politics, were trained in Mackinder geopolitics.

In his book, *The Grand Chessboard*, Brzezinski trumpeted the US victory in the Cold War against his life-long geopolitical foe, Soviet Russia. His view of America's presumed allies in Western Europe, however, expressed the arrogance of power. He declared:

> *In brief, for the United States, Eurasian geo-strategy involves the purposeful management of geo-strategically dynamic states...To put it in a terminology that harkens back to the more brutal age of ancient empires, the three grand imperatives of imperial geo-strategy are to prevent collusion and to maintain security dependence among the vassals, to keep tributaries pliant and protected, and to keep the barbarians from coming together.*[23]   .

Brzezinski was declaring openly the unspoken viewpoint of victorious American policy elites towards the nations of the European Union and Eurasia in the wake of their Cold War victory. Translated into plain English, Brzezinski asserted that America's sole superpower status would be maintained by preventing 'collusion'— a crass word for bilateral cooperation — among sovereign Eurasian states. This meant, in effect, precluding Eurasian countries from developing their own defense pillars or security structures independent of US-controlled NATO. The 'barbarians' were a clear reference by Brzezinski to Russia, China and the nations of Central Asia.

Mackinder Gives The Cold War Blueprint To The Usa

During the Second World War, Brzezinski's intellectual mentor, Mackinder, had been invited by *Foreign Affairs*, the Council on Foreign Relations' prestigious journal, to outline his thoughts on post-war geopolitics.

The resulting article, published in 1943, ominously presaged the Cold War to come. Even before the outcome of World War Two was clear, Mackinder wrote:

[T]he conclusion is unavoidable that if the Soviet Union emerges from this war as conqueror of Germany, she must rank as the greatest land Power on the globe. Moreover, she will be the Power in the strategically strongest defensive position. The Heartland is the greatest natural fortress on earth. For the first time in history, it is manned by a garrison sufficient both in number and quality.[24]

In 1919 in a work prepared for British negotiators at the Versailles peace talks, Mackinder set forth his most famous dictum of geopolitics. In his view, the strategy of the British Empire had to be to prevent, at all costs, a convergence of interests between the nations of Eastern Europe — Poland, Czechoslovakia, Austria-Hungary — and the Russia-centered Eurasian 'Heartland.' Mackinder summed up his ideas with the following dictum:

Who rules East Europe commands the Heartland;

Who rules the Heartland commands the World-Island;

Who rules the World-Island commands the world.[25]

Mackinder's Heartland was the core of Eurasia—Russia and Ukraine. The World-Island was all of Eurasia, including Europe, the Middle East and Asia. Great Britain, in Mackinder's world view, was never a part of Continental Europe; it was a separate naval and maritime power, and should remain so whatever the cost.

The Mackinder geopolitical perspective shaped Britain's entry into the 1914 Great War. It shaped her entry into World War Two. It shaped Churchill's calculated provocations to entice Soviet Russia into a 'Cold War' with Britain, beginning already in 1943. By forcing Washington to join with Britain against the USSR, Britain cynically calculated that Washington would be forced to rely on London's superior global political capabilities. Britain would thereby remain 'in the game.'

In 1997, in his role as former US National Security Adviser, Zbigniew Brzezinski, drew on Mackinder's geopolitics by name, as the principal strategy to enable the United States to remain the sole Superpower following the collapse of the Soviet Union.[26]

Just two years after Mackinder's 1943 *Foreign Affairs* article outlining his geopolitical plan for United States' global dominance, Prime Minister Winston Churchill added another Mackinder voice to the chorus. In April 1945, Churchill began agitating General Dwight Eisenhower and President Roosevelt to launch an immediate full-scale war against the Soviet Union, using up to 12 captured German divisions — prisoners of war — as cannon fodder to destroy Russia once and for all.

Ironically, in light of US policy after 1990, Washington rejected Churchill's proposal out of hand as being "too risky."[27] In point of fact, it seems that Washington had already reached the conclusion that its interests in dominating the entire non-communist world were better served by a hostile Soviet Union. So long as Western Europe and a Japan-centered Asia felt militarily threatened by the Soviet Union or the People's Republic of China, they would more or less bow, however reluctantly, to Washington's dictates, like Brzezinski's 'vassals.'

In 1945, when President Harry S. Truman ordered General Eisenhower and his Joint Chiefs to prepare secret plans for a surprise nuclear strike on some 20 cities of the Soviet Union, it was known that the Soviet Union posed no direct or immediate threat to the United States.[28]

The secret nuclear war plan, code-named, "Strategic Vulnerability of the U.S.S.R.to a Limited Air Attack," was the first American war plan whose goal was to obliterate the Russian Heartland. It would by no means be the last.

Moscow shocked Washington by testing its own atomic bomb in 1949 and hydrogen bombs soon thereafter. When the Russians demonstrated the ballistic missile delivery capability to deploy them by its bold launch of the Sputnik space satellite in 1957, US policy elites were forced to put their dream of nuclear first strike, called 'nuclear primacy,' on ice. It was to remain on ice for more than a half century until Donald Rumsfeld, Dick Cheney, Paul Wolfowitz and a small clique of neo-conservative war hawks in the Administration of George W. Bush resurrected it after September 11, 2001. The 'Bush doctrine,' the policy of pre-emptive war, now included the doctrine of pre-emptive nuclear strike.

From that point on, a powerful segment of the US military-industrial leadership and its policy elites were ready to renew efforts to attain nuclear 'first strike' superiority. That was the real reason the conflict in tiny Georgia in August 2008 had such terrifying potential for most informed European governments. Most Americans were kept blissfully ignorant of those awesome stakes by a largely controlled media and a barrage of disinformation from the White House.

The New Cold War— Encircling Russia And China

The first Pentagon war plan for nuclear first strike was never implemented. The Soviet Union's detonation of its own atomic bomb in August 1949 caught the United States planners completely by surprise. The swift development of the Russian atomic bomb changed the calculus of a first strike for the coming decades, and what would have been a hot war came to be the Cold War.

In 2007, however, a number of leading US policy makers saw it as unfinished business to accomplish the utter and complete dismemberment of Russia as an independent pivot for Eurasia. Nuclear missiles were but one tool in a vast arsenal of weapons and deceptive campaigns being deployed to encircle Russia. Their goal was ultimately to destroy the one remaining power that could prevent a total global American Century — the realization of Full Spectrum Dominance, as the Pentagon called it.[29]

At the time of President Putin's 2007 speech in Germany, the world was already deep in a New Cold War. The New Cold War had not been initiated by Moscow. But, inevitably, at a certain point Moscow was moved to react. Ever since Putin ordered the arrest of Russian oil oligarch, Mikhail Khodorkovsky in 2003, the Kremlin had

Russia's Vladimir Putin drew the line against NATO's advance at the 2007 Munich conference

been putting the engines of economic control into state hands once again. The US Missile Defense decision shifted those Kremlin motors into high gear.

The dynamic set in motion by Washington's announcement of a 'pre-emptive' nuclear policy had made nuclear war by miscalculation a far higher risk than even during the deepest tensions of the Cold War, including the October 1962 Cuban Missile Crisis. The closer Washington got to operational capability of its Polish and Czech missile defense systems, the greater the chance that Kremlin strategists would see their only hope of surviving in a pre-emptive nuclear strike against select targets in Poland or the EU before it was too late to respond effectively.

The debacle in Iraq, or the prospect of a US tactical nuclear pre-emptive strike against Iran, were ghastly enough. But they paled in comparison to worldwide US military build-up against Russia, its most formidable remaining global rival.

US military policies since the end of the Soviet Union and emergence of the Republic of Russia in 1991 were in need of close examination in this context. Only then did Putin's frank remarks on February 10, 2007 at the Munich Conference on Security make sense.

Putin spoke in Munich in general terms about Washington's vision of a "unipolar" world, with one center of authority, one center of force, one center of decision-making, calling it a "world in which there is one master, one sovereign. And at the end of the day this is pernicious not only for all those within this system, but also for the sovereign itself because it destroys itself from within."[30]

Putin was not, of course, talking about Russia, but about the sole superpower, the USA. Then the Russian President got to the heart of the matter:

> *Today we are witnessing an almost uncontained hyper use of force – military force – in international relations, force that is plunging the world into an abyss of permanent conflicts. As a result we do not have sufficient strength to find a comprehensive solution to any one of these conflicts. Finding a political settlement also becomes impossible.*

We are seeing a greater and greater disdain for the basic principles of international law. And independent legal norms are, as a matter of fact, coming increasingly closer to one state's legal system. One state and, of course, first and foremost the United States, has overstepped its national borders in every way. This is visible in the economic, political, cultural and educational policies it imposes on other nations. Well, who likes this? Who is happy about this?[31]

Putin's words began to touch on what Russia had been concerned about in US foreign and military policy since the end of the Cold War, citing explicit military policies that were of particularly urgent concern.

He warned of the destabilizing effect of space weapons:

[I]t is impossible to sanction the appearance of new, destabilising high-tech weapons...a new area of confrontation, especially in outer space. Star wars is no longer a fantasy – it is a reality.... In Russia's opinion, the militarization of outer space could have unpredictable consequences for the international community, and provoke nothing less than the beginning of a nuclear era.

Plans to expand certain elements of the anti-missile defence system to Europe cannot help but disturb us. Who needs the next step of what would be, in this case, an inevitable arms race?[32]

What was he referring to? Few people were aware that the US, at the beginning of 2007, had announced it was building massive anti-missile defense installations in Poland and the Czech Republic. It had surrounded this announcement with bogus claims of protecting to protect itself against the risk of 'rogue state' nuclear missile attacks from the likes of North Korea or perhaps, one day, Iran.

Poland? Ballistic Missile Defense? What was that all about? In order to grasp the extremely provocative and dangerous nature of Washington's nuclear policy, it was necessary to analyze a few very basic military concepts.

'Using The Right Hand To Reach The Left Ear'

On January 29, 2007 US Army Brigadier General Patrick J. O`Reilly, Deputy Director of the Pentagon`s Missile Defense Agency, had announced US plans to deploy an anti-ballistic missile defense system in Europe by 2011. The Pentagon claimed that the deployment was aimed at protecting American and NATO installations against threats from enemies in the Middle East, not from Russia.

Following Putin's Munich remarks, the US State Department issued a formal comment noting that the Bush Administration was "puzzled by the repeated caustic comments about the envisaged system from Moscow."[33]

On February 28, two weeks after Putin's speech, the head of the US Missile Defense Agency, General Henry Obering, arrived in Europe from Washington to 'explain' the new US missile plans for Poland and Eastern Europe. Meeting in Belgium with the 26 ambassadors from NATO's members and with Russia, Obering insisted that the planned missile system was entirely defensive in nature, and that its purpose was to provide protection against a possible attack from Iran.[34]

The argument that a hypothetical Iranian missile threat to the United States required deployment of US anti-missile defenses in Poland was not quite convincing, especially if the imagined targets were actually on US territory or critical US installations in Europe.[35]

Serious analysts were wondering why Washington did not ask its long-time NATO ally Turkey if the US can place its missile shield there? Wasn't Turkey far closer to Iran? Or maybe Kuwait? Qatar? Or Israel?' As Putin pointed out in his Munich speech:

> *Missile weapons with a range of about five to eight thousand kilometres that really pose a threat to Europe do not exist in any of the so-called problem countries. And in the near future and prospects, this will not happen and is not even foreseeable. And any hypothetical launch of, for example, a North Korean rocket to American territory through Western Europe obviously contradicts the laws of ballistics. As we say in Russia, it would be like using the right hand to reach the left ear.[36]*

Speaking at NATO headquarters in March 2007, General Obering said that Washington also wanted to base an anti-missile radar systems in the Caucasus, most likely in the former Soviet Republics of Georgia and Ukraine, neither of which were members of NATO at that time.

The Obering declaration prompted an immediate and sharp response from Russian Foreign Ministry spokesman, Mikhail Kamynin, reported by Itar-Tass news agency:

> *This statement is another proof that the American side will continue to enlarge its missile defense potential, which will increasingly concern the Russian security. Russia has repeatedly expressed concern about the US missile defense plans. We think that the scale of US preparations is disproportionate to the declared missile threat. The US intention to deploy missile defense components, which will become strategic military facilities in direct proximity to Russian borders, is the source of special concern. We will have to bear in mind the prospective facilities in further Russian military-political steps and military planning. Such plans contradict NATO commitment to restrain the deployment of forces, which was made in the Russia-NATO Founding Act.*[37]

Washington had listed more than 20 states that produce ballistic missiles. Aside from Russia and China, none of them had missiles that could remotely pose a danger for Europe or the United States. And, except for North Korea and Iran, all of them either cooperated with the US, like Russia or India or Israel, or were longstanding US allies like France or the UK. Moreover, Iran was several years from developing long-range missiles tipped with nuclear warheads and North Korea's alleged nuclear potential was essentially hot air and not a real threat, according to Western military experts.

Pyongyang's Taepodong-2 ballistic missile had an estimated range of 4,300 kilometers. When North Korea tested a long-range missile in July 2006, President Bush ordered Fort Greely in Alaska to be put on high alert. In the end, the missile splashed into the Pacific only 40 seconds after liftoff. It was unclear even when North Korea would be able to fit reliable projectiles with nuclear warheads.

Iran, as of early 2008, had only tested missiles with a range of up to 1,600 kilometers. Even the country's supposedly cutting-edge model Shahab-5, likely a derivative of a North Korean Taepodong type missile, was estimated to have a range of only 3,000 kilometers. The radar stations in Eastern Europe would therefore not be detecting any Iranian missiles hurtling towards America for some time to come.

According to retired US Lieutenant General Robert Gard, the US missile defense program was an effort to provide security against Iranian missiles that did not yet exist, and that might hypothetically use warheads that also did not yet exist. Furthermore, he added, the Iranians were fully aware that the US would annihilate them were they ever to fire missiles at America.[38]

Washington was clearly not being very forthcoming about its new missile defense strategy.

Moscow Reacts

Moscow lost little time in reacting to the announcement of US plans for its ballistic missile defense (BMD) systems in Eastern Europe. The commander of Russia's strategic bomber force, Lt. Gen. Igor Khvorov, said on March 5, 2007 that his forces could easily disrupt or destroy any missile defense infrastructures in Poland and the Czech Republic – precisely where the United States is preparing to install them.

Two weeks earlier, similar statements by Strategic Rocket Forces commander Col. Gen. Nikolai Solovtsov left little doubt that Moscow would target US Ballistic Missile Defense sites with its nuclear arsenal if Washington pushed ahead with its plans.[39]

On March 10, 2007, Russia's President Putin delivered a speech at a military awards ceremony in the Kremlin where he announced that Russia would spend $190 billion over the next eight years, some 5 trillion rubles, to equip the Army and Navy with modern weapons by 2015. Putin said the "global situation" dictated the need to improve Russia's military structure. "We cannot fail to notice the constant attempts to resolve international disputes by force, the threat of international conflicts, terrorism, the escalation of local conflicts and the spread of weapons of mass destruction," he said.[40] It was a verbatim repeat of his February remarks in Munich where he had referred to the USA by name.

Putin noted that a considerable part of the funds would be allocated to buy state-of-the-art weapons and hardware, and to develop military science and technology. "We are trying to integrate the defense industry with the civilian sector of the economy, primarily with the high tech sectors," he added. "The Armed Forces once and for all must resume the [permanent] practice of large scale military exercises, missile launches and remote marine missions," the Russian President concluded.[41]

In clear words, Putin was responding to the escalating Washington provocations by declaring openly that a New Cold War was on. It was not a new Cold War initiated by Russia, but one where Russia, out of national survival considerations, was forced to respond.

The world was at the beginning of a new arms race. By the spring of 2007, some 17 years after the supposed end to the US-Soviet Cold War, a new, nuclear-based arms race was in full bloom.

One of the few Western leaders to voice alarm over the US announcement of its plans to build missile defenses in Poland and the Czech Republic was former German Chancellor Gerhard Schroeder. Schroeder had earned the status of de facto 'enemy' of the Bush Administration after his vocal opposition to the Iraq war in 2003. Speaking in Dresden on March 11, 2007, several days after President Putin's Munich remarks, Schroeder declared that the efforts of the United States to establish its anti-missile systems in Eastern Europe were part of an attempt to pursue "an insane encirclement policy against Russia." Schroeder warned that it risked a new global arms race.[42]

USA Missile Defense Act Of 1999

US policy since 1999 had called for building some form of active missile defense, despite the end of the Cold War and the lack of any articulated threat from Soviet or Russian ICBM or other missile launches. The USA National Missile Defense Act of 1999 stipulated:

It is the policy of the United States to deploy as soon as is technologically possible an effective National Missile Defense system capable of defending the territory of the United States against limited ballistic missile attack, whether accidental, unauthorized, or deliberate, with funding subject to the annual authorization of appropriations and the annual appropriation of funds for National Missile Defense.[43]

Missile defense was one of Donald Rumsfeld's obsessions as Defense Secretary. Was that an aberration of an excessively militarist clique around Bush and Cheney? Or, was it part of a far more dangerous strategy for world domination by a powerful financial and political elite bent on world hegemony? The answer was buried in policies and programs which, considered separately, appeared harmless enough, but when put in the context of policies implemented by Washington since September 2001, were anything but harmless.

To implement their long-term strategic agenda to maintain dominance of the world as Sole Superpower, the leading circles in and around the US Pentagon and State Department required deployment of a revolutionary new technique of regime change to impose or install 'US-friendly' regimes throughout the former Soviet Union and across Eurasia. The American strategists would borrow a page from the book of the bees—'swarming'—as a method of covert warfare and regime change. 'Swarming' was the term given by the RAND Corporation to a new mode of military conflict. Based on the communication patterns and movements of insect swarms applied to military conflict, it depended on using networked technologies and communication flows.[44]

Text messaging and revolutionary new information technologies would be applied to the task of advancing Washington's agenda of Full Spectrum Dominance.

Endnotes:

[1] George F. Kennan, Policy Planning Study, PPS/23: Review of Current Trends in U.S. Foreign Policy, Memorandum by the Director of the Policy Planning Staff (Kennan)2 to

the Secretary of State and the Under Secretary of State (Lovett), in Foreign Relations of the United States, Washington DC, February 24, 1948, Volume I, pp. 509-529.

[2] Arnold L. Horelick and Myron Rush, Strategic Power and Soviet Foreign Policy, The RAND Corporation, Santa Monica, California, R-434-PR, A Report Prepared for the United States Air Force Project RAND, August, 1965, pp. 202-204. The US missile deployment in Turkey was kept top secret, so that the American public was unaware of how provocative US policies against the Soviet Union had been. The US missiles in Turkey were mentioned briefly in a RAND study three years after, but the facts were only declassified three decades later. In the October 26 International Herald Tribune of 1996, 'Chiefs Urged War in '62 Missile Crisis,' the article reported details of just-declassified tapes from the John Kennedy White House. It reported, "Mr Kennedy worried that Mr Khrushchev's offer to remove Soviet missiles from Cuba if the United States removed its nuclear missiles from Turkey seemed so reasonable that it would turn world public opinion to the Soviet side.' The article cited Kennedy: 'If we don't take it we're going to be blamed, and if we do take it we're going to be blamed..." It then gave the reply of the Pentagon: 'We don't have any choice but military action', General Curtis Lemay, Air Force Chief of Staff insisted October 19, three days before the public knew about the crisis. In the end, Mr Kennedy accepted the (Soviet Turkey for Cuba missile) deal, though he managed to keep it a secret.' Cited in International Herald Tribune, October 26-27, 1996.

[3] At the annual G7 summit of leading Western industrial nations, meeting in Houston, Texas in June 1990, the Bush Administration demanded that the IMF, an institution which Washington and the US Treasury controlled since 1944, would be the sole dictator of the economic transformation of the states of the former Soviet Union. It was to prove a colossal blunder and one which made the emerging Russia increasingly skeptical of Washington's true motives at the end of the Cold War. In a true sense IMF shock therapy and its forced imposition by Washington on Russia laid the first seeds of a new phase in the Cold War back in 1990.

[4] Philip Zelikow and Condoleezza Rice, Germany Unified and Europe Transformed , Cambridge, Harvard University Press, 1995, pp. 180-184. US Ambassador to Moscow at that time, Jack Matlock, confirmed in personal discussions with German researcher Hannes Adomeit of the Stiftung Wissenschaft und Politik of the German Institute for International and Security Affairs that he had been present and noted in his diary that US Secretary of State James Baker III had agreed in talks with Soviet President Mikhail Gorbachev that 'Any extension of the zone of NATO is unacceptable.' Curiously, Baker omitted the pledge entirely in his memoirs.

[5] Dimitri K. Simes, Losing Russia: The Costs of Renewed Confrontation, Foreign Affairs, Vol. 86. no. 6, Nov/Dec 2007.

[6] Press Secretary, The White House, ABM Treaty Fact Sheet, Announcement of Withdrawal from the ABM Treaty, December 13, 2001, accessed in http://www.whitehouse.gov/news/releases/2001/12/20011213-2.html.

[7] Zbigniew Brzezinski, Second Chance: Three Presidents and the Crisis of American Superpower, New York, Basic Books, 2007, pp. 1-2.

[8] Zbigniew Brzezinksi, The Grand Chessboard: American Primacy and Its Geostrategic Imperatives (New York: Basic Books, 1997), passim.

[9] Brzezinski, Second Chance.

[10] Olesya Vartanyan and Ellen Barry, Ex-Diplomat Says Georgia Started War With Russia, The New York Times, November 25, 2008.Former Georgian Ambassador to Moscow, and onetime close ally of President Saakashvili, Erosi Kitsmarishvili, told a special Georgian Parliamentary Commission investigating the background to the war that Georgian officials had told him in April that they planned to start a war in Abkhazia, one of two breakaway regions at issue in the war, and had received a green light from the United States government to do so. He said the Georgian government later decided to start the war in South Ossetia, the other region, and continue into Abkhazia. Two days later, on November 28 at the same Parliamentary Commission, President Saakashvili himself blurted out, "We did start military action to take control of Tskhinvali and other unruly areas...The issue is not about why Georgia started military action - we admit we started it. The issue is about whether there was another chance when our citizens were being killed? We tried to prevent the intervention and fought on our own territory."

[11] Lieutenant General Henry A. "Trey" Obering III, Director Missile Defense Agency, briefing in Brussels, Belgium, March 1, 2007, United States Mission to NATO, accessed in http://nato.usmission.gov/News/Obering_030107.htm.

[12] George W. Bush, Presidential Letter, September 19, 2003, accessed in http://www.whitehouse.gov/news/releases/2003/09/20030919-1.html.

[13] Vladimir Putin, Rede des russischen Präsidenten Wladimir Putin auf der 43. Münchner ‚Sicherheitskonferenz,' München, 10.2.2007.

[14] George F. Kennan, Op. Cit.

[15] Peter Grose, Continuing the Inquiry: The Council on Foreign Relations from 1921 to 1996, New York, Council on Foreign Relations Press, 1996, pp.23-26.

[16] Ibid. This official Council on Foreign Relations account describes the then-secret 1939-1942 CFR War & Peace Studies project. One of the project leaders, Johns Hopkins University President Isaiah Bowman, a geographer and student of British geopolitician Halford Mackinder, once referred to himself as 'America's Haushofer,' a reference to Hitler's geopolitical adviser, until he realized that it played poorly among the American public that was being mobilized to war against Nazi Germany. Describing the War & Peace Studies, Bowman wrote, 'The matter is strictly confidential because the whole plan would be 'ditched' if it became generally known that the State Department was working in collaboration with any outside group.' Bowman was being disingenuous. It was working not just with 'any' outside group, but with the most powerful group of the American power establishment, the CFR. The CFR project was directly financed by a significant contribution of $350,000 from the Rockefeller Foundation. The project's leading members were quietly sent to senior positions inside the State Department to implement the CFR postwar agenda for a Pax Americana or US global empire. The Bowman group explicitly rejected using the term "empire" in order to deceive the rest of the world as well as the naïve American public that America was 'something different.' The idea of the United Nations was a centerpiece of their postwar design.

[17] Michio Kaku and Daniel Axelrod, To Win a Nuclear War: The Pentagon's Secret War Plans, Boston, South End Press, 1987, pp. 30-31.

[18] The plan, called JIC 329/1, envisioned a nuclear attack on the Soviet Union with 20 to 30 atomic-bombs. It earmarked 20 Soviet cities for obliteration in a first strike: Moscow, Gorki, Kuibyshev, Sverdlovsk, Novosibirsk , Omsk, Saratov, Kazan, Leningrad , Baku, Tashkent, Chelyabinsk, Nizhni Tagil, Magnitogorsk, Molotov, Tbilisi, Stalinsk, Grozny, Irkutsk, and Jaroslavl." Detailed in Michio Kaku and Daniel Axelrod, To Win a Nuclear War: The Pentagon's Secret War Plans, Boston, South End Press, 1987, pp. 30-31. The secret Pentagon strategy since the end of the Cold War to use modernization of its nuclear strike force and deployment of missile defense technology is but a modern update of a policy established in 1945—Full Spectrum Dominance of the world, via the destruction of the only power capable of resisting that dominance—Russia.

[19] Sir Halford J. Mackinder, The Geographical Pivot of History, in Democratic Ideals and Reality, pp. 241-42, 255, 257-58, 262-64.

[20] Ibid.

[21] Brooks Adams, The New Empire, New York, MacMillan Co, 1900.

[22] William Appleman Williams, The Frontier Thesis and American Foreign Policy, in Henry W. Berger (ed.), A William Appleman Williams Reader, Chicago, Ivan R. Dee, 1992, pp. 90-96.

[23] Brzezinski, The Grand Chessboard, p. 40..

[24] Halford J. Mackinder, The Round World and the Winning of the Peace, Foreign Affairs, New York, Vol. 21, No. 4, July 1943, pp.597-605.

[25] Halford J. Mackinder, Democratic Ideals and Reality: A study in the politics of reconstruction, New York, Henry Holt & Co., 1919, p. 150.

[26] Zbigniew Brzezinski, Op. Cit., pp. 38-39.

[27] Valentin M. Falin, Russia Would Have Faced World War III Had it Not Stormed Berlin, Novosti Russian Information Agency, March 28, 2005, in en.rian.ru/rian/index.cfm?.

[28] Michio Kaku and Daniel Axelrod, Op. Cit., p.30.

[29] Inderjeet Parmar, To Relate Knowledge and Action: The Impact of the Rockefeller Foundation on Foreign Policy Thinking During America's Rise to Globalism 1939-1945, Minerva, Vol.40, Kluwer Academic Publishers, 2002.

[30] Vladimir Putin, Rede des russischen Präsidenten Wladimir Putin auf der 43. Münchner, Sicherheitskonferenz,' München, February 10, 2007.

[31] Ibid.

[32] Ibid.

[33] David Gollust, US Reiterates Missile-Defense Plan Not Directed at Russia, US State Department, Voice of America, 15 February 2007

[34] Der Spiegel, Europe Divided over US Missile Defense Plan, March 5, 2007, Spiegel Online, English in www.spiegel.de.

[35] [35] Richard L. Garwin, Ballistic Missile Defense Deployment to Poland and the Czech Republic, A Talk to the Erice International Seminars, 38th Session, August 21, 2007, in

www.fas.org/RLG/. Garwin, a senior US defense scientist demonstrated the fraudulent nature of the US Government's motivation for its missile policy, p.17. Garwin asked, 'Are there alternatives to the Czech-Polish deployment? Yes...An Aegis cruiser deployed in the Baltic Sea and another in the Mediterranean could thus provide equivalent protection of Europe against Iranian missiles.' Garwin, as well, reached the same conclusion as Putin: the US missiles were being aimed directly at Russia.

[36] Putin, Rede des russischen, München, February 10, 2007.

[37] Today.az, Diplomat: US ABM in Caucasus will affect Russian relations with neighbors, March 10, 2007, in www.today.az.

[38] Ralf Beste, et al, America's Controversial Missile Shield: Where Does Germany Stand? [http://www.spiegel.de/international/spiegel/0,1518,473952,00.html]. SPIEGEL ONLINE, March 26, 2007.

[39] Viktor Lotovkin, ABM: Washington trying to use Europe as a cover, in RAI Novosti, [http://en.rian.ru/analysis/20070406/63267224.html], April 6, 2007.

[40] Today.az,, Putin says $190 bln funding for military equipment, March 10, 2007, in www.today.az.

[41] Ibid.

[42] Der Spiegel Online, Schröder geißelt Bushs Raketenabwehr, 11 March 2007. www.spiegel.de.

[43] US Congress, USA National Missile Defense Act of 1999, 106th Congress, 1st Session, S. 269, Washington D.C., Library of Congress, accessed in http://thomas.loc.gov/cgi-bin/query/C?c106:./temp/~c106f0Hcte.

[44] John Arquilla and David Ronfeldt, Swarming and the Future of Conflict, (Santa Monica, CA: RAND, MR-311-OSD, 2000).

CHAPTER TWO

Controlling Russia
Color Revolutions and Swarming Coups

The operation - engineering democracy through the ballot box and civil disobedience - is now so slick that the methods have matured into a template for winning other people's elections.
     – Ian Traynor, London Guardian, November 26, 2004

Washington Perfects A Method For Staging Coups

In the year 2000, a strange new political phenomenon emerged in Belgrade, the capital of Serbia in the former Yugoslavia. Although it appeared seemingly out of the blue, it signalled a change in the course of US covert warfare. On the surface, it seemed to be a spontaneous and genuine political 'movement.' In reality, it was the product of techniques that had been under study and development in the US for decades. The RAND Corporation's military strategists had been analyzing the patterns of successful political protest movements such as the 1968 student uprisings in Paris. They characterized the techniques as 'swarming.' because they were decentralized but connected, like a swarm of bees.[1]

In Belgrade, several specific organizations were key players: the National Endowment for Democracy and two of its offshoots, the National Republican Institute, tied to the Republican party, and the National Democratic Institute, tied to the Democrats. While claiming to be private Non-Government Organizations (NGOs), they were, in fact, financed by the US Congress and State Department. Armed with millions in US taxpayer dollars, they were moved into place to create a synthetic movement for 'non-violent change.'[2]

Washington Post writer, Michael Dobbs, provided a first-hand description of what took place in Belgrade. The beginnings went back to a secret closed-door meeting in October 1999, more than a year earlier:

(Belgrade)—*In a softly lit conference room, American pollster Doug Schoen flashed the results of an in-depth opinion poll of 840 Serbian voters onto an overhead projection screen, sketching a strategy for toppling Europe's last remaining communist-era ruler.*

> *His message, delivered to leaders of Serbia's traditionally fractious opposition, was simple and powerful. Slobodan Milosevic—survivor of four lost wars, two major street uprisings, 78 days of NATO bombing and a decade of international sanctions—was "completely vulnerable" to a well-organized electoral challenge. The key, the poll results showed, was opposition unity.*

> *Held in a luxury hotel in Budapest, the Hungarian capital, in October 1999, the closed-door briefing by Schoen, a Democrat, turned out to be a seminal event, pointing the way to the electoral revolution that brought down Milosevic a year later. It also marked the start of an extraordinary U.S. effort to unseat a foreign head of state, not through covert action of the kind the CIA once employed in such places as Iran and Guatemala, but by modern election campaign techniques.*

> *While the broad outlines of the $41 million U.S. democracy-building campaign in Serbia are public knowledge, interviews with dozens of key players, both here and in the United States, suggest it was much more extensive and sophisticated than previously reported.*

> *Regarded by many as Eastern Europe's last great democratic upheaval, Milosevic's overthrow may also go down in history as the first poll-driven, focus group-tested revolution. Behind the seeming spontaneity of the street uprising that forced Milosevic to respect the results of a hotly contested presidential election on Sept. 24 was a carefully researched strategy put together by Serbian democracy activists with active assistance of Western advisers and pollsters.* [3]

Dobbs reported that the United States government had 'bought' the removal of Milosevic for $41 million. The operation was run out of the offices of US Ambassador Miles, he reported, with specially trained agents coordinating networks of naïve students who were convinced they were fighting for a better world, the 'American way of life.'

The *Washington Post* noted that "U.S.-funded consultants played a crucial role behind the scenes in virtually every facet of the anti-Milosevic drive, running tracking polls, training thousands of opposition activists and helping to organize a vitally important parallel vote count. US taxpayers paid for 5,000 cans of spray paint used by student activists to scrawl anti-Milosevic graffiti on walls across Serbia.."[4] As many as 2.5 million stickers with the slogan 'Gotov Je' ('He's Finished') were plastered all over Serbia; 'Gotov Je' became the revolution's catchphrase. The group was called Otpor, which means 'resistance.'

This remarkable first-hand account from one of America's most respected establishment newspapers revealed what had been at work in Serbia to topple Milosevic. Initially, the US role had been to support Milosevic during the early 1990s; but later, US official propaganda had demonized Milosevic as the heir to Hitler in terms of atrocities. This complete reversal suggested a hidden Washington agenda.

Behind Otpor had been the US State Department which, in Belgrade, was led by US Ambassador to Serbia, Richard Miles. The US Agency for International Development (USAID) had channeled the funds through commercial contractors and through the so-called NGOs – NED, NDI, and IRI.[5]

According to Dobbs, the IRI paid for some two dozen Otpor leaders to attend a seminar on nonviolent resistance at the Hilton Hotel in Budapest. There the Serbian students received training in such matters as how to organize a strike, how to communicate with symbols, how to overcome fear, and how to undermine the authority of a dictatorial regime. The principal lecturer was retired US Army Col. Robert Helvey, former Defense Intelligence Agency analyst, who trained and then used the Otpor activists to distribute 70,000 copies of a manual on nonviolent resistance. Helvey had worked with Gene Sharp, founder of the controversial Albert Einstein Institution in Boston where the Pentagon learned to conceal its coup d'etats under the guise of non-violence. Sharp was described by Helvey as "the Clausewitz of the nonviolence movement," referring to the renowned Prussian military strategist.[6]

The non-violent tactics that the Otpor! youth had been trained in were reportedly based on RAND corporation analyses of the warfare methods of Ghengis Kahn upgraded with modern networking technologies that connected people like swarming bees.[7] Using GPS satellite images, special agents could direct their hand-picked, specially trained leaders on the ground to maneuver 'spontaneous' hit-and-run protests that always eluded the police or military. Meanwhile, CNN would be carefully and conveniently pre-positioned to project images around the world of these youthful non-violent 'protestors.'

What was new in the Belgrade coup against Milosevic was the use of the Internet – particularly its chat rooms, instant messaging, and blog sites — along with mobiles or cell phones, including SMS text-messaging. Using these high tech capabilities that had only emerged in the mid-1990s, a handful of trained leaders could rapidly steer rebellious and suggestible 'Generation X' youth in and out of mass demonstrations at will.[8]

Otpor!, the US hand behind the Belgrade coup d'etat of 2000, was the first successful civilian application of what would become the hallmark of US Defense policies under Secretary Donald Rumsfeld at the Pentagon.

Reliance on new communications networking technologies to rapidly deploy small groups was the civilian counterpart of Rumsfeld's 'Revolution in Military Affairs' doctrine — the deployment of highly mobile, weaponized small groups directed by 'real time' intelligence and communications. A perceptive US analyst of the process described the relationship:

> *Squads of soldiers taking over city blocks with the aid of 'intelligence helmet' video screens that give them an instantaneous overview of their environment, constitute the military side. Bands of youth converging on targeted intersections in con-*

stant dialogue on cell phones, constitute the doctrine's civilian application.[9]

If the US invasion of Iraq in 2003 was the violent form of Rumsfeld's military doctrine, then Serbia's coup, followed by Georgia's 'Rose Revolution' and Ukraine's 'Orange Revolution,' were examples of the non-violent, civilian application of the doctrine. As the debacles of Iraq and Afghanistan deepened, many US strategists were increasingly convinced that the 'civilian' application was far more effective than the overtly military.

It was no accident that there was such a similarity between the civilian and military models for regime change. Andrew Marshall, former RAND strategist and the reclusive head of the Pentagon Office of Net Assessments since 1974, had overseen the development of both from his Pentagon office. Through slick Madison Avenue marketing techniques and careful study of genuine protest movements, the US Government had, in effect, perfected techniques for 'democratically' getting rid of any opponent, while convincing the world they were brought down by spontaneous outbursts for freedom. It was a dangerously effective weapon.

The Serbian *Otpor!* revolution had been founded, guided and financed covertly by the US Government via select NGOs. It marked the modern perfection of techniques which, according to Jonathan Mowat, had been under study for years in the Pentagon and its various think-tanks, most notably the Santa Monica, California RAND corporation.[10]

Early CIA Crude Measures

In the early days of its existence, the Central Intelligence Agency deployed what were comparatively crude measures to effect regime change when Washington wanted somebody out of its way. The toppling of the popular and democratically elected Premier Mohammed Mossadegh in Iran was pulled off mainly by covert CIA agents sent into the country with cash which they doled out to phony protesters, supplying them with slogans and banners in support of the Shah. This emboldened the Shah's reactionary monarchist opposition forces. Mossadeq was arrested and US oil interests were again protected. In Guatemala, the CIA acted on behalf of and at the of request of the United Fruit Company to get rid of the elected President Arbenez, a nationalist whose measures of economic betterment for Guatemalan peasants threatened the profits of the US banana producer.[11]

In those early years, the pattern of US 'informal imperialism' as some called it, was repeated frequently. All manner of cover and illegal interventions into the sovereign affairs of other nations could be justified in terms of the Cold War against the 'threat' of communism. American business interests abroad might be threatened even by non-communist leaders who were popular or democratically elected because they favored land reform, stronger unions, and redistribution of wealth. Also threatening to US interests were leaders who nationalized local resources and limited foreign-owned industry, or sought to regulate business to protect workers or consumers.

On behalf of American businesses, and often with their help, the CIA would mobilize the internal opposition. First it would identify right-wing groups within the country, usually tied to the military, and then offer them a deal: 'We'll put you in power if you maintain a favorable business climate for us.' Typically, to grease the process, huge payoffs and bribes were involved.

The CIA would then work with them to overthrow the existing government, usually a democracy. It used a vast array of tricks and tactics: propaganda, stuffed ballot boxes, bought elections, extortion, blackmail, sexual intrigue, false stories about opponents in the local media, transportation strikes, infiltration and disruption of opposing political parties, kidnapping, beating, torture, intimidation, economic sabotage, death squads and even assassination.[12]

These efforts would typically culminate in a military coup, installing a 'pro-American' right-wing dictator. The CIA would then train the dictator's security apparatus to crack down on the traditional enemies of big business, often using interrogation, torture and murder. The victims were called 'communists,' but almost always were just peasants or liberals, moderates, labor union leaders, students, nationalists, political opponents and advocates of free speech and democracy. Widespread human rights abuses, often involving the use of 'death squads,' typically followed.[13] The victims often became known as 'the disappeared.'

The bloody histories of Chile and Argentina, and countless other 'pro-US' dictatorships during the Cold War, were cut from that crude mold.

Truman Creates The 'National Security State'

The early career of Wall Street lawyer and intelligence operative Frank Wisner exemplified the old methods. In 1947 President Harry Truman had signed the statute creating the Central Intelligence Agency as an arm of the Executive Branch, an agency largely immune from Congressional oversight, and completely hidden from public scrutiny. The two words, 'national security' were used to cloak everything. It was the birth of what was to become the American National Security State, a world in which every crime imaginable would be justified in the name of 'national security' and the purported threat of 'global communist subversion.'

Frank Wisner had been recruited in 1948, at the birth of the CIA, to head the deceptively named Office of Policy Coordination (OPC). In reality, OPC was the covert operations arm of the agency. Under the terms of its top secret charter, its responsibilities would encompass "propaganda, economic warfare, preventive direct action, including sabotage, anti-sabotage, demolition and evacuation procedures; subversion against hostile states, including assistance to underground resistance groups, and support of indigenous anti-communist elements in threatened countries of the free world."[14]

In late 1948, Wisner established Operation Mockingbird, a project designed to illegally influence the domestic and foreign media. In 1952, he became head of the Directorate of Plans where he controlled 75% of the CIA budget. He was thus instrumental in bringing about the fall of Mohammed Mossadeq in Iran and Jacobo Arbenz Guzmán in Guatemala.[15]

In other coup operations the CIA deployed hit-men, crude assassins with little more sophistication than the mob's killers — even in some cases, actually using the mob.[16]

The problem was that the CIA's methods for eliminating popular heads of state during the 1950's and 1960's, all justified in the name of the 'war against the spread of Godless communism,' were not only inefficient, but they often resulted in a blowback against the United States that cost more than it gained for Washington. Invariably, America's 'Beacon of Liberty' would be tarnished by exposure of its covert operations, whether by jealous FBI Director J. Edgar Hoover, by foreign media, or by local opponents in the target countries.

The CIA's operations were virtually uncontrolled; it went to extreme lengths to advance its version of an American Century. Beginning in the 1950s, for example, with covert funding from Nelson Rockefeller's Department of Health Education and Welfare, the CIA engaged in a program given the code name "MK-ULTRA." Alleged to be necessary in response to claims of 'brainwashing' of American soldiers by North Korea, the CIA began experiments in "mind control." The allegations of North Korean brainwashing were fabricated, as later research revealed, in order to justify this program after the fact. At the time, there was no evidence of such brainwashing, nor has there been any since.

The CIA's program involved administering LSD and other drugs to American subjects without their knowledge or against their will, causing several to commit suicide.

The MK-ULTRA operation was secretly co-funded by the Rockefeller Foundation,[17] as well as by funds specifically earmarked for MK-ULTRA front projects by Nelson Rockefeller – then President Eisenhower's Under Secretary for Health, Education and Welfare, and later his Special Assistant on Cold War Strategy and Psychological Warfare. In addition to attempts at 'mind control' with drugs, MK-ULTRA involved research on methods of effective propaganda, brainwashing, public relations, advertising, hypnosis, and other forms of suggestion.[18]

Beginning in the 1960's, some in the US intelligence community started to see possibilities for an entirely new form of covert regime change.

From Tavistock To Rand

In 1967, the head of the Tavistock Institute of Human Relations in London was a man named Dr. Fred Emery, an expert on the 'hypnotic effects' of television. Dr. Emery was particularly struck by what he observed of crowd behavior at rock concerts, which were a relatively new phenomenon at that time. Emery referred to the audiences as 'swarming adolescents.' He was convinced that this behavior could effectively be refined and used to bring down hostile or uncooperative governments. Emery wrote an article about this for the Tavistock Institute's journal, *Human Relations,* which he confidently titled, "The Next Thirty Years: Concepts, Methods and Anticipations." The article detailed ways in which to safely channel or directly manipulate what he termed 'rebellious hysteria.' This is precisely what the RAND studies later observed, and manufactured, as 'swarming.'[19]

Following World War I, the British Military had created the Tavistock Institute to serve as its psychological warfare arm. The Institute received its name from the Duke of Bedford, Marquis of Tavistock, who donated a building to the Institute in 1921 to study the effect of shell-shock on British soldiers who had survived World War I. Its purpose was not to help the traumatized soldiers, however, but instead to establish the 'breaking point' of men under stress. The program was under the direction of the British Army Bureau of Psychological Warfare. For a time Sigmund Freud worked with Tavistock on psychoanalytical methods applied to individuals and large groups.

After World War II, the Rockefeller Foundation moved in to finance the Tavistock Institute and, in effect, to co-opt its programs for the United States and its emerging psychological warfare activities.[20] The Rockefeller Foundation provided an infusion of funds for the financially strapped Tavistock, newly reorganized as the Tavistock Institute for Human Relations. Its Rockefeller agenda was to undertake "under conditions of peace, the kind of social psychiatry that had developed in the army under conditions of war."[21]

That was a fateful turn.

Tavistock immediately began work in the United States, sending its leading researcher, the German-born psychologist, Kurt Lewin, to the Massachusetts Institute of Technology in 1945 to establish the Research Center for Group Dynamics. Lewin was interested in the scientific study of the processes that influence individuals in group situations, and is widely credited as the founder of 'social psychology.' After Lewin's death, the Center moved to the University of Michigan in 1948 where it became the Institute for Social Research.[22]

Tavistock's work over the next two decades was to co-opt legitimate psychological insights into social groups and social dynamics in order to refine techniques for social manipulation.

Then, Fred Emery's 1967 insights about 'swarming' crowds seemed validated by massive student uprisings in Paris during May 1968. Thousands of 'swarming adolescents' grew into a movement of millions, destabilizing the French government and eventually toppling President Charles de Gaulle.[23] That spontaneous outpouring was closely studied by Tavistock and by various US intelligence agencies for methods, patterns and tactics that would be developed and implemented over the ensuing three and a half decades by the US intelligence community.

Rock Videos In Katmandu

In late 1989, another piece of the 'new regime change' program emerged at a conference at Case Western Reserve University in Ohio. The university's 'Program for Social Innovations in Global Management' featured Dr. Howard Perlmutter, Professor of Social Architecture, a curious new academic field located at the Wharton School of Finance in Philadelphia. Perlmutter, a disciple of Tavistock's Emery, boldly announced that "rock video in Katmandu" was the paradigm for destabilizing traditional cultures, enabling powerful states to create what Perlmutter called a "global civilization."[24]

According to Perlmutter, two things were necessary for such destabilizing transformations: "building internationally committed networks of international and locally committed organizations" (the equivalent of today's human rights organizations and other NGOs) and "creating global events through the transformation of a local event into one having virtually instantaneous international implications through mass-media."[25]

Perlmutter's idea contained the core blueprint for the 'new and improved' US-made regime change, the modern form of US-staged coup d'etat. In Central Europe after 2000, these became known as the 'Color Revolutions.'

Perlmutter's core blueprint for destabilization was supplemented in the mid-1990's by more groundbreaking research at the RAND Corporation on the application of the Information Revolution to covertly fomenting regime change. In 1997, RAND researchers John Arquilla and David Ronfeldt published their work on exploiting the information revolution for the US military. By taking advantage of network-based organizations linked via email and mobile phones to enhance the potential of swarming, IT techniques could be transformed into key methods of warfare. [26]

Swarming From Serbia To Georgia

The US success in removing the tenacious Slobodan Milosevic as Serbia's President in 2000 proved to the US State Department and intelligence community that their new model for covert regime change via non-violent coup d'etats worked. It seemed to be the perfect model for eliminating regimes opposed to US policy. It did not matter if a regime had been popular or democratically elected. Any regime was vulnerable to the Pentagon's new methods of warfare — the 'swarming' and 'color revolution' techniques of RAND.

Within months of his success in overseeing the creation of the Serb Otpor! Revolution, US Chief of Mission to Belgrade, Ambassador Richard Miles, was sent to his next assignment, the tiny Republic of Georgia in the Caucasus mountains of Central Asia.[27]

Normally, a post in Georgia — a small state on the Black Sea run by a tight-fisted Soviet era veteran, Edouard Shevardnadze — would have been considered a step down in a typical State Department career path.

Not for Miles. His assignment was to oversee a repeat of the Belgrade revolution in Tbilisi, Georgia.[28] In Tbilisi, Miles was introduced to his star Georgian pupil, Mikheil Saakashvili, a product of Columbia University Law School, George Washington University Law School, and a US State Department Fellow. At the time, 2002, Saakashvili was Georgia's Justice Minister under President Eduard Shevardnadze; Miles would coach Saakashvili on how to bring down his boss.[29]

Miles got ample assistance from US Government linked or financed NGOs, including the National Endowment for Democracy, the organization that seemed to be present in every major US coup or regime change operation since the 1980's.[30] Also prominent in Georgia, according to Mowat, was the Open Society Foundation run by American billionaire, George Soros, and the Washington-based Freedom House which had been set up in the 1940s as a NATO propaganda organization and in 2001 was headed by former CIA chief, James Woolsey.

The US State Department had often used NGOs in its coup machinery over the years: in the overthrow of President Fernando Marcos of the Philippines in 1986, or in the Tiananmen Square destabilization in 1989, and Vaclav Havel's 'velvet revolution' in Czechoslovakia in 1989. Now, the somewhat crude tactics of previous decades were augmented by the refinements of RAND swarming techniques, SMS text messaging and mobile phones, and Gene Sharp's studies of what he termed 'nonviolence as a method of warfare.'[31]

In and around the student nonviolent protests in Tiananmen Square in 1989, both Gene Sharp's Albert Einstein Institution and George Soros' Fund for the Reform and Opening of China, had apparently been present. Gene Sharp actually admitted to being in Beijing just prior to the outbreak of the nonviolent student protests at Tiananmen Square.[32] The Chinese Government at the time openly accused the Soros' foundation of having ties to the CIA, forcing it to leave the country.[33]

Sharp's Albert Einstein Institution apparently played a key role in training and educating youth movements across former Warsaw pact countries and also in Asia.[34] According to researcher Jonathan Mowat, Sharp's organization was funded in part by the Soros foundations and the US Government's National Endowment for Democracy, among others.[35]

On its own website, Sharp's institute admitted to being active with opposition 'pro-democracy' groups in a number of countries, including Burma, Thailand, Tibet, Latvia, Lithuania, Estonia, Belarus, as well as Serbia.[36] Conveniently, his target countries entirely coincided with the US State Department's targets for regime change over the same time period. The word 'democracy,' as the ancient Greek oligarchs well knew, was a double-edged sword that could be manipulated against one's opponents, with the directed fury of an enraged mob.

Among the advisors to Sharp's institute at the time of the Serbia Otpor! Operation, in addition to Colonel Helvey, was a high-ranking US intelligence specialist, Major General Edward B. Atkeson, US Army (Ret.).[37] A former Deputy Chief of Staff Intelligence, US Army Europe, and member of the National Intelligence Council under the Director of the CIA, General Atkeson also served with the Bureau of Politico-Military Affairs, Department of State. Another advisor to Sharp's Albert Einstein Institution was former US Admiral Gene R. La Rocque, head of the Center for Defense Information.[38]

Just as things were getting hot in Georgia, where the Albert Einstein Institution was playing a role, another vital part of the old Soviet Union was suddenly added to Washington's 'hit list.' Ukraine, at the very heart of ethnic Russia, was now also made a target of a US-backed Color Revolution.

Ukraine's Orange Revolution And Pipeline Geopolitics

Ukraine and Russia were so intertwined economically, socially and culturally, especially in the east of the country, that they were almost indistinguishable from one another. Most of Russia's natural gas pipelines from West Siberia flowed through Ukraine on their way to Germany, France and other West European states. In military strategic terms, a non-neutral Ukraine in NATO would pose a fatal security blow to Russia. In the age of advanced US nuclear weapons and anti-missile defenses, that was just what the Bush Administration wanted.

A look at a map of Eurasian geography revealed a distinct pattern to the Washington-sponsored Color Revolutions after 2000. They were clearly aimed at isolating Russia and ultimately cutting her economic lifeline—her pipeline networks that carried Russia's huge reserves of oil and natural gas from the Urals and Siberia to Western Europe and Eurasia – straight through Ukraine.

Russia is being surrounded by NATO states and if Ukraine joins NATO it would deal a devastating blow to Russian economic and military security

The transformation of Ukraine from independent former Russian republic to pro-NATO US satellite was accomplished by the so-called 'Orange Revolution' in 2004 overseen by John Herbst, appointed US Ambassador to Ukraine in May 2003. As the US State Department euphemistically described his activities:

> *During his tenure, he worked to enhance US-Ukrainian rela-*
> *tions and to help ensure the conduct of a fair Ukrainian*
> *presidential election. In Kiev, he witnessed the Orange Revo-*

lution. Prior to that, Ambassador John Herbst was the U.S. Ambassador to Uzbekistan, where he played a critical role in the establishment of an American base to help conduct Operation Enduring Freedom in Afghanistan.[39]

The man Washington decided to back in its orchestrated regime change in Ukraine was Viktor Yushchenko, a fifty-year old former Governor of Ukraine's Central Bank. Yushchenko's wife, Kateryna, an American citizen born in Chicago, had been an official in both the Reagan and George H.W. Bush administrations, and in the US State Department. She had come to Ukraine as a representative of the US-Ukraine Foundation whose Board of Directors included Grover Norquist, one of the most influential conservative Republicans in Washington. Norquist had been called "the managing director of the hard-core right" backing the George W. Bush Presidency.[40]

The central focus of Yushchenko's slick campaign for President was to advocate membership for Ukraine in NATO and the European Union. His campaign used huge quantities of orange colored banners, flags, posters, balloons and other props, leading the media inevitably to dub it the 'Orange Revolution.' Washington funded 'pro-democracy' youth groups that played a particularly significant role organizing huge street demonstrations that helped him win the re-run of a disputed election.

In Ukraine the pro-Yushchenko movement worked under the slogan *Pora* ('It's Time') and they brought in people who had helped organize the 'Rose Revolution' in Georgia: Chair of Georgia's Parliamentary Committee on Defense and Security, Givi Targamadze; former member of the Georgian Liberty Institute; as well as members of Georgia's youth group, Kmara. The Georgians were consulted by Ukrainian opposition leaders on techniques of non-violent struggle. Georgian rock bands Zumba, Soft Eject and Green Room, which had supported the 'Rose Revolution' now organized a solidarity concert in central Kiev to support Yushchenko's campaign in November 2004.[41]

A Washington-based PR firm called Rock Creek Creative also played a significant role in branding the Orange Revolution by developing a pro-Yushchenko website around the orange logo and color theme.[42]

On the ground, several elements worked in concert to create an aura of fraud around the election of 2004 that Yuschchenko had lost, and to mobilize popular support for a new run-off. Using the Pora and other youth groups, especially election monitors, in coordination with key western media such as CNN and BBC, a second election was organized that allowed Yushchenko to squeak out a narrow margin of victory in January 2005 and declare himself President. The US State Department spent some $20 million for the Ukraine Presidency.[43]

The same US Government-backed NGOs that had been in Georgia also produced the results in Ukraine: the George Soros Open Society Institute; Freedom House; and the National Endowment for Democracy, along with its two subsidiaries, the National Republican Institute and the National Democratic Institute. According to Ukrainian reports, the US-based NGOs, along with the conservative US-Ukraine Foundation, were active throughout Ukraine, feeding the protest movement of Pora and Znayu, and training poll watchers.[44]

At a certain point in 2004 following Washington's successes in Georgia and in Ukraine, Russia's Putin moved to centralize control over the one strategic asset Russia possessed that the Western European NATO countries badly needed—energy. Russia was far and away the world's largest producer of natural gas.

The Eurasia Pipeline Wars

The unspoken agenda of Washington's aggressive Central Asia policies after the collapse of the Soviet Union could be summed up in a single phrase: control of energy. So long as Russia was able to use its strategic trump card — its vast oil and gas reserves — to win economic allies in Western Europe, China and elsewhere, it could not be politically isolated. The location of the various Color Revolutions was aimed directly at encircling Russia and cutting off, at any time, her export pipelines. With more than sixty percent of Russia's dollar export earnings coming from its oil and gas exports, such an encirclement would amount to an economic chokehold on Russia by US-led NATO.

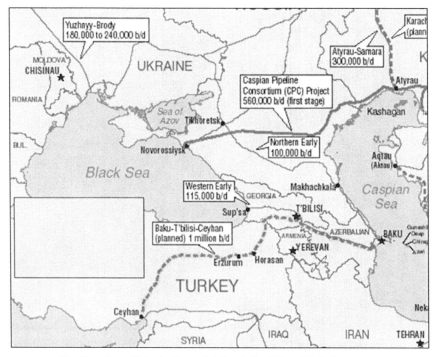

Pipeline Geopolitics in Central Asia pit the US and Britain against
Russia and China with high conflict potential

The color revolution in the tiny Republic of Georgia and the effort to draw Georgia into NATO under the new President, US-trained Mikheil Saakashvili, was in part aimed at securing a new oil pipeline route to get the vast oil reserves of the Caspian Sea near Baku in Azerbaijan. British Petroleum had secured the lead role in developing huge offshore oil fields near Baku soon after the dissolution of the Soviet Union in the early 1990s.

With Washington's backing as early as the Clinton Administration, BP had sought to build an oil pipeline that would somehow avoid transit through Russia. Owing to the mountainous terrain, the only such route was from Baku across Georgia via Tbilisi, and then across the Black Sea to NATO member Turkey where it would connect with a pipeline to the Mediterranean Turkish port of Ceyhan.

The oil riches of Russia and Central Asia depend on pipelines to get to market a point where NATO is aiming to control Russian access via Ukraine and Georgia

The Baku-Ceyhan pipeline was originally proclaimed by BP and others as 'The Project of the Century.' Zbigniew Brzezinski was a consultant to BP during the Clinton era, lobbying Washington to support the BP project. It was Brzezinski who went to Baku in 1995, unofficially, on behalf of President Clinton to meet with Azeri President Haidar Aliyev, and to negotiate the new independent Baku pipeline routes, including what became the B-T-C or Baku-Tbilisi-Ceyhan pipeline.

By 2003, Russia had become the world's second largest producer of crude oil, after Saudi Arabia. During the Soviet era the economies of Ukraine, Georgia, Russia, Kazakhstan, Azerbaijan and the other Republics of the USSR had been fully integrated economically. After the Soviet Union collapsed in the early 1990s, its gas and oil pipelines and export routes across Eurasia continued to operate. Moreover, the former Soviet regions, including Ukraine, continued to receive Russian gas via the state gas monopoly, Gazprom, at highly subsidized prices below that charged in Western Europe.

US-Sponsored Ngos

Zbigniew Brzezinski sits on the Board of Directors of a rather impressive if little-known organization, the US-Azerbaijan Chamber of Commerce (USACC). The chairman of USACC in Washington had been Tim Cejka, President of ExxonMobil Exploration. USACC Board members, in addition to Brzezinski, included Henry Kissinger, Brent Scowcroft, and James Baker III. Scowcroft had been advisor on national security to Presidents Nixon, Ford, Bush, Sr, and Bush, Jr. Baker was the man who traveled to Tbilisi in 2003 to tell Shevardnadze in person that Washington wanted him to step aside in favor of the US-trained Shaakashvili. Dick Cheney was a former USACC board member before he became Vice President.

A heavier Washington power team of geopolitical fixers would be hard to imagine. It suffices to say Washington's power elites would not waste their time, nor focus their concentration in such a manner unless an area was of utmost geopolitical strategic importance.

Another so-called NGO that invariably turned up in each of Color Revolution regime changes was Freedom House. Along with the Open Society Institutes of George Soros, the US-funded NED and others, the curiously named Freedom House turned up everywhere.

Freedom House was an organization with a noble-sounding name and a long history. It had been created in the late 1940s as a US lobby to organize public opinion in favor of establishing NATO. The chairman of Freedom House at the time of the Georgia and Ukraine Color Revolutions was James Woolsey, former CIA director and a neo-conservative who proclaimed to the world that September 11, 2001 was the start of "World War IV."[45] Woolsey defined the Cold War as World War III.

Other trustees and financial backers of Freedom House included Zbigniew Brzezinski and Anthony Lake, foreign policy advisors to Presidents Carter, Clinton and Obama. Freedom House also listed among its financial contributors the US State Department, USAID, US Information Agency, Soros Open Society Foundations, and the ubiquitous National Endowment for Democracy (NED). [46]

The NED, along with Freedom House, had been at the center of all the major 'color revolutions' in Eurasia since 2000. It had been created during the Reagan Administration to function as a *de facto* CIA, privatized so as to allow more freedom of action.[47] Allen Weinstein, who helped draft the legislation establishing NED, said in an interview in 1991, "A lot of what we do today was done covertly 25 years ago by the CIA."[48]

NED President since 1984 was Carl Gershman who had previously been a Freedom House Scholar. NATO General and former Presidential candidate Wesley Clark, the man who led the US bombing of Serbia in 1999, also sat on the NED Board.

The majority of the historic figures linked to clandestine CIA actions have at some time been members of the Board of Directors or the Administrative Council of the NED, including Otto Reich, John Negroponte, Henry Cisneros and Elliot Abrams. The Chairman of the NED Board of Directors in 2008 was Vin Weber, founder of the ultraconservative organization, Empower America, and campaign fundraiser for George W. Bush in 2000.[49]

Gershman, head of the NED since its creation to the present, was no ordinary civil servant. He had been a leading member during the 1970's of something called Social Democrats-USA, where he worked closely with Richard Perle, Elliott Abrams and Frank Gaffney. Gershman was in a sense 'present at the creation' of the political-intelligence faction known later as neo-conservativism. The NED by 2007 was involved in distributing US Government funds to select groups in more than 90 countries. The neo-conservative think-tank, the American Enterprise Institute, and former Senator Bill Frist (R-TN) were among those on the NED Board of Directors.[50]

Under Gershman's leadership the NED was countless times involved in operations to promote regime change in governments whose policies in one way or another clashed with a particular Washington priority. In 2004, the NED was involved in a US-sponsored coup attempt against Venezuela's new democratically-elected President, Hugo Chavez. After Hugo Chavez had easily won a referendum in August 2004 on his presidency, accusations emerged about the NED's role in supporting anti-

Chavez groups. A key figure in the attempted coup had been Bush's Assistant Secretary of State for the Western Hemisphere, Cuban-born Otto Juan Reich. Reích, a former Washington lobbyist for military contractors such as McDonnell Douglas and Lockheed-Martin, was also a board member of the controversial Western Hemisphere Institute for Security Cooperation, better known as the School of the Americas, where the Pentagon trained most of the Latin American death squads.[51]

The National Endowment for Democracy was the vehicle that was used in country after country to advance a Washington agenda of Full Spectrum Dominance.

Eurasian Political Geography

A close look at the map of Eurasia began to suggest what was at stake for Washington in Eurasia. The goal was not only the strategic encirclement of Russia through a series of NATO bases ranging from Camp Bond Steel in Kosovo, to Poland, to the Czech Republic, and possibly Georgia, and possibly Ukraine. All of this had the overarching goal of enabling NATO to control energy routes and networks between Russia and the EU.

The Washington strategy of 'democratic' coups — the color revolutions in Georgia and Ukraine — were designed strategically to cut China off from access to the vital oil and gas reserves of the Caspian Sea, including Kazakhstan and, ultimately, Russia.

Asia's ancient trades routes, and specifically The Great Silk Road, went through Tashkent in Uzbekistan and Almaty in Kazakhstan. In a region surrounded by major mountain ranges, geopolitical control of Uzbekistan, Kyrgystan, and Kazakhstan would enable control of any potential pipeline routes between China and Central Asia. So, too, the encirclement of Russia would allow for control of pipelines and other ties between it and Western Europe and the Middle East.

In this context, a *Foreign Affairs* article by Zbigniew Brzezinski in September 1997 revealed the true Washington geopolitical strategy towards Eurasia:

Eurasia is home to most of the world's politically assertive and dynamic states. All the historical pretenders to global power originated in Eurasia. The world's most populous aspirants to regional hegemony, China and India, are in Eurasia, as are all the potential political or economic challengers to American primacy. After the United States, the next six largest economies and military spenders are there, as are all but one of the world's overt nuclear powers, and all but one of the covert ones. Eurasia accounts for 75 percent of the world's population, 60 percent of its GNP, and 75 percent of its energy resources. Collectively, Eurasia's potential power overshadows even America's.

Eurasia is the world's axial super-continent. A power that dominated Eurasia would exercise decisive influence over two of the world's three most economically productive regions, Western Europe and East Asia. A glance at the map also suggests that a country dominant in Eurasia would almost automatically control the Middle East and Africa. With Eurasia now serving as the decisive geopolitical chessboard, it no longer suffices to fashion one policy for Europe and another for Asia. What happens with the distribution of power on the Eurasian landmass will be of decisive importance to America's global primacy....[52]

A New Cold War Begins Over Oil

After the bungled occupation of Iraq in 2003, Brzezinski's geopolitical 'chessboard' presented a number of challenges for the US: the question of war or not against Iran; the issue of Georgia and the Baku-Tbilisi-Ceyhan oil pipeline; the question of China's emergence as a global economic superpower. All were linked to the issue of geopolitics. The future of the United States as sole superpower had been intimately linked to its ability to control global oil and gas flows, the economic artery system of the modern economy. That was the real reason for the invasion of Afghanistan, the violent occupation of Iraq, the Kosovo war in 1999, the sabre-rattling over Iran, and the efforts of Washington to oust Hugo Chavez in Venezuela.

Russia, following almost a decade of economic devastation and state debt default in 1998, had begun to emerge as a functioning economy under the Presidency of Vladimir Putin. Russia's oil and gas exports benefited from a world market where energy prices had increased significantly after the Iraq invasion of 2003. The expanded revenues allowed Russia to pay down its IMF loans and build substantial foreign exchange reserves. The Russian economy had begun to grow for the first time in decades.

Beginning in the first decade of the millennium, the new Russia was gaining in influence not through arms, but by strategic moves using its geopolitical assets in energy—its oil and natural gas. Russia's leaders during the Putin presidency realized that if they did not act decisively, Russia soon would be encircled and entrapped by a military rival, the USA.

China, meanwhile, would not be able to emerge as a truly independent global power over the coming decades unless it could resolve two strategic vulnerabilities— its growing dependence on energy imports for its economic growth, and its inability to pose a credible nuclear deterrence to a US nuclear first strike.

Russia was the only power with enough strategic nuclear deterrence potential, as well as sufficient energy reserves, to make a credible counterweight to global US military and political primacy. Moreover, A Eurasian combination of China and Russia, plus allied Eurasian states, presented an even greater counterweight to unilateral USA dominance. Following the 1998 Asia Crisis, Beijing and Moscow formed a mutual security agreement with surrounding states, Kazakhstan and Tajikistan. In 2001, Uzbekistan joined, and the group renamed itself the Shanghai Cooperation Organization,

Washington's New Oil Geopolitics

Since the Bush-Cheney Administration took office in January 2001, controlling the major oil and natural gas fields of the world had been the primary, though undeclared, priority of US foreign policy. The battle was for the highest stakes. Washington's power elites were determined to deconstruct Russia as a functioning power in their pursuit of global domination, their New World Order. It became increasingly clear that not only the invasion of Iraq, but also the toppling of the Taliban in Afghanistan, had nothing to do with 'democracy,' and everything to do with pipeline control across Central Asia and the militarization of the Middle East.[53]

After 1999, the United States, which already maintains between 600 and 800 military bases around the world, built even more bases ranging geographically from Camp Bondsteel in Kosovo, to Sao Tome/Principe off the coast of West Africa. It attempted 'regime change' of the democratically elected President of oil-rich Venezuela, while shamelessly proclaiming itself the champion of democracy. And the US put massive pressure on a nervous Germany and France to bring the tiny but strategic Republic of Georgia into NATO to secure oil flows from Baku to the Mediterranean.

President George W. Bush himself made a trip to Tbilisi on May 10, 2005 to address a crowd in Freedom Square, promoting Washington's 'war on tyranny' campaign for the region. He praised the US-backed 'color revolutions' from Ukraine to Georgia, in the process opportunistically attacking Roosevelt's Yalta division of Europe in 1945. Bush then made the curious declaration:

> We will not repeat the mistakes of other generations, appeasing or excusing tyranny, and sacrificing freedom in the vain pursuit of stability," the president said. "We have learned our lesson; no one's liberty is expendable. In the long run, our security and true stability depend on the freedom of others. . . .Now, across the Caucasus, in Central Asia and the broader Middle East, we see the same desire for liberty burning in the hearts of young people. They are demanding their freedom — and they will have it. [54]

Bush's remarks were calculated to fan the flame of further regime destabilizations across Eurasia where the National Endowment for Democracy (NED) and its related NGO's were now coordinating accusations of 'human rights' violations across the region.

Cheney's Energy Strategy

The Bush-Cheney Presidency had, from the outset, been based on a clear consensus among various factions of the US power establishment. That consensus was that US foreign policy should aim to secure what the Pentagon termed 'Full Spectrum Dominance.'

The strategists of Full Spectrum Dominance envisioned control of pretty much the entire universe, including outer and inner-space, from the galaxy to the mind. The control of energy, particularly global oil and gas resources, by the Big Four Anglo-American private oil giants— ChevronTexaco, ExxonMobil, BP and Royal Dutch Shell—was the cornerstone of their global strategy.

The Bush Administration implemented the consensus of the US establishment that the US required a drastic change in its foreign policy — to an extremely aggressive grab for global oil resources —- in order for the US to continue to control world economic growth and to prevent the emergence of rival economic groups, especially China.

It was clear in Washington policy circles that in order to control those global oil and gas flows, the United States needed to project its military power far more aggressively, to achieve a total military supremacy, which was what Full Spectrum Dominance was actually about.

Dick Cheney was ideally suited to weave the US military and energy policies together into a coherent strategy of dominance. During the early 1990s, Cheney had been Secretary of Defense under Bush, Sr. And when Cheney left Government in 1993, he became CEO of Halliburton Corporation (formerly Texas-based, now based in Dubai to avoid paying US taxes). Halliburton was the largest oil and gas services company in the world. At the same time, through its Kellogg, Brown & Root subsidiary, it was the Pentagon's largest constructor of military facilities, as well as prisons. The Bush-Cheney Administration was a fusion of the interests, and the owners, of the military-industrial complex and Big Oil.

'Where The Prize Ultimately Lies'

In September 1999, a little more than a year before he became the most powerful Vice President in US history, Cheney gave a revealing speech to the London Institute of Petroleum. Reviewing the outlook for Big Oil, Cheney made the following comment:

> *By some estimates there will be an average of two per cent an-*
> *nual growth in global oil demand over the years ahead along*
> *with conservatively a three per cent natural decline in produc-*
> *tion from existing reserves. That means by 2010 we will need*
> *on the order of an additional fifty million barrels a day. So*
> *where is the oil going to come from? Governments and the na-*
> *tional oil companies are obviously controlling about ninety*
> *per cent of the assets. Oil remains fundamentally a govern-*
> *ment business. While many regions of the world offer great oil*
> *opportunities, the Middle East with two thirds of the world's*
> *oil and the lowest cost, is still where the prize ultimately lies . .*
> *. [55]*

Cheney estimated that the world must come up with a staggering 50 million new barrels of oil per day by 2010— 50% of 2008 total world output, the equivalent of five new Saudi Arabias.

The second point of Cheney's London speech was his statement that "the Middle East. . . is still where the prize ultimately lies." However, he noted, the oil 'prize' of the Middle East was in national or government hands, not open to exploitation by the private market. Yet.

Cheney, it turned out, was also part of a powerful group determined to take Middle East oil out of state hands. At the time of his 1999 London speech, he was a member of an extremely influential think-tank, the Project for the New American Century (PNAC). A group within PNAC, including Donald Rumsfeld, Paul Wolfowitz, and others who went into the Bush Administration, issued a policy paper in 2000 titled, '*Rebuilding America's Defenses.*'

Cheney fully endorsed the PNAC paper. It advocated the doctrine of pre-emptive war, and all but called on the new US President to find a pretext to declare war on Iraq, in order to occupy it and take direct control of the second largest oil reserves in the Middle East.[56] The PNAC report stated bluntly, "the need for a substantial American force presence in the Gulf transcends the issue of the regime of Saddam Hussein . . . ." [57]

It was what Cheney had alluded to in his 1999 London speech. The problem, as Cheney saw it, was that the vast untapped oil reserves of the Middle East were largely under local government control and not in private hands. The military occupation of Iraq was the first major step in this US strategy to move oil into select private hands, Anglo-American Big Oil hands.

However, while ultimate US military control over the vast oil resources of the Persian Gulf, was necessary to the Pentagon's agenda of Full Spectrum Dominance (unchallenged domination of the entire planet), it was not at all sufficient. So long as Russia remained a free agent and not yet under the thumb of US military domination, US control of Eurasia would remain impossible. Ultimate dismemberment or deconstruction of Russia's remaining nuclear arsenal and control of Russia's vast oil and gas resources remained the strategic priority of Washington.

De-Construction Of Russia: The 'Ultimate Prize'

For obvious military and political reasons, Washington could not admit openly that since the fall of the Soviet Union in 1991, its strategic goal had been to dismember or de-construct Russia, thereby gaining effective control of its huge oil and gas resources.

However, the Russian Bear still had formidable military means, even though somewhat dilapidated, and she still had nuclear teeth.

Beginning in the mid-1990s Washington initiated a deliberate process of bringing former satellite Soviet states into not only the European Union, but also into a Washington-dominated NATO. By 2004 Poland, the Czech Republic, Hungary, Estonia, Latvia, Lithuania, Bulgaria, Romania, Slovakia and Slovenia were all in NATO, with the Republic of Georgia being groomed to join.

The spread of NATO to the immediate perimeter of Russia was a major objective of the PNAC members. Since 1996, PNAC member and Cheney crony, Bruce Jackson, Vice President for Strategy and Planning at US defense giant, Lockheed Martin Corporation, headed the US Committee on NATO, a powerful Washington lobby. He then founded the "Project for Transitional Democracies" which aimed specifically at bringing former Soviet Republics into NATO.

The NATO encirclement of Russia, the Color Revolutions across Eurasia, and the war in Iraq, were all aspects of one and the same American geopolitical strategy: a grand strategy to de-construct Russia once and for all as a potential rival to a sole US Superpower hegemony.

The end of the Yeltsin era put a slight crimp in Washington's grand plans, however. Following the IMF-guided looting of Russia by a combination of Western banks and corrupt Russian oligarchs, a shrewder and more sober Putin cautiously emerged as a dynamic nationalist force, committed to rebuilding Russia.

Concurrently, Russian oil output had been steadily rising since the collapse of the Soviet Union to the point that, by the time of the 2003 US invasion of Iraq, Russia was the world's second largest oil producer behind Saudi Arabia.

The Real Meaning Of The Yukos Affair

A defining event in Russian energy geopolitics took place in 2003. Just as Washington proclaimed its intent to militarize Iraq and the Middle East, regardless of world protest or international law, Putin ordered the spectacular public arrest of Russia's billionaire oligarch, Mikhail Khodorkovsky, on charges of tax evasion. Putin then surprised Western observers by freezing shares of Khodorkovsky's giant Yukos Oil group, in effect, putting it under state control.

What had triggered Putin's dramatic action?

Khodorkovsky was arrested four weeks before a decisive election in the Russian Duma, or lower house. It was reliably alleged that Khodorkovsky, using his vast wealth, had bought the votes of a majority. Control of the Duma was the first step by Khodorkovsky in a plan to run against Putin the next year as President. The Duma victory would have allowed him to change election laws in his favor, as well as to alter a controversial law being drafted in the Duma, "The Law on Underground Resources." That law would prevent Yukos Oil and other private companies from gaining control of underground raw materials, or from developing private pipeline routes independent of Russia's state pipelines.[58]

Khodorkovsky had violated the pledge the oligarchs had made to Putin — that if they stayed out of Russian politics and repatriated a share of their stolen money (in effect, stolen from the state in rigged bidding under Yeltsin) they would be allowed to keep their assets.

Khodorkovsky's arrest came shortly after reports of an unpublicized Washington meeting that July between Khodorkovsky and Vice President Dick Cheney. After the Cheney meeting, Khodorkovsky began talks with ExxonMobil and ChevronTexaco (US Secretary of State Condoleezza Rice's old firm) about acquiring a major stake of up to 40% in Yukos.[59]

In other words, Khodorkovsky, the most powerful oligarch at the time, was evidently serving as the vehicle for a Washington-backed putsch against Putin.

The 40% stake in Russia's Yukos would have given Washington, via US oil giants, a *de facto* veto power over future Russian oil and gas pipelines and oil deals. Just days before his October 2003 arrest, Khodorkovsky had entertained George H.W. Bush, who had come to Moscow on behalf of the powerful Carlyle Group, to discuss the US buy-in of Yukos. Bush discreetly resigned his position with Carlyle just after the arrest of Khodorkovsky and his partner, Platon Lebedev, chairman of Group Menatep.[60]

Khodorkovsky also served as an energy consultant to the same Washington Carlyle Group whose partners included former US Defense Secretary Frank Carlucci and former US Secretary of State, James Baker III.[61] Carlyle was known as a power firm in Washington for good reason.

At the time of Khodorkovsky's arrest, Yukos had just begun steps to acquire Sibneft, one of Russia's largest oil producing and refining groups. The combined Yukos-Sibneft enterprise, with 19.5 billion barrels of oil and gas, would then have owned the second-largest oil and gas reserves in the world after ExxonMobil. The Exxon or Chevron buy-up of Yukos-Sibneft would have been a literal energy coup d'etat. Cheney knew it; Bush knew it; Khodorkovsky knew it. Above all, Vladimir Putin knew it and moved decisively to block it.

Khodorkovsky's arrest signalled a decisive turn by the Putin government towards rebuilding Russia and erecting strategic defenses. It took place in the context of the brazen US grab for Iraq in 2003. Putin's bold move was also less than two years after the Bush Administration announced that the USA was unilaterally abrogating its treaty obligations with Russia under the earlier Anti-Ballistic Missile (ABM) Treaty in order to go ahead with development of new US missiles. This was viewed in Moscow as a clearly hostile act aimed at her security.

By 2003, it took little strategic military acumen to realize that the Pentagon hawks, and their allies in the armaments industry and Big Oil, had a vision of a United States unfettered by international agreements and acting unilaterally in its own best interests, as defined, of course, by the neo-conservative PNAC. The events in Russia were soon followed by Washington-financed covert destabilizations in Eurasia — the Color Revolutions against governments on Russia's periphery.

By the end of 2004 it was clear to Moscow that a new Cold War — this one over strategic energy control and unilateral nuclear primacy — was looming.

After 2003, Russian foreign policy, especially its energy policy, reverted to the axioms of 'Heartland' geopolitics as defined by Sir Halford Mackinder, politics which had been the basis of earlier Soviet Cold War strategy since 1946.

Putin began to make a series of defensive moves to restore some tenable form of equilibrium in the face of Washington's increasingly obvious policy of encircling and weakening Russia. Subsequent US strategic blunders made the job a bit easier for Russia. Now, with the stakes rising on both sides—NATO and Russia—Putin's Russia moved beyond simple defense to a new dynamic offensive aimed at securing a more viable geopolitical position by using its energy as the lever.

Russian Energy Geopolitics

In terms of its standard of living, mortality rates and economic prosperity, Russia in 2004 was not a world class power. In terms of energy, it was a colossus. In terms of landmass it was still the largest nation in the world, spanning from the Pacific to the door of Europe. It had vast territory, vast natural resources, and the world's largest reserves of natural gas. In addition, it was the only power on the face of the earth with the potential military capabilities to match those of the United States despite the collapse of the USSR and the deterioration in the Russian military since then.

A look at the map makes clear why the Pentagon has a geopolitical interest in bases in Afghanistan and Pakistan and in Iraq—the military control of Central Asia oil flows

Russia had more than 130,000 oil wells and some 2000 oil and gas deposits. Oil reserves had been estimated at 150 billion barrels, similar to Iraq. They could be far larger, but had not yet been exploited owing to the difficulty of drilling in remote arctic regions. Oil prices anywhere above $60 a barrel, however, made it economical to explore in those remote regions.

Russia's state-owned natural gas pipeline network, the 'unified gas transportation system,' included a vast network of pipelines and compressor stations extending more than 150,000 kilometers across Russia. By law, only the state-owned Gazprom was allowed to use the pipeline. The network was perhaps the most valued Russian state asset other than the oil and gas itself. Here was the heart of Putin's new energy geopolitics.

Already in 2001, as it became clear that the Baltic republics were about to join NATO, Putin backed development of a major new oil port on the Russian coast of the Baltic Sea in Primorsk. This Baltic Pipeline System (BPS), completed in March 2006, greatly lessened export dependency on new NATO states Latvia, Lithuania and Poland. The Baltic was Russia's main oil export route from the West Siberian and Timan-Pechora oil provinces. The BPS was now able to carry more than 1.3 million barrels/day of Russian oil to western markets.

In March 2006, former German Chancellor Gerhard Schroeder was named chairman of a private-public Russian-German consortium building a 1200 km natural gas pipeline under the Baltic.

Majority shareholder in the North European Gas Pipeline (NEGP) was the Russian state-controlled Gazprom, the world's largest natural gas company. Germany's BASF and E.On each held 24.5%. The €5 bn project was started in late 2005 and would connect the gas terminal at the Russian port city of Vyborg near St. Petersburg with Greifswald in eastern Germany. It was classic Russian geopolitics—the attempt by the Heartland to link with Central Europe. The aim of Churchill and later Truman's Cold War had been to drive a wedge, an 'iron curtain,' between central Europe and the Russian Heartland. Their aim was to make Great Britain the indispensable geopolitical mediator or power broker between the two.

The joint venture between Gazprom and BASF was Schroeder's last major act as German Chancellor. It provoked howls of protest from the pro-Washington Polish government, as well as from Ukraine, both of which stood to lose control over pipeline flows from Russia. Despite her close ties to the Bush Administration, Germany's new conservative Chancellor, Angela Merkel, was forced to swallow hard and accept the project. Russia was by far the largest supplier of natural gas to Germany—more than 40% of its total gas imports.

The giant Shtokman gas deposit in the Russian sector of the Barents Sea, north of Murmansk harbor, would also become a part of the gas supply of the NEGP. When completed in two parallel pipelines, NEGP would supply Germany with up to 55 billion cubic meters more Russian gas annually.

In April 2006, the Putin government began an East Siberia-Pacific Ocean Pipeline (ESPO), a $14 billion oil pipeline from Taishet in East Siberia, to Russia's Pacific coast. Transneft, the Russian state-owned pipeline company, was to build it. When finished, it would pump up to 1.6 million barrels a day from Siberia to the Russian Far East and from there to the energy-hungry Asia-Pacific region, mainly to China and Japan.

Additionally, China was intensely discussing with Putin a branch pipe between Blagoveshchensk and Daqing. The Taishet route provided a roadmap for energy cooperation between Russia and China, Japan and other Asia-Pacific countries.

Sakhalin: Russia Reins In Big Oil

In late September 2006, a seemingly minor dispute exploded and resulted in the revocation of the environmental permit for a Royal Dutch Shell Sakhalin II Liquified Natural Gas project, which had been due to deliver LNG to Japan, South Korea and other customers by 2008. Shell was lead energy partner in an Anglo-Japanese oil and gas development project on Russia's Far East island of Sakhalin, a vast island north of Hokkaido Japan.

The Putin government announced that environmental requirements had not been met by ExxonMobil for their oil terminal on Sakhalin as part of its Sakhalin I oil and gas development project. Sakhalin I contained an estimated 8 billion barrels of oil and vast volumes of gas, making the field a rare Super-Giant oil find, in geologists' terminology.

In the early 1990s, the Yeltsin government had made a desperate bid to attract needed Western investment capital and technology into exploiting Russian oil and gas regions at a time when the Russian government was broke and oil prices were very low. In a bold departure, Yeltsin granted US and other western oil majors generous exploration rights to two large oil projects, Sakhalin I and Sakhalin II, both under a so-called PSA or Production Sharing Agreement.

Under the terms of the PSA's, Russia would be paid for the oil and gas rights in shares of the oil or gas eventually produced, but only after all production costs had first been covered. PSA agreements with Western oil majors had previously only been made with weak Third World governments unable to demand fairer terms.

Shortly before the Russian government told ExxonMobil that it had problems with its terminal on Sakhalin, ExxonMobil had announced a 30% cost increase in the project. ExxonMobil, whose attorney, James Baker III, maintained a close partnership with the Bush-Cheney White House, knew that such a cost increase would further postpone any Russian oil flow share from the PSA. The Russian Environment Ministry in turn threatened to halt production by ExxonMobil.

Britain's Shell held rights, under another PSA, to develop oil and gas resources in Sakhalin II region, and to build Russia's first Liquified Natural Gas project. The $20 billion project employed over 17,000 people and was the world's largest integrated oil and gas project. It included Russia's first offshore oil production, as well as Russia's first offshore integrated gas platform.

The clear Russian government moves against ExxonMobil and Shell were interpreted in the energy industry as an attempt by the Putin government to regain control of Russia's oil and gas resources that Yeltsin had given away during his era.

Russia-Turkey Gas Project

In November 2005 Russia's Gazprom completed the final stage of its 1,213 kilometer, $3.2 billion Blue Stream gas pipeline. It brought Russian gas from fields in Krasnodar by way of underwater pipelines across the Black Sea to the Turkish Black Sea coast. From there, the pipeline supplied Russian gas to Ankara.

Greece, Italy and Israel all were engaged in talks with Gazprom to tap gas from the Blue Stream pipeline across Turkey. Another Russian gas route, a South-European Gas Pipeline, was being developed via Eastern and Central Europe, to establish a new international gas transmission system. Putin was using Russia's energy trump card to build economic ties across Eurasia from West to East, North to South. Washington was not at all pleased.

Moscow's Military Status

In his May 2003 Russian State of the Nation Address, Vladimir Putin spoke of strengthening and modernizing Russia's nuclear deterrent by creating new types of weapons, including some for Russia's strategic forces, which would ensure the defense capability of Russia and its allies in the long term. After the Bush Administration unilaterally declared an end to the Anti-Ballistic Missile Treaty, and *de facto* nullified the Start II Treaty in 2001, Russia stopped withdrawing and destroying its SS-18 MIRV-ed missiles.

Russia had never stopped being a powerful entity that produced state-of-the-art military technologies. While its army, navy and air force were in derelict condition at the end of the Cold War in 1990, the elements for Russia's resurgence as a military powerhouse were still in place. Russia had consistently fielded top-notch military technology at various international trade shows, using the world arms export market to keep its most vital military technology base intact.

According to a 2004 analysis by the Washington-based think tank, Power and Interest News Report (PINR), for example, one of Russia's best achievements after the dissolution of the Soviet Union had been its armored fighting vehicle, BMP-3, which was chosen over Western vehicles in contracts for the United Arab Emirates and Oman.

Russia's surface-to-air missile systems, the S-300, and its more powerful successor, the S-400, were reported to be more potent than American-made Patriot systems. A once-anticipated military exercise between the Patriot and the S-300 never materialized, leaving the Russian complex with an undisputed, yet unproven, claim of superiority over the American system.

Russia's Kamov-50 family of military helicopters incorporated the latest cutting-edge technologies and tactics, making them an equal to the best Washington had, according to European helicopter industry sources.

In 2006, joint Indo-American air force exercises, where the Indian Air Force was equipped with modern Russian-made Su-30 fighters, the Indian Air Force out-maneuvered American-made F-15 planes in a majority of their engagements, prompting US Air Force General Hal Homburg to admit that Russian technology in Indian hands gave the US Air Force a 'wake-up call.' The Russian military establishment was continuing to design other helicopters, tanks and armored vehicles that were on a par with the best that the West has to offer.[62]

Weapons exports, in addition to oil and gas, had been one of the best ways for Russia to earn much-needed hard currency in the 1990s and into the new century. Russia was the second-largest worldwide exporter of military technology after the United States. Russia's modern military technology was more likely to be exported than supplied to its own armies. That had implications for America's future combat operations since practically all insurgent, guerrilla, breakaway or armed formations across the globe — the very formations that the United States would most likely face in its future wars — were fielded with Russian weapons or their derivatives.

The Russian nuclear arsenal had also played an important political role since the end of the Soviet Union, providing fundamental security for the Russian state. In 2003, Russia had to buy from Ukraine strategic bombers and ICBMs that were warehoused there.

Since then, however, strategic nuclear forces have been a priority. By 2008, the finances of the Russian state, ironically enough, owing to extremely high prices of oil and gas exports, were on a strong footing. The Russian Central Bank had become the world's third largest dollar reserve holder behind China and Japan, with reserves of more than $500 billion.

The gradual re-emergence of a dynamic Russia in the Heartland of Eurasia, one that was growing economically closer to China and to key nations of Continental Western Europe, was the very development that Brzezinski had warned could mortally threaten American dominance. It was Halford Mackinder's worst nightmare. Ironically, Washington's bungled invasions of Iraq and of Afghanistan and its crude elaboration of its 'War on Terror' had directly helped to bring that Eurasian cooperation about. It also created the backdrop for the Georgia conflict in August 2008.

Washington obviously had encouraged the hot-headed Georgian President, Mikheil Saakashvili to invade South Ossetia, clearly knowing that Russia would be forced to intervene to draw the line in the sand against America's relentless encirclement.[63] Washington was deliberately fanning the flames of a New Cold War with Russia to drive an iron wedge between Russia and Germany, and bring the geopolitical world order back to Mackinder's original scheme, the order of the Cold War. For both America's domination of Western Europe and for Russia, Germany was a vital partner. German industry had become the major European importer of Russian natural gas and its industry depended on Russian energy. There was no viable substitute in sight.

To achieve its Full Spectrum Dominance, Washington needed not only the resources of its Color Revolutions across Central Europe to encircle Russia. The Pentagon also needed to draw the rope tight around the emerging economic colossus of Asia, namely China. There, a different approach was required, given the extreme US financial dependence on China and its economic ties and investments there. For control of China, a form of 'human rights' as a weapon of US foreign policy was to play the central role.

Endnotes:

[1] John Arquilla and David Ronfeld, *Swarming and the Future of Conflict*, Santa Monica, Ca., RAND/National Defense Research Institute, 2000, in www.rand.org/pubs/documented_briefings/2005/RAND_DB311.pdf.

[2] *Michael Dobbs,* US Advice Guided Milosevic Opposition Political Consultants Helped Yugoslav Opposition Topple Authoritarian Leader, *Washington Post, December 11, 2000.*

[3] Ibid.

[4] Ibid.

[5] Ibid.

[6] Ibid.

[7] Jonathan Mowat, *Coup d'État in Disguise: Washington's New World Order 'Democratization' Template,* February 9, 2005, in http://globalresearch.ca/articles/MOW502A.html. The author is indebted to Mowat's groundbreaking research on the role of Emery, RAND and others in creating the Color Revolution model for US-led regime coups in Eurasia.

[8]Ibid.

[9] Ibid.

[10] Ibid.

[11] William Blum, *Killing Hope: U.S. Military and CIA Interventions since World War II,* Monroe, Maine, Common Courage Press, 1995.

[12] Ibid.

[13] Steve Kangas, *A Timeline of CIA Atrocities,* accessed in www.huppi.com/kangaroo/CIAtimeline.html.

[14] William Blum, Op. Cit., p.259 discusses the CIA's immunity from prosecution for crimes including assassination and bribery.

[15] Ibid., pp.72-83.

[16] Ibid.

[17] John Marks, *The Search for the 'Manchurian Candidate': The CIA and Mind Control—The Secret History of the Behavioral Sciences,* New York, W.W. Norton & Co., 1979, p. 141.

[18] Gerard Colby and Charlotte Dennett, *Thy Will Be Done: The Conquest of the Amazon: Nelson Rockefeller and Evangelism in the Age of Oil,* New York, HarperCollins, 1995, p. 256.

[19] Jonathan Mowat, Op. Cit.

[20] Bill Cooke, *Foundations of Soft Management: Rockefeller, Barnard, and the Tavistock Institute of Human Relations,* Lancaster University Management School, accessed in http://209.85.129.132/search?q=cache:f-itMuENYSIJ:www.ncl.ac.uk/nubs/research/centres/mhrg/papers/paper13.pdf+tavistock+institute+rockefeller+foundation&hl=en&ct=clnk&cd=6.

Cooke notes, 'While Tavistock histories have been previously written, this is the first to draw on archival material which sets out the early relations between the Rockefeller and TIHR founder ATM "Tommy" Wilson in the 1930s, and shows how the Tavistock's development into a centre of social and organizational science was supported by the Rockefeller's medical research program up until the 1950s. It also situates the rise of the Tavistock in a nexus of transatlantic inter-personal relationships on the one hand, and changing UK, US, and world politics on the other.'

[21] Eric Trist and Hugh Murray, *The Social Engagement of Social Science—A Tavistock Anthology: The Foundation and Development of the Tavistock Institute to 1989*, quoted in http://everything2.com/e2node/The%2520Tavistock%2520Institute.

[22] University of Michigan Institute for Social Research, Research Center for Group Dynamics, *History*, in http://www.rcgd.isr.umich.edu/history/.

[23] A curious tiny group named Situationist International played in inordinately large role behijnd the student uprisings in May 1968 leading some researchers to posit that it was backed or steered by US intelligence. Even the powerful French Communist trade union, CGT, attempted to quell the student unrest to no avail. De Gaulle was considered a 'friend' of the Soviet Union for his opposition to US-run NATO.

[24] Jonathan Mowat, Op. Cit.

[25] Howard Perlmutter was one of the leading strategists of the US model of globalization from his work at the Wharton School of Finance at University of Pensylvania. At Wharton, he led the internationalization process as Chairman of the Multinational Enterprise Unit and Founder-Director of the Worldwide Institutions Research Center.During this time with his colleague, Tavistock's Eric Trist, he formulated his vision the Social Architecture of the Global Societal enterprise, based on this paradigm for organizations in the 21st Century.

At Wharton, he introduced research and teaching on the global social architecture of the multinational enterprise, multinational organization development, global strategic alliances, global cities, and the globalization of education, in a course called Cross cultural management in the context of the First Global Civilization. Cited in http://www.deepdialog.com/dr_perlmutter/index.html.

[26] John Arquilla and David Ronfeldt, *In Athena's Camp: Preparing for Conflict in the Information Age*, Santa Monica, CA: RAND, MR-880-OSD/RC, 1997.

[27] Mark Ames, *Georgia Update: The Not-So-Great Game*, accessed in http://www.mail-archive.com/srpskainformativnamreza@yahoogroups.com/msg07366.html.

[28] Ibid.

[29] Jonathan Mowat, Op. Cit.

[30] Ibid.

[31] Ibid.

[32] Amitabh Pal, *Gene Sharp: The Progressive Interview*, The Progressive, March 1, 2007.

[33] Ibid.

[34] SourceWatch, *Open Society Institute*, cited in
http://www.sourcewatch.org/index.php?title=Soros_Foundation.

[35] Jonathan Mowat, Op. Cit.

[36] The Albert Einstein Institution, in http://www.aeinstein.org/.

[37] Albert Einstein Institution, *Report on Activities*, 1993-1999, accessed in
http://www.aeinstein.org/organizationsda9f.html.

[38] SourceWatch, *Albert Einstein Institution*, in
http://www.sourcewatch.org/index.php?title=Albert_Einstein_Institution#Advisors_.281
993-1999.29.

[39] US Department of State, *John E. Herbst Biography*, accessed in
http://www.state.gov/r/pa/ei/biog/67065.htm.

[40] Kateryna Yushchenko, *Biography*, on My Ukraine: Personal Website of Viktor Yushchenko, 31 March 2005, accessed in
http://www.yuschenko.com.ua/eng/Private/Family/2822/.

[41] Orange Revolution in Wikipedia, accessed in
http://en.wikipedia.org/wiki/Orange_Revolution.

[42] Andrew Osborn, *We Treated Poisoned Yushchenko, Admit Americans*, The Independent
U.K., March 12, 2005, accessed in http://www.truthout.org/article/us-played-big-role-
ukraines-orange-revolution.

[43] Dmitry Sudakov, *USA Assigns $20 million for Elections in Ukraine, Moldova*, Pravda.ru,
11 March 2005.

[44]'Nicholas,' *Forces Behind the Orange Revolution*, Kiev Ukraine News Blog , January 10,
2005 accessed in http://blog.kievukraine.info/2005/01/forces-behind-orange-
revolution.html.

[45] James R. Woolsey, World *War IV: A speech by the Honorable James R. Woolsey* former
Director of the Central Intelligence Agency, November 16, 2002, accessed in
http://www.globalsecurity.org/military/library/report/2002/021116-ww4.htm.

[46] Freedom House, *2004 Annual Report, Our Partners*, p. 37.

[47] Nicholas Thompson, This Ain't Your Mama's CIA, Washington Monthly, March 2001.
Thompson describes the creation of the National Endowment for Democracy and the
Reagan Administration's related 'Project Democracy: *'Ronald Reagan loved subversion,
and he empowered CIA director William Casey to covertly organize a war in Nicaragua.
But Reagan's more lasting legacy comes from his recognition that the weakness of communism could be exploited by international institution building. Reagan proclaimed in
1982 that "The march of freedom and democracy will leave Marxism-Leninism on the ash
heap of history," and set in motion a major movement that led to the creation of a number
of QUANGOs (quasi-nongovernmental organizations) like the National Endowment for
Democracy (NED) that worked to build democratic opposition abroad. In a way, NED was
chartered to do what the CIA used to do, only working bottom up and helping activists
instead of working top down and lopping off heads.*

'Reagan also worked inside the White House, pulling Walt Raymond, a top-ranking CIA official, over from Langley to organize what the president called "Project Democracy."As part of the project, the United States Information Agency (USIA) began to cook up plans that, except for their openness, seemed like the old CIA. In the summer of 1982, USIA organized democracy-building seminars for African colonels, voting technique lessons for Peruvians, and conferences on freedom for the press in the Philippines and Romania. Cultural ambassadors were even sent by USIA from universities to travel around and preach Reagan's gospel of democracy, and in what Vaclav Havel would say was the most important thing the United States did for his country, USIA beamed the Voice of America and Radio Free Europe into Czechoslovakia. Simultaneously, the CIA sent millions of dollars to the Solidarity movement in Poland by way of the international arm of the AFL-CIO.'

[48] David Ignatius, *Openness Is the Secret to Democracy*, Washington Post National Weekly Edition, 30 September-6 October,1991, 24-25.

[49] Eva Golinger, *The Proof is in the Documents: The CIA Was Involved in the Coup Against Venezuelan President Chavez*, accessed in http://www.venezuelafoia.info/english.html.

[50] Political Research Associates, Right Web, *Profile Carl Gershman*, accessed in http://rightweb.irc-online.org/profile/1199.html.

[51] Scoop Independent News, *Otto Reich Named on Board to Oversee SOA*, May 3, 2002, accessed in http://www.scoop.co.nz/stories/WO0205/S00006.htm.

[52] Zbigniew Brzezinski, *A Geostrategy for Eurasia*, Foreign Affairs, September/ October 1997.

[53] F. William Engdahl, *A Century of War: Anglo-American Oil Politics and the New World Order*, London, Pluto Press, 2004, pp.253-255.

[54] George W. Bush, *President Addresses and Thanks Citizens in Tbilisi, Georgia*, May 10, 2005, accessed in http://www.state.gov/p/eur/rls/rm/45891.htm

[55] Dick Cheney, *Remarks to the London Institute of Petroleum Autumn Lunch*, September 1999, published by the Institute of Petroleum June 8, 2004 and subsequently removed from their own website. Archived and reprinted in full at http://www.energybulletin.net/node/559.

[56] Donald Kagan et al, *Rebuilding America's Defenses: Strategy, Forces and Resources For a New Century*, September 2000, The Project for the New American Century (PNAC), Washington, D.C., p. 61, in www.newamericancentury.org/RebuildingAmericasDefenses.pdf.

[57] Ibid.

[58] Dmitry Slobodanuk, *The State Determined to Own Oil and Gas*, Pravda, September 23, 2003.

[59] Tanvir Ahmad Khan, *Russia's Return to Centre Stage*, Dawn, February 26, 2007, accessed in http://www.dawn.com/2007/02/26/op.htm

[60] Greg Schneider, *Arrested Russian Businessman Is Carlyle Group Adviser*, November 10, 2003, The Washington Post.

[61] Ibid.

[62] Yvgeny Bendersky, *"Keep a Watchful Eye on Russia's Military Technology,"* Power & Interest News Report, July 21, 2004.

[63] Russia Today, *Saakashvili: we started the war*, November 28, 2008, Russia Today, accessed in http://www.russiatoday.com/news/news/33939. See also, Oleysa Vartanyan and Ellen Barry, Ex-Diplomat Says Georgia Started War With Russia, November 25, 2008, The New York Times, accessed in http://www.nytimes.com/2008/11/26/world/europe/26georgia.html?_r=1&partner=rss&emc=rss. The Times reports that, 'Erosi Kitsmarishvili, Tbilisi's former ambassador to Moscow, testifying before a Georgian Congressional Commission, 'said Georgian officials told him in April that they planned to start a war in Abkhazia, one of two breakaway regions at issue in the war, and had received a green light from the United States government to do so. He said the Georgian government later decided to start the war in South Ossetia, the other region, and continue into Abkhazia.'

CHAPTER THREE

Controlling China
with Synthetic Democracy

'What happens with the distribution of power on the Eurasian landmass will be of decisive importance to America's global primacy....'
  – *Zbigniew Brzezinski*

'Different Strokes For Different Folks...'

Fundamental US military and geopolitical strategy towards the People's Republic of China never deviated from its core purpose in the entire period from 1945 until 2008. Its tactics varied considerably, however, between what could be called 'big stick' diplomacy and 'carrot-and-stick' diplomacy. The former used direct military threats; the latter involved something slightly more seductive, but every bit as dangerous in the long run for Chinese sovereignty. The overall American strategy of 'divide and conquer' remained at all times.

That strategy had its roots in the axioms of geopolitics, the axioms of British Royal Geographer, Sir Halford Mackinder. For Mackinder, the prime objective of both British and later, of United States, foreign policy and military policy was to prevent a unity, whether natural or un-natural, between the two great powers of the Eurasian landmass—Russia and China.[1]

Most leading American policy elites in and around the influential Council on Foreign Relations (CFR) were schooled in Mackinder's geopolitical strategy. They included former Beijing ambassador Winston Lord, a former aide to Henry Kissinger who prepared Nixon's policy change toward China in 1972; former CIA Director and Ambassador to

Beijing, George Herbert Walker Bush; and Bush's longtime CIA crony, China Ambassador, James R. Lilley. Both Secretary of State Henry Kissinger and former National Security Adviser, Zbigniew Brzezinski were advocates of Mackinder geopolitics. For obvious reasons, their debt to Mackinder was rarely admitted openly.[2]

Post-war American policy makers were drawn from a relatively small number of privileged families. Most of them were part of the influential circle around the Rockefeller family, especially John D. III and his banker brother, David Rockefeller. It was this particular group that determined postwar US-China policy.

Their goal was always to maintain a strategy of tension across Asia, and particularly in Eurasia. For example, the US would threaten Japan with the loss of US military protection if it did not follow US policy wishes, and it would seduce China by outsourcing US manufacture to China, while actually providing failing American manufacturers with huge profits.

Regardless of the tactics used, the end goal of US China Policy was the maintenance of control over China as the potential economic colossus of Asia—over its energy development, its food security, its economic development, its defense policy...its very future.

By 2007, US control of China was becoming increasingly difficult, as the military forces of the United States were badly over-committed in ill-conceived wars and occupations in Iraq and Afghanistan.

Washington policy, while still based on advancing US military hegemony, increasingly shifted to masquerading behind the issues of human rights and 'democracy' as weapons of psychological and economic warfare in its ongoing attempt to contain and control China and its foreign policy.

Africom: Pentagon's 'Resource War' Strategy

In November 2006, China hosted an unprecedented summit on economic cooperation, investment and trade with at least 45 African heads of state. Washington would not be long in responding to the new Chinese interest in Africa. By June 2007 the Bush Administration and senior Pentagon officials had authorized creation of the special Africa division, AFRICOM, to be headquartered in Stuttgart, Germany.

Why, after neglecting Africa – other than South Africa, or oil rich Nigeria, Angola and Mozambique — for more than five decades did Washington now place such a high priority on Africa? And why did the US commitment require the added expense of an autonomous military command for the continent?

Was 'terrorism' a reason for the US to deploy a separate military command within striking range of some 53 countries on the African subcontinent? No. The creation of AFRICOM was Washington's response to its increasing loss of control over Africa's raw materials. China, not terrorism, was the unspoken reason for the new US military concern over Africa.

On October 1, 2008, amid the chaos of collapsing US financial markets, the Pentagon launched its separate new military Command, USAFRICOM or simply, AFRICOM.

The United States Africa Command (AFRICOM), was a new Unified Combat Command of the United States Department of Defense. It was to be responsible for US military operations and military relations with 53 African nations.

Resource Wars: The '2008 Army Modernization Strategy'

Full explanation for this new deployment lay in the Pentagon document, *2008 Army Modernization Strategy.* That document stated that the objective of US Army strategy was to span and dominate the entire universe, not just the globe. It called for "an expeditionary, campaign-quality Army capable of dominating across the full spectrum of conflict, at any time, in any environment and against any adversary—for extended periods of time." [3] The document went on, "the Army must concentrate its equipping and modernization efforts on two mutually supporting ends—restoring balance and achieving full-spectrum

Dominance." [4]

No other army in history had had such ambitious goals.

Most relevant, *Army Modernization* envisioned that the United States, for at least the next "thirty to forty years," would be engaged in continuous wars to control raw materials.

Moreover, in a clear reference to China and Russia, the Pentagon's strategic plan declared: "We face a potential return to traditional security threats posed by emerging near-peers as we compete globally for depleting natural resources and overseas markets."[5]

In terms of economic growth, the only "emerging near peer" on the planet in 2008 was China, which was scrambling and scouring the earth for secure sources of oil, metals, and other raw materials to sustain its dramatic growth projections.

In terms of military and energy supplies, the only potential "emerging near peer" would be Russia. Russia played a strategic role in delivering virtually every vital resource required for an advanced industrial economy – everything from oil and gas to metals and raw materials. Russia was the key supplier, outside South and southern African states, of strategic resources not under the direct control of the United States. Russia's increasing role in Africa had been a major factor behind Washington's confrontational military policy of using NATO to encircle Russia since 1991.

The major concern in Pentagon and Washington policy circles was that Russia and China would deepen their economic and even military cooperation, most likely within the framework of the Shanghai Cooperation Organization. Were that to happen, as Zbigniew Brzezinski had stated, the global supremacy of the United States would be fundamentally challenged.[6]

The Pentagon's *2008 Army Modernization Strategy* was an extension of the doctrine elaborated by the DOD's reclusive futuristic strategic planner, Andrew Marshall. Marshall, a senior RAND Corporation analyst brought into the Pentagon in 1973, had been named by President Nixon to head a specially created, strategic Office of Net Assessments in the Pentagon. Marshall was given a unique and unheard-of status in the chain of command: he reported only to the Secretary of Defense, with no intermediaries in the Pentagon chain-of-command.

Over the years, Marshall, still in charge of long-term Pentagon strategy despite his 87 years of age, had spawned cadre of disciples to implement his so-called Revolution in Military Affairs (RMA). He numbered among his proteges Dick Cheney, Donald Rumsfeld, Paul Wolfowitz, Richard Perle and numerous other war hawks. It was Marshall who had convinced Rumsfeld and Cheney in 2001 that strategic ballistic missile defense installations on the borders of Russia would give the United States its long-dreamed-of Nuclear Primacy, the ability to launch a nuclear first strike attack on Russia and destroy their ability to retaliate.[7]

The pursuit of Nuclear Primacy by the US was the real reason why Russia responded so strongly in August 2008 to a seemingly peripheral provocation in South Ossetia; it was also behind the US desire to bring Ukraine into NATO.

Marshall was the architect of Rumsfeld's disastrous 'electronic battlefield' strategy in the Iraq war—using 'networked' soldiers wired to the Internet and equipped with GPS reconnaissance. Yet when criticism forced the President to dump Rumsfeld, Marshall remained at the Pentagon, untouched; such was his power.

US Plans 'Perpetual Resource Warfare'

The Pentagon's *2008 Army Modernization Strategy* revealed a number of profoundly significant strategic principles and operating assumptions that had already been adopted as official doctrine by the US military. In its preamble, it predicted a post-Cold War future of 'perpetual warfare.'

The Pentagon official responsible for the document, General Stephen Speakes, asserted in the Foreword:

> *This 2008 document is radically different from previous years. This year we get right to the heart of things with a brief description of our modernization strategy—with the ends, ways and means of how we intend to use the Army Equipping Enterprise to reach end of state defined as: Soldiers equipped with the best equipment available, making the Army the most*

dominant land power in the world, with full spectrum capa-bilities.

America is engaged in an era of persistent conflict that will continue to stress our force. To win this fight, we need an Army that is equipped for the long haul—that has what it needs for soldiers to accomplish their missions across the full spectrum of conflict.[8]

The Pentagon paper emphasized, "We have entered an era of persistent conflict . . . a security environment much more ambiguous and unpredictable than that faced during the Cold War."

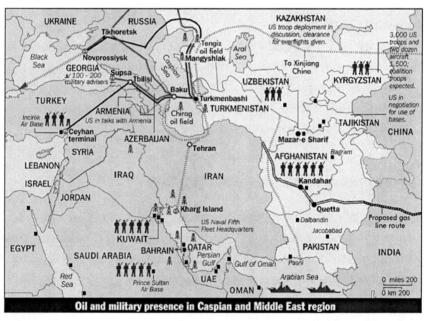

Oil and military presence in Caspian and Middle East region

Mideast Oil Pipelines and Bases

It described the key features of its planned era of continuous warfare, including, the usual rhetoric about terrorists using weapons of mass destruction. Significantly, and for the first time since Henry Kissinger's National Security Strategic Memorandum-200 during the Ford Administration, the US Army stated that among its official 'missions' was the control of population growth in raw material rich countries.[9]

The 2008 document cited 'population growth' as the predominant threat to the security of the US and its allies, and it called for wars to control raw material resources. It linked the two:

> *Population growth—especially in less-developed countries— will expose a resulting 'youth bulge' to anti-government and radical ideologies that potentially threaten government stability.*
>
> *Resource competition induced by growing populations and expanding economies will consume ever increasing amounts of food, water and energy. States or entities controlling these resources will leverage them as part of their security calculus. (emphasis added-w.e.)[10]*

The two official priorities for the Pentagon — controlling the population 'youth bulge' in resource-rich developing countries, and preventing China and Russia from controlling the food, water and energy of the developing world — were the motives for the creation of AFRICOM.

Never before had US foreign policy contemplated or imagined that such a force would be necessary; the United States had thought it controlled Africa's resources. But within weeks of Beijing's 2006 reception for heads of more than 40 African nations, George W. Bush signed the Presidential Order creating AFRICOM.

During the Cold War, US control of Africa and its vast mineral wealth had relied on assassination and civil wars which it covertly fuelled, or the cooperation of brutal former colonial powers such as Britain, France, Portugal or Belgium. Washington was more than alarmed to see 43 African heads of state treated with respect and dignity by China, who offered them billions of dollars worth of trade agreements rather than IMF conditions or US-imposed austerity programs.[11]

From Darfur, where China's state oil company had won a major oil exploration concession from the Sudan government, to Nigeria and Chad and South Africa, Washington was moving to try to counter growing Chinese influence across Africa.

Having identified increasing populations in the developing world as a threat, the 2008 Pentagon strategy document highlighted specific paradigm shifts in the way future wars were to be conducted:

> *The Army recently unveiled its newest doctrine, FM 3-0 Operations, which provides a blueprint for operating in an uncertain future, and serves as a principal driver for changes in our organizations, training, leader development, personnel policies, facilities and materiel development.*
>
> *FM 3-0 institutionalizes how commanders employ offensive, defensive and stability or civil support operations simultaneously. FM 3-0 acknowledges the fact that 21st Century operations will require Soldiers to engage among populations and diverse cultures instead of avoiding them.*[12]

In a sense the Pentagon was officially announcing the end of the 'Vietnam war syndrome' which dictated that US soldiers not be put at risk on the ground, leaving combat restricted primarily to air strikes, as had been the case in both Iraq wars, and Afghanistan in early 2002.

'Human Rights' As A Weapon Of War

Unlike the US policy of sabre rattling against Russia's potential threat, US policy towards China's economic emergence across Asia, Africa and beyond, incorporated unexpected weapons of war—'Human Rights' and 'Democracy.' Atypical as weapons of warfare, 'Democracy' and 'Human Rights' were a 21st Century version of the 1840 Opium Wars— tactics aimed at forcing China to open itself up to full US Superpower domination.[13] That was something, of course, the Chinese Government did not welcome in any way.

Between 1999 and 2006, the United States government "made available or authorized roughly $110 million for democracy-related programs in China," according to an official US Congressional report.[14]

The Congressional Research report added,

The consolidated appropriations act for FY2000 (P.L. 106-113) provided $1 million for U.S.-based NGOs (to preserve cultural traditions and promote sustainable development and environmental conservation) in Tibet as well as $1 million to support research about China, and authorized ESF for NGOs to promote democracy in China. For FY2001 (P.L. 106- 429), Congress authorized up to $2 million for Tibet. In FY2002 (P.L. 107-115), Congress made available $10 million for assistance for activities to support democracy, human rights, and the rule of law in China and Hong Kong, including up to $3 million for Tibet. In FY2003 (P.L. 108-7), Congress provided $15 million for democracy-related programs in China, including up to $3 million for Tibet and $3 million for the National Endowment for Democracy (NED).[15]

According to this report, US aid, appropriated by Congress to promote democracy in China, including Tibet, ballooned from $2,435,000 in Fiscal Year 2000 to $33,695,000 by FY2006. That was an increase of well over 1400% within six years. Clearly Washington was getting ever keener to promote its special version of 'democracy' in China, especially in Tibet.

Significantly, in 2004, within the US State Department, "the Bureau of Democracy, Human Rights and Labor became the principal administrator of China democracy programs."[16] That Bureau lay within the domain of the US State Department's Under Secretary for Democracy and Global Affairs, headed by Dr. Paula J. Dobriansky. As the official website for the US Department of State noted:

Since her appointment in 2001, Under Secretary Dobriansky has also served concurrently as the Special Coordinator for Tibetan Issues. In this capacity, she is the US government's point person on Tibet policy matters, including: support for dialogue between the Chinese and the Dalai Lama or his representatives; promotion of human rights in Tibet; and efforts to preserve Tibet's unique cultural, religious and linguistic identity.[17]

Paula Dobriansky received her doctorate from Harvard University in Soviet military and political affairs. She came to her State Department position from her post as Senior Vice President and Director of the Washington Office of the Council on Foreign Relations, where she was the first George F. Kennan Senior Fellow for Russian and Eurasian Studies. She had also been awarded a National Endowment for Democracy (NED) 'Democracy Service Medal' and the International Republican Institute's 'Jeanne Kirkpatrick Award.' Both the NED and IRI, as documented earlier, were the US State Department's primary vehicles to promote pro-US regime changes around the world.

Dobriansky's ties to the NED had not been casual. Her official biography noted that she had served as NED Vice Chairman before coming to the State Department, as well as serving as a member of the Board of Directors of Freedom House, headed in 2006 by former CIA Director James Woolsey and including Zbigniew Brzezinski on its board. Moreover, Dobriansky had been a senior Fellow of the Hudson Institute, one of the most strident neo-conservative and hawkish think-tanks in Washington.

Paula Dobriansky was also a member of another neo-conservative think-tank, the Project for a New American Century (PNAC).[18] In that capacity, Dobriansky, echoing PNAC, "championed America's 'unique role in preserving and extending an international order friendly to our security, our prosperity, and our principles.'"[19]

Dobriansky also signed PNAC's January 26, 1998, letter to President Bill Clinton which urged the President to attack Iraq at that time, almost five years before Operation Shock & Awe, arguing that containment had failed. The PNAC letter bluntly asserted:

> *The only acceptable strategy is one that eliminates the possibility that Iraq will be able to use or threaten to use weapons of mass destruction. In the near term, this means a willingness to undertake military action as diplomacy is clearly failing. In the long term, it means removing Saddam Hussein and his regime from power.'[20]*

Dobriansky's fellow co-signers of PNAC's Open Letter on Iraq included a Who's Who of senior officials in the post-Clinton Administration of George W. Bush, including: Secretary of Defense Donald Rumsfeld; US Trade Representative, later World Bank head, Robert Zoellick; Deputy Secretary of State Richard Armitage; Deputy Secretary of

Defense Paul Wolfowitz and later World Bank president; Under Secretary of State John Bolton; Assistant Secretary of Defense Peter Rodman; and National Security Council senior officials Elliott Abrams and Zalmay Khalilzad. [21]

From her post in the State Department, not surprisingly, Dobriansky was an aggressive public supporter of the (US Government-financed) Color Revolutions. Dobriansky was fond of quoting George W. Bush's Inauguration speech calling for spreading "democratic movements and institutions in every nation and culture ... [and] ending tyranny in our world."[22] In late February 2005, reacting to anti-Syria demonstrations in Lebanon, Dobriansky claimed: "As the president noted in Bratislava just last week, there was a rose revolution in Georgia, an orange revolution in Ukraine and, most recently, a purple revolution in Iraq. In Lebanon, we see growing momentum for a cedar revolution."[23]

Paula Dobriansky's role after 2004 was, among other things, to control US State Department activities and organizations, including US-based NGOs, in Tibet. The focus on Tibet had clearly been part of a long-term Washington strategy of upping the pressure on Beijing.

Democracy And Raw Materials

The main US targets in the new 'Opium War' against China, euphemistically termed 'promotion of democracy,' were China's vital sources of raw materials. Specifically, the US targeted Myanmar, Sudan, and China itself – through the Dalai Lama organizations in Tibet and the Falun Gong 'religious' sect inside China. To accomplish their goal, the US clandestine intelligence services turned to an arsenal of NGOs they had carefully built up, using the battle cry of 'human rights violations' and weakening of 'democracy.'

This approach was part of a highly effective method of 'soft warfare' developed since the 1980's by US intelligence agencies to disarm and destabilize regimes it deemed 'uncooperative.' Countries to be targeted were singled out and repeatedly charged — typically in a massive international media assault led by CNN and BBC — as violators of 'human rights.' The definition of human rights, of course, was contrived by the accusing country, the United States, which itself remained immune to similar charges. It was a controlled game in which US agencies, from the State Department to the intelligence community, worked behind the façade of a handful of extremely influential, allegedly 'neutral' and 'nonpartisan' NGOs.

In the 1980s, during the presidency of Ronald Reagan, US intelligence agencies and the State Department spent billions of dollars to create an elaborate and sophisticated global network of NGOs and ostensibly philanthropic organizations. NGOs and 'foundations' would serve US strategy as a flank in its effort to bring the entire planet under its Full Spectrum Dominance. One Australian researcher of the process, Michael Barker, called it "the Project for a New American Humanitarianism, a human rights offensive."[24]

The project had evolved by the dawn of the new Century into one of the most effective weapons to extend the influence of American global dominance. It had also managed to avoid major media scrutiny in the Western press. Barker described the concerted US deployment of various 'human rights and pro-'democracy' front organizations it funded, from the National Endowment for Democracy to Human Rights Watch and the Open Society Institutes:

> *The loose collection of concerned activists that coalesce within the Project for a New American Humanitarianism help sustain imperialism by both providing it with 'moral cover' and sanctioning the abandonment of the rule of law in the purported interest of human rights.*[25]

That was the weapon unleashed by Washington to force regime change in Myanmar, in a destabilization modelled on the color revolutions that Washington had used to bring corrupt, Washington-friendly despots to power in Georgia and Ukraine in 2004.

It was to become known as the 'Saffron Revolution' in Mayanmar, in reference to the saffron robes of the protesting Buddhist monks. In Tibet, it was called the 'Crimson Revolution.' In Sudan it was called simply 'genocide.' In each case, the power of the Pentagon and US intelligence services, in coordination with the State Department and select Non-Government Organizations such as the National Endowment for Democracy, were involved in the 'weaponizing' of human rights to extend the control of US interests and prevent the rise of 'emerging near-peers,' specifically China and Russia.

Endnotes:

[1] By far the most influential foreign policy strategist of both Great Britain and later the United States from 1904 until his death in 1947, Halford Mackinder formulated the famous Heartland Theory which argued that the geography of the heart of the Eurasian continent, centered on Russia, was the key threat to Britain's continued domination. An ardent British imperialist, Mackinder wrote a little-known but enormously influential policy recommendation for the emerging American empire in the magazine of the New York Council on Foreign Relations, its July 1943 issue, titled *The Round War and the Winning of the Peace*. In that article, as it was clear the United States would emerge as the successor to the British Empire as global hegemon, Mackinder cites his landmark 1904 thesis, *The Geographical Pivot of History*, describing the threat to British hegemony of a unification of either Germany with Russia (something British diplomacy avoided by encouraging Hitler to march east). He then went on to argue that were another power to replace that central or 'pivot' role as he termed it, of Russia as Heartland, the effect for British hegemony would be equal: 'Were the Chinese, for instance...to overthrow the Russian Empire and conquer its territory, they might constitute the yellow peril (sic) to the world's freedom just because they would add an oceanic frontage to the resources of the great continent.' While in 1943 Mackinder and his US colleagues who drafted the United Nations structure, saw China playing a key role as a counter to the Soviet Union Heartland, that changed significantly when the Peoples' Republic of China was established in October 1949. US policy then shifted to containment using a fabricated war in Korea beginning 1950 and the Vietnam or Second Indochina War which began in 1959 and ended in humiliating defeat for the United States in 1975. The shift in policy that began with the 1972 Nixon-Kissinger trip to Beijing was an attempt to influence China through economic dependency on US and Western investment and capital goods. By the end of the Century, some circles in the US elites began to fear that economic strategy risked creating an economic superpower in Asia that the United States could not control. Beginning the Bush-Cheney Administration in 2001 US China policy began a marked shift to a more aggressive confrontation course. The US NATO bombing of the Chinese Embassy in Belgrade in May 1999 was a deliberate strike to signal changing US policy, ever so gradually, towards China.

[2] *In his revealing 1997 book,* The Grand Chessboard: American Primacy and its Geo-strategic Imperatives, *Brzezinski, who was a life-long Polish revanchist against Russia, openly praised Mackinder, though, amusingly enough, he carelessly misstated his first name as Harold instead of Halford Mackinder. In the book, Brzezinski, a decades-long part of the Rockefeller faction and in 2008 foreign policy adviser to Barack Obama, wrote,* "...the three grand imperatives of imperial geostrategy are to prevent collusion and

maintain security dependence among the vassals (sic), to keep tributaries pliant and protected, and to keep the barbarians from coming together." *(Brzezinski, Op. Cit., p.40.). For Brzezinski, the most worrisome 'barbarians' he sought to prevent coming together were the two Eurasian powers, China and Russia.*

[3] Stephen M. Speakes, Lt. Gen., 2008 *ARMY MODERNIZATION STRATEGY*, 25 July 2008, Department of the Army, Washington D.C., 7.

[4] Ibid., 9.

[5] Ibid., 5,6.

[6] Brzezinski, Op. Cit.

[7] See Chapter Seven: *A Revolution in Military Affairs?* for a full listing of Marshall's protégés.

[8] Ibid., Foreword.

[9] For a more detailed description of Kissinger's 1975 document, NSSM-200, see F. William Engdahl, *Seeds of Destruction: The Hidden Agenda of Genetic Manipulation*, pp.56-60.

[10] Ibid., 6.

[11] *China Daily*, "China offers package of aid measures for Africa," November 4, 2006, in www.chinadaily.com.cn.

[12] Ibid., 7.

[13] During the 1840's, the private British merchant company, the British East India Company, backed by the military power of the Royal Navy, launched a series of military operations to literally force opium addiction on the Chinese population as a part of a colonialization strategy that left the Chinese state bankrupt and morally devastated. By the 1880's China had an estimated 40 million addicts. It was far the most lucrative business in the world for the select City of London and US merchants and banks. The scars of that humiliation according to discussions with numerous Chinese intellectuals still shape Chinese perceptions of Western morality.

[14] Thomas Lum, *US-Funded Assistance Programs in China*, Congressional Research Service, Washington, D.C., RS22663, May 18, 2007.

[15] Ibid., CRS-3.

[16] Ibid., CRS-3.

[17] US Department of State, *Under Secretary for Democracy and Global Affairs*. http://www.state.gov/g/.

[18] See Appendix A for details on the PNAC, which included as members Dick Cheney, Jeb Bush, Donald Rumsfeld and Paul Wolfowitz when PNAC issued a controversial September 2000 report, *Rebuilding America's Defenses*, which among other items called for regime change against Saddam Hussein, one year prior to September 11, 2001, and for US missile defense.

[19] *Right Web,* "Profile: Paula Dobriansky," http://rightweb.irc-online.org/profile/1120.html.

[20] Project for the New American Century, "Letter to President Bill Clinton," January 26, 1998, http://web.archive.org/web/20070810113947/www.newamericancentury.org/iraqclintonletter.htm.

[21] Ibid.

[22] Bureau of International Information Programs, U.S. Department of State: http://usinfo.state.gov. http://usinfo.org/wf-archive/2005/050510/epf204.htm.

[23] Timothy Garton Ash, "Cedar Revolution," *Guardian* [UK], March 3, 2005 (http://www.guardian.co.uk/ politics/2005/mar/03/foreignpolicy.syria).

[24] Michael Barker, "The Project for a New American Humanitarianism," *Swans Commentary*, August 25, 2008 (www.swans.com/library/art14/barker04.html).

[25] Ibid.

CHAPTER FOUR

Weaponizing Human Rights: Darfur to Myanmar to Tibet

"A lot of what we do today was done covertly 25 years ago by the CIA."
  — *-Allen Weinstein, who helped create the National Endowment for Democracy (NED).*[1]

Myanmar: The Saffron Revolution

By the time of the US decision to force regime change in Iraq — a decision actually made well before the September 11, 2001 attacks — US policy was already beginning to change towards China. However, as noted earlier, unlike US policy towards an economically weakened but still militarily formidable Russia, US policy towards China pursued what some called 'soft power' options. The main weapons of US pressure on China would be assertions regarding 'democracy' and 'human rights.' It sounded paradoxical. It wasn't.

A major application of Washington's new human rights offensive against China focused on Myanmar, on Tibet, and on Darfur in oil-rich southern Sudan.

A major US 'human rights' destabilization campaign to try to tighten the noose around China first came in September-October 2007, aimed at Myanmar, formerly the British colony, Burma. (The US government still prefers to call it Burma, despite the official rejection of that name by the government of Myanmar.) At that time, CNN ran images of saffron-robed Buddhist Monks streaming through the streets of Myanmar's former capital city Rangoon (Yangon) and calling for more democracy. Behind the scenes, however, was a battle of major geopolitical consequence.

The tragedy of Myanmar/Burma, whose land area was about the size of George W. Bush's Texas ranch, was that its population was being used as a human stage prop in a drama that had been scripted in Washington. The spectacle unfolding on CNN had been written and produced by the combined efforts of the National Endowment for Democracy (NED), George Soros's Open Society Institute, Freedom House, and Gene Sharp's Albert Einstein Institution. These NGOs functioned as US military and intelligence-connected assets. They were used to train cadre in 'non-violent' regime change around the world on behalf of the US strategic agenda. They were the same NGOs and organizations that had been used in the Color Revolutions surrounding Russia — in Georgia, Ukraine, and Serbia.

Burma's 'Saffron Revolution,' like Ukraine's 'Orange Revolution' or Georgia's 'Rose Revolution,' was a well-orchestrated exercise in Washington-run regime change. It replicated the methods and gimmicks of the prior Color Revolutions: using 'hit-and-run' protests by 'swarming' mobs of Buddhists in saffron robes; creating internet blogs and mobile text-messaging links among protest groups; deploying well-organized protest cells which dispersed and re-formed on command.

CNN blundered at one point during a September 2007 broadcast, by mentioning the active presence of the NED behind the protests in Myanmar.[2] In fact the US State Department admitted to supporting the activities of the NED in Myanmar. The NED was a US Government-funded 'private' entity, as previously noted, whose activities were designed to support US foreign policy objectives. The idea was to accomplish what the CIA had done during the Cold War, but under the cover of a seemingly innocent NGO.

On October 30, 2003 the State Department issued a formal Press Release stating:

> *The restoration of democracy in Burma is a priority US policy objective in Southeast Asia. To achieve this objective, the United States has consistently supported democracy activists and their efforts both inside and outside Burma...The United States also supports organizations such as the National En-*

dowment for Democracy, the Open Society Institute and In-
ternews, working inside and outside the region on a broad
range of democracy promotion activities.[3]

A priority US policy objective in Southest Asia? It all sounded very noble and self-effacing of the State Department. Their 'democracy promoting activities' however had a sinister hidden agenda. They were aimed directly at Beijing's regional security, including energy security.

As in the Balkans and Central Asia, the US State Department had recruited and trained key opposition leaders from numerous antigovernment organizations in Myanmar. It had poured the huge sum (for Myanmar) of more than $2.5 million annually into NED activities promoting regime change in Myanmar since at least 2003. The US regime change operation, its 'Saffron Revolution,' was run — according to the State Department's own admission – primarily out of the US Consulate in nearby Chiang Mai, Thailand, where the government was more hospitable to US military and intelligence presence.[4]

The State Department and the NED funded key opposition media, including the *New Era Journal, Irrawaddy* and the Democratic Voice of Burma radio.[5]

The concert-master — or more correctly perhaps, theoretician — of the non-violent regime change by Saffron-clad monks was Gene Sharp, founder of the deceptively-named Albert Einstein Institution in Cambridge Massachusetts. Sharp's Albert Einstein Institution was itself, as previously noted, funded by an arm of the US Congress' NED; its purpose was to foster US-friendly regime change in key spots around the world.[6]

Sharp's institute had been active in Burma since 1989, just after the regime massacred some 3000 protestors to silence the opposition. CIA special operative and former US Military attaché in Rangoon, Col. Robert Helvey, an expert in clandestine operations, introduced Sharp to Burma in 1989. Helvey wanted Sharp to train the Burmese opposition in non-violent tactics.

According to the Institution, Sharp's book, *From Dictatorship to Democracy*, was "originally published in 1993 in Thailand for distribution among Burmese dissidents. *From Dictatorship to Democracy* has since spread to several parts of the world. It is a serious introduction to the use of nonviolent action to topple dictatorships."[7]

At the time of the attempted Saffron Revolution in 2007, London's *Financial Times* described Gene Sharp's role in the Burma events, which Sharp's Institution quoted at length on its own website. According to the *Financial Times*:

> *Over the last three years, activists from the exile movement's 'political defiance committee' have trained an estimated 3,000 fellow-Burmese from all walks of life – including several hundred Buddhist monks – in philosophies and strategies of non-violent resistance and community organising. These workshops, held in border areas and drawing people from all over Burma, were seen as 'training the trainers,' who would go home and share these ideas with others yearning for change.*

> *That preparation – along with material support such as mobile phones – helped lay the groundwork for dissident Buddhist monks in September to call for a religious boycott of the junta, precipitating the biggest anti-government protests in two decades. For 10 dramatic days, monks and lay citizens, infuriated by deepening impoverishment and pervasive repression, poured into the streets in numbers that peaked at around 100,000 before the regime crushed the demonstrations, killing at least 15 and arresting thousands.*

> *The inspiration for the training was Mr Sharp, whose 'From Dictatorship to Democracy' – a short, theoretical handbook for non-violent struggle against repressive regimes – was published in Burmese in 1994 and began circulating among exiles and surreptitiously among dissidents inside the country. Some were imprisoned for years for possessing it.[8]*

The British financial daily further noted that:

> *Gene Sharp, the Oxford-educated, Harvard-affiliated theoretician on peaceful resistance to repression, urged the rebels to embrace non-violent means to fight the junta. His acolyte, re-*

tired colonel Robert Helvey, a US military attaché in Rangoon in the 1980s, expounded on how to use military-style planning and strategizing for peaceful dissent.[9]

Interestingly, Sharp was also in China just days before the dramatic events at Tiananmen Square in June 1989. Was that just a coincidence? One wondered.[10]

The relevant question was why the US Government had such a keen interest in fostering regime change in Myanmar in 2007. It clearly had little to do with concerns for democracy, justice, or human rights for the oppressed population there. Iraq and Afghanistan were sufficient testimony to the fact that Washington's paean to 'democracy' was propaganda cover for another agenda.

The question was, what would motivate such engagement in a place as remote as Myanmar?

Geopolitical control was clearly the answer; control, ultimately, of strategic sea lanes from the Persian Gulf to the South China Sea. The coastline of Myanmar provided shipping and naval access to one of the world's most strategic waterways, the Strait of Malacca, the narrow ship passage between Malaysia and Indonesia.

The Pentagon had been trying to militarize this region since September 11, 2001 on the pretext of defending against possible 'terrorist attack.' When that did not materialize, they shifted to alleged 'defense against pirates.' The US managed to gain an airbase on Banda Aceh, the Sultan Iskandar Muda Air Force Base on the northernmost tip of Indonesia. The governments of the region, including Myanmar, however, adamantly refused US efforts to militarize the region. A glance at a map confirmed the strategic importance of Myanmar.

The Strait of Malacca, linking the Indian and Pacific Oceans, was the shortest sea route between the Persian Gulf and China. It was the key chokepoint in Asia.

More than 80% of all China's oil imports were shipped by tankers passing the Malacca Strait. The narrowest point was the Phillips Channel in the Singapore Strait, only 1.5 miles wide at its narrowest. Supertankers carried more than 12 million barrels of oil daily through the narrow passage, most en route to the world's fastest-growing energy market: China.

If the Malacca Strait were closed, nearly half of the world's tanker fleet would be required to sail thousands of miles farther. Closing the Strait would immediately raise freight costs worldwide. More than 50,000 vessels per year transited the Strait of Malacca.

Whoever controlled the waterways at this strategic chokepoint — the region from Maynmar to Banda Aceh in Indonesia - would controll China's energy supply and therefore its life-line.

Once it became clear to China that the US was embarked on a unilateral militarization of Middle East oil fields beginning in 2003, Beijing quite lawfully stepped up its engagement in Myanmar. Chinese energy and military security, not human rights concerns, drove their policy.

Beijing poured billions of dollars of military assistance into Myanmar, including fighter and transport aircraft, tanks and armored personnel carriers, naval vessels and surface-to-air missiles. China built up Myanmar's railroads and roads and won permission to station its troops in Myanmar. China, according to Indian defense sources, also built a large electronic surveillance facility on Myanmar's Coco Islands and was building naval bases for access to the Indian Ocean.

Myanmar was an integral part of what some in the Pentagon referred to as China's 'string of pearls,' its strategic design of establishing military bases in Myanmar, Thailand and Cambodia in order to counter US control over the Strait of Malacca chokepoint. There was also energy on and offshore Myanmar, and lots of it.

Oil and gas had been produced in Myanmar since the British set up the Rangoon Oil Company in 1871, later renamed Burmah Oil Co. The country had produced natural gas since the 1970s, and in the 1990s it granted gas concessions to ElfTotal of France and Premier Oil of the UK in the Gulf of Martaban. Later Texaco and Unocal (now Chevron) won concessions at Yadana and Yetagun as well. Yadana alone had an estimated gas reserve of more than 5 trillion cubic feet with an expected life of at least 30 years. Yetagun was estimated to have about a third the gas of the Yadana field. In 2004 a large new gas field, Shwe field, off the coast of Arakan was discovered.

By 2002 both Texaco and Premier Oil withdrew from the Yetagun project following UK government and NGO pressure. Malaysia's Petronas bought Premier's 27% stake. By 2004 Myanmar was exporting Yadana gas, via pipeline to Thailand, worth annually $1 billion to the Myanmar regime.

In 2005 China, Thailand and South Korea invested in expanding the Myanmar oil and gas sector, with export of gas to Thailand rising 50%. Gas export by 2007 was Myanmar's most important source of income. Yadana was developed jointly by ElfTotal, Unocal, PTT-EP of Thailand and Myanmar's state MOGE, operated by the French ElfTotal. Yadana supplied some 20% of Thailand's natural gas needs.

The Yetagun field was operated by Malaysia's Petronas along with MOGE and Japan's Nippon Oil and PTT-EP. The gas was piped onshore where it linked to the Yadana pipeline. Gas from the Shwe field was to come online beginning 2009. China and India had both been in strong contention over the Shwe gas field reserves.

India Lost, China Won

In the summer of 2007, shortly before Washington launched its 'Saffron Revolution,' Myanmar had signed a Memorandum of Understanding with PetroChina to supply large volumes of natural gas from reserves of the Shwe gas field in the Bay of Bengal. The contract ran for 30 years. India, which had become a military cooperation partner of Washington, was the main loser.

Myanmar had earlier given India a major stake in two offshore blocks to develop gas that would have been transmitted via pipeline through Bangladesh to India's energy-hungry economy. Political bickering between India and Bangladesh brought the Indian plans to a standstill, however.

Beijing took advantage of the stalemate. China deftly trumped India with an offer to invest billions in building a strategic China-Myanmar oil and gas pipeline across Myanmar from its deepwater port at Sittwe in the Bay of Bengal to Kunming in China's Yunnan Province—-a stretch of more than 2,300 kilometers. China planned an oil refinery in Kunming, as well.

The Myanmar-China pipelines would allow oil and gas to be transported from Africa (Sudan and other sources) and the Middle East (especially Iran and Saudi Arabia) without needing to go through the vulnerable chokepoint of the Malacca Strait.

Myanmar would become China's 'bridge' linking Bangladesh and countries westward to the China mainland independent of any possible future moves by Washington to control the Strait. That bridge would be a geopolitical disaster for the US that Washington was determined to prevent by all means.

The 'Saffron Revolution' of 2007 was that attempt. It did not quite reach its goal, however. In May 2008 another attempt was made to destabilize the regime in Myanmar as the devastating Cyclone Nargis pounded the country leaving thousands dead in its wake. The Bush Administration threatened to send in military troops under the guise of bringing international rescue relief to the country, using the humanitarian argument to maximize pressure on the regime in a time of genuine crisis.

In July 2008, President Bush renewed his call for the Myanmar regime to release opposition leader Aung San Suu Kyi from house arrest. Bush stated to the press, "I'm deeply concerned about that country."[11] His sincerity was put in doubt, however, as the world looked at his record in Iraq and in backing prisoner torture in Guantanamo and elsewhere, despite world criticism and international laws prohibiting it.

Nonetheless, the humanitarian ploy was a clear attempt by Washington to use the vehicle of 'human rights' as a weapon of regime change in Myanmar and an extension of what could only be termed American imperialism.

India's Dangerous Alliance Shift

It was no wonder China was taking precautions. Ever since the Bush Administration decided in 2005 to recruit India to the Pentagon's 'New

Framework for US-India Defense Relations,' India had been pushed into a strategic alliance with Washington, explicitly in order to counter the growing influence of China in Asia.

Defense Secretary Donald Rumsfeld had commissioned a study by Andrew Marshall's Pentagon Office of Net Assessments. The report was called "The India-US Military Relationship: Expectations and Perceptions." It was released in October 2002. Approximately forty senior US officials and around the same number of serving and retired Indian officials were interviewed for the study. Among the report's observations was that Indian armed forces could be used "for low-end operations in Asia such as peacekeeping operations, search and rescue operations...." The study concluded:

We want a friend in 2020 that will be capable of assisting the US military to deal with a Chinese threat. We cannot deny that India will create a countervailing force to China.[12]

That October 2002 Pentagon report stated further that the reason for the India-USA defense alliance would be to have a "capable partner who can take on more responsibility for low-end operations" in Asia, i.e. low-end operations directed at China, and to "ultimately provide basing and access for US power projection," also aimed at China. Washington was quietly negotiating a base on Indian territory as part of the new deal, a severe violation of India's traditional non-aligned status.

The Pentagon report echoed the September 2002 Bush Administration National Security Strategy document declaring that the US would not allow any other country to equal or surpass its military strength. It announced that the US would use its military power to dissuade any potential aspirant. The strategic review pointed to China as the potential power that could threaten US hegemony in the region.

As far as India was concerned, the report stated:

The United States has undertaken a transformation in its bilateral relationship with India based on a conviction that US interests require a strong relationship with India. We are the two largest democracies, committed to political freedom pro-

tected by representative governments. India is moving to-
wards greater economic freedom as well.[13]

To sweeten the military ties, the Bush Administration offered India to
end its 30 year nuclear sanctions and to sell advanced US nuclear
technology, legitimizing India's open violation of the Nuclear Non-
Proliferation Treaty. This, at the same time Washington accused Iran of
violating the same, an exercise in political hypocrisy to say the least.

Notably, just as the Saffron-robed monks of Myanmar took to the
streets, the Pentagon opened joint US-Indian naval exercises, Malabar
07, along with armed forces from Australia, Japan and Singapore. The US
showed the muscle of its 7th Fleet, deploying the aircraft carriers USS
Nimitz and USS Kitty Hawk, the guided missile cruisers USS Cowpens
and USS Princeton, and no less than five guided missile destroyers.[14]

The danger of US-backed regime change in Myanmar, together with
Washington's growing military power projection into India and other
allies in the region, was clearly a factor in Beijing's policy vis-à-vis
Myanmar's military junta.

Within India itself there was a deep split among the country's leaders
and in its Parliament over the new strategic alliance with Washington.
The split was such that in January 2008 the Prime Minister of India,
Manmohan Singh, made his first official visit to China where he declared, "I have made it clear to the Chinese leadership that India is not
part of any so-called 'contain China' effort."[15] Whether he was sincere
was not clear. It was clear that his government was feeling pressure from
both Washington and Beijing.

As was often the case, from Darfur to Caracas to Rangoon, the rally-
ing call of Washington for 'democracy' and 'human rights' had to be
taken with at least a large grain of salt. Most often the taste was beyond
bitter; it was un-palatable.

That was very much the case with Washington's 'democracy' and
'human rights' operations in Darfur in southern Sudan, a region of vital
strategic importance for China's oil supplies.

Sudan: The Significance Of Darfur

A curious thing about the human rights campaign against what Secretary of State, Colin Powell termed 'genocide' in the southern Sudan province of Darfur, near the border with Chad, was its timing. The massive, Hollywood-backed 'human rights' campaign began soon after the Sudanese Government in Khartoum announced it had discovered huge potential new oil reserves in that region. Chinese oil companies had been involved in the discovery.

Prior to that oil discovery, the United States had been arming and training anti-Khartoum rebels in southern Sudan, including the late John Garang, trained at the notorious School of the Americas, Fort Benning, Georgia.[16] It was that region where, in 1999, the Chinese state oil company began building a major pipeline to bring oil to a new harbor at Port Sudan. From Port Sudan it was destined to fuel China's economic growth.

Neither the discovery of huge oil reserves in Darfur nor the fact that Khartoum had granted major exploration rights to China's state oil company were ever mentioned in US Government pronouncements or US mainstream media. Nor did Washington mention that it had secretly been supplying arms to Idriss Deby, the dictator of neighboring Chad, and encouraging Deby to launch military strikes into Darfur.

Washington then blamed Deby's strikes on Khartoum, declaring them part of a systematic Sudanese 'genocide' against the Christian Darfur peoples. As will be shown, the claim of genocide was a huge orchestrated charade, another exercise in a new American 'human rights' offensive, every bit as brutal, violent, and oil driven, as Operation Shock and Awe in Iraq.[17]

The US focus on Darfur, a forbidding piece of sun-parched real estate in the southern part of Sudan, exemplified the Pentagon's new Cold War over oil, in which China's dramatically increased need for oil to fuel its booming growth had led Beijing to embark on an aggressive policy of - ironically - dollar diplomacy.

With more than US $1.8 trillion, mostly in US dollar reserves at the Peoples' National Bank of China from export trade surpluses, Beijing was actively engaging in petroleum geopolitics. Africa was a major focus of its search for oil. In Africa, the central region between Sudan and Chad was a US priority because it was the location of vast untapped reservoirs of petroleum.

By 2007 China was drawing an estimated 30% of its crude oil imports from Africa — clearly the motive for China's extraordinary series of diplomatic initiatives that left Washington furious.

Beijing's Effective Economic Diplomacy

The Beijing Government began using no-strings-attached dollar credits to gain access to Africa's vast raw material wealth, leaving Washington's typical control game via the World Bank and International Monetary Fund (IMF) out in the cold. Who needed the painful medicine of the IMF when China would give easy terms, and build roads and schools to boot?

In November 2007, when Beijing hosted its extraordinary summit, China literally rolled out the red carpet for 43 African heads of state. They included among them the leaders of Algeria, Nigeria, Mali, Angola, Central African Republic, Zambia and South Africa.

China had just concluded an oil deal that linked it with Nigeria and South Africa, two of the continent's largest nations. China National Offshore Oil Corporation (CNOOC) would extract oil from Nigeria via a consortium that also included South African Petroleum Co, giving China access to some 175,000 barrels a day by 2008. It was a $2.27 billion deal that gave state-controlled CNOOC a 45% stake in a large off-shore oil field in Nigeria.

Previously, Washington had considered Nigeria to be an asset of the Anglo-American oil majors, ExxonMobil, Shell and Chevron.

China was very generous in dispensing its aid to some of the poorest debtor states of Africa; it did so via soft loans at no interest, or as outright grants. The loans went into infrastructure, including highways, hospitals, and schools – in stark contrast to the brutal austerity demands of the IMF and World Bank. In 2006 China committed more than $8 billion to

Nigeria, Angola and Mozambique. Meanwhile, Ghana was negotiating a $1.2 billion Chinese electrification loan.

By contrast, the World Bank loaned just $2.3 billion to all of sub-Saharan Africa. Unlike the World Bank, a de facto arm of US foreign economic policy, China wisely attached no strings to its loans.

China's oil-related diplomacy in Africa led to the bizarre accusation from Washington that Beijing was trying to "secure oil at the sources,"[18] something Washington foreign policy had itself been preoccupied with for at least a century. No source of oil was more the focus of China-US oil conflict than Sudan, home of Darfur's vast reserves.

Sudan's Oil Riches

China National Petroleum Company (CNPC) had become Sudan's largest foreign investor, with some $5 billion in oil field development. Since 1999 China had invested at least $15 billion overall in Sudan. It co-owned 50% of an oil refinery near Khartoum with the Sudanese government. The oil fields were concentrated in the south, site of a long-simmering civil war — a civil war covertly financed, in part, by the United States to divide the oil-rich south Sudan from the Islamic Khartoum-centered north.

CNPC built an oil pipeline from southern Sudan to a new terminal at Port Sudan on the Red Sea, where the oil was loaded on tankers bound for China. By 2006, Sudan had become China's fourth largest foreign oil source; by 2007, 8% of China's oil came from southern Sudan. China took 65-80% of Sudan's 500,000 barrels/day production

In 2006 China surpassed Japan as the world's second largest importer of oil after the United States, importing 6.5 million barrels a day of the black gold. With its oil demand growing by an estimated 30% a year, China would clearly pass the US in oil import demand in a few years. That reality was the driving force behind Beijing's foreign policy in Africa, as well as the Pentagon's AFRICOM counter strategy, and the State Department's 'genocide' campaign in Darfur.

The Darfur Genocide Game

China's CNPC held rights to 'Bloc 6,' which straddled the Darfur regionof Sudan near the border with Chad and the Central African Republic. In April 2005, when Sudan announced that it had found oil in Southern Darfur, it was estimated to be able to pump 500,000 barrels per day when developed. The world press forgot to report that vital fact in discussing the Darfur conflict that subsequently developed.

Genocide was the preferred theme, and Washington was the orchestra conductor. Curiously, while all neutral observers acknowledged that Darfur had seen a large and tragic human displacement and human misery, with tens of thousands or even as many as 300,000 deaths in the last several years, only Washington and the NGOs close to it used the emotionally charged term 'genocide' to describe the situation in Darfur.[19]

If the US were able to get popular acceptance of the charge of genocide, it opened the possibility of using that as a pretext for drastic regime changing intervention by NATO - i.e., Washington — into Sudan's sovereign affairs, and of course into its oil relations with China.

Sudanese Information Minister Abdel Basit Sabdarat told the *Los Angeles Times* in 2005 that the US had pushed Khartoum to limit its ties with Chinese oil companies. "But we refuse such pressures," he said. "Our partnership with China is strategic. We can't just disband them because the Americans asked us to do so."[20]

Failing in its attempt to pressure Sudan to break its ties with China, Washington then turned its human rights and other guns on Khartoum directly. They launched a massive campaign to 'save Darfur.'

The genocide theme was being used, with full-scale Hollywood backing from stars like George Clooney, to orchestrate the case for *de facto* NATO occupation of the region. Not surprisingly the Sudanese government politely declined to accept the assault on its sovereignty.

The US government repeatedly used the term 'genocide' in reference to Darfur. It was the only government to do so. US Assistant Secretary of State Ellen Sauerbrey, head of the Bureau of Population, Refugees and Migration, said during a USINFO online interview in November 2006: "The ongoing genocide in Darfur, Sudan - a gross violation of human rights - is among the top international issues of concern to the United States." [21] The Bush administration insisted that genocide had been going on in Darfur since 2003, despite the fact that a five-person UN mission led by Italian Judge Antonio Cassese reported in 2004 that while 'grave human rights abuses' were being committed, genocide had not been committed in Darfur. He therefore called for war crime trials instead.[22]

Merchants Of Death

The United States, acting through its proxies Chad, Eritrea and neighboring states, trained and armed the Sudan People's Liberation Army (SPLA). A man named John Garang, trained at the US Special Forces School of the Americas at Fort Benning, Georgia, headed the SPLA until his death in July 2005.[23]

By pouring arms first into southeastern Sudan and then, since the discovery of oil in Darfur, into that region as well, Washington fueled the conflicts that led to tens of thousands dying and several million being driven from their homes. Eritrea, a de facto US client state, hosted and supported the SPLA, the umbrella NDA opposition group, and both the Eastern Front and Darfur rebels.

In Sudan's Darfur region, two rebel groups — the Justice for Equality Movement (JEM) and the larger Sudan Liberation Army (SLA) were fighting against the Khartoum government of President Omar al-Bashir.

In February 2003, the SLA, reportedly with arms covertly provided via proxies from the Pentagon, launched attacks on Sudanese government positions in the Darfur region.[24] SLA secretary-general Minni Arkou Minnawi called for armed struggle, accusing the government of ignoring Darfur. The objective of the SLA was to create a united democratic Sudan.[25] In other words, regime change in Khartoum.

The US Senate adopted a resolution in February 2006 that requested NATO troops in Darfur, as well as a stronger UN peacekeeping force with a robust mandate. A month later, President George W. Bush called for additional NATO forces in Darfur.

Genocide, Or Oil?

Meanwhile, the Pentagon had been busy training African military officers in the US, much as it had trained Latin American officers and their death squads for decades. Its International Military Education and Training program recruited military officers from Chad, Ethiopia, Eritrea, Cameroon and the Central African Republic.

Many of the weapons that fueled the killing in Darfur and the south had been brought in via murky, private 'merchants of death' such as Victor Bout, a notorious former KGB operative who, after the collapse of the Soviet Union found protection and a new home in the United States. Bout had been accused repeatedly of selling weapons across Africa. US government officials, significantly enough, left his arms dealing operations in Texas and Florida untouched despite the fact he was on the Interpol wanted list for money laundering.

US development aid for all Sub-Saharan Africa, including Chad, had been cut sharply in recent years while its military aid rose. Oil and the scramble for strategic raw materials were clearly the reason. It turned out that the enormous oil reserves of southern Sudan, from the Upper Nile to the Chad border, had been known to American oil executives long before they were known to the Sudanese government.

Chevron's 1974 Sudan Project

US oil majors had known about Sudan's vast oil wealth at least since the early 1970s. In 1979, Jafaar Nimeiry, Sudan's then-head of state, broke ties with the Soviets and invited Chevron to develop Sudan's oil industry. UN Ambassador George H. W. Bush had personally told Nimeiry about satellite photos indicating oil in Sudan. Nimeiry took the bait and invited Chevron in. That proved to be a fatal mistake.Wars over Sudan's oil had been the consequence ever since.

Chevron spent $1.2 billion exploring and testing in southern Sudan and in 1979, found big oil reserves in Abu Jabra. That oil triggered what was called Sudan's second civil war in 1983. Chevron was the target of repeated attacks and killings and it suspended the project in 1984. In 1992, Chevron sold its Sudanese oil concessions. Then, seven years later, in 1999, China began to develop the abandoned Chevron fields with notable results.

But Chevron was not far from Darfur even in 2007.

Chad Oil And Pipeline Politics

Condoleezza Rice's former oil company, Chevron, had moved to neighboring Chad, across the border from the Darfur region of Sudan. Early in 2007, together with ExxonMobil, Chevron completed a $3.7 billion oil pipeline that would carry 160,000 barrels per day from Doba in central Chad, near Darfur, via Cameroon to Kribi on the Atlantic Ocean. The oil was destined for US refineries.

To accomplish the pipeline, the US oil giants worked with Chad's 'President for life' Idriss Deby, a corrupt despot who had been accused of feeding US-supplied arms to the Darfur rebels. Deby joined Washington's Pan Sahel Initiative run by the Pentagon's US-European Command, to train his troops to fight 'Islamic terrorism.' The Pan Sahel Initiative, a precursor of the AFRICOM command, used US Army Special Forces to train military units from Mali, Mauritania, Niger and Chad.

Supplied with US military aid, training and weapons, and using his elite Presidential Guards recruited from Darfur, Deby launched the initial assault in 2004 that triggered the major conflict in Darfur. Borders between Chad and Darfur are virtually non-existent. Deby provided the elite troops with all-terrain vehicles, arms and anti-aircraft guns to aid Darfur rebels fighting the Khartoum government in southwestern Sudan.

Thus, US military support to Deby had been the trigger for the Darfur bloodbath. Khartoum retaliated, and the ensuing debacle was unleashed with full, tragic force.[26]

Washington and its NGOs then swung into full action, charging Khartoum with genocide, as a pretext for bringing UN/NATO troops into the oil fields of Darfur and southern Sudan. Oil, not human misery, was behind Washington's new interest in Darfur.

The 'Darfur genocide' campaign began, significantly, the same time Chevron's Chad-Cameroon oil pipeline began to flow. The US now had a military base in Chad from which to go after Darfur oil and, potentially, to take over China's new oil sources if NATO 'peacekeeper troops' could be brought in.

US military objectives in Darfur—and the Horn of Africa more widely—were being served by US and NATO backing for African Union (AU) troops in Darfur, the successor organization to the Organization of African Unity that included more than 50 African states as members. NATO provided ground and air support for AU troops who were categorized as 'neutral' and 'peacekeepers.'

By early 2008 Sudan was at war on three fronts—against Uganda, Chad, and Ethiopia. Each had a significant US military presence and ongoing US military programs. The war in Sudan involved both US covert operations and US trained 'rebel' factions coming in from south Sudan, Chad, Ethiopia and Uganda.

In May 2008, Chad-backed mercenaries commanded by Khalil Ibrahim, head of the Justice and Equality Movement (JEM), managed to launch a bold attack directly on the Sudanese capital Khartoum before being repelled. The Sudanese government accused Chad of being behind the provocation.

The London *Times* confirmed the direct ties between Chad's Deby and the JEM:

> *Chad and Sudan accuse each other of supporting rival rebel movements to destabilise their regimes. Although JEM fighters deny support from Chad, their ties to President Déby – who is from the same Zaghawa tribe as the JEM leader – are well known. In February, JEM forces traveled from Darfur to Chad to protect Mr Déby from rebels pouring into the capital, Ndjamena. Chadian rebels are a common sight on the Sudanese side of the border, buying supplies in the West Darfur capital of El Geneina. Last month The Times saw rebels from Chad speaking French – a giveaway in Darfur – and driving freely through the town's market in their roofless pickup trucks.[27]*

Deby Looks To China Too

The US and World Bank-financed oil pipeline from Chad to the Cameroon coast was one part of a far grander Washington scheme to control the oil riches of Central Africa from Sudan to the Gulf of Guinea. The geological belt was rumored to hold oil reserves on a scale that would rival the oil-rich region of the Persian Gulf.[28]

But Washington's erstwhile friend, Chad's Deby, at a certain point began to feel unhappy with his small share of US-controlled oil profits. When he and his parliament decided, in early 2006, to take more of the oil revenues to finance military operations and beef up their army, the new World Bank president - and Iraq war architect - Paul Wolfowitz suspended loans to Chad.

In August 2006, after Deby had won re-election, he created Chad's own oil company, SHT, and threatened to expel Chevron and also Malaysia's Petronas for not paying the required taxes. He demanded a 60% share of the Chad oil pipeline. Eventually, he came to terms with the oil companies, but winds of change were blowing.

Deby also faced growing internal opposition from a Chad rebel group, United Front for Change, known under its French name as FUC, which he claimed was being covertly funded by Sudan. The FUC based itself in Darfur.

Into this unstable situation, Beijing appeared in Chad with a buckets of aid money in hand. Earlier, in January 2006, Chinese President Hu Jintao had made a state visit to Sudan and Cameroon, as well as other African states. During that year, in fact, China's leaders visited no fewer than 48 African states. Such attention to Africa from a non-African head of state was unprecedented.

In August 2006, Beijing hosted Chad's foreign minister for talks and to resume formal diplomatic ties that had been cut in 1997. China began to import oil from Chad as well as from Sudan.

Keeping in mind that Washington had considered Deby 'one of theirs,' this development was not greeted well in Washington.

*In April 2007, Chad's foreign minister, Allawi, announced in
Beijing that talks over increasing China's participation in
Chad's oil development were "progressing well." Referring to
China's terms for oil development, he said:*

*The Chinese are open; they are win-win partners. As they say,
it is not about monopolies. These are much more equal part-
nerships than those we are used to having.*[29]

The Chinese economic presence in Chad, ironically, was more effective in calming the fighting and reducing displacement in Darfur than
any AU or UN troop presence ever could. That was not welcome for some
people in Washington and at Chevron headquarters, since it meant that
US oil companies would not be able to secure the oil.

Chad and Darfur were part of a significant Chinese effort to secure oil
at the source, all across Africa. Oil - or, more precisely, control of oil at its
sources — was also the prime factor determining US-Africa policy as
China's activity expanded.

George W. Bush's interest in Africa included a new US military base
in Sao Tome/Principe, 124 miles off the Gulf of Guinea, from which it
could control oil fields from Angola in the south to the Democratic
Republic of Congo, Gabon, Equatorial Guinea, Cameroon and Nigeria.[30]
That just happened to be the very same area where China had also
focused its diplomatic and investment activity.

"West Africa's oil has become of national strategic interest to us,"
stated US Assistant Secretary of State for Africa, Walter Kansteiner, in
2002.[31]

US actions in Darfur and Chad were extensions of US Iraq policy, but
with other means— instead of direct military assault, a callous enflaming
of internal violence. But the control of oil — all oil, everywhere - was the
goal. China was challenging that control 'everywhere,' especially in
Africa. It was an undeclared, but very real, New Cold War—over oil.

Tibet: An Old CIA Asset Is Unleashed

By early 2008, the US establishment had determined that it was time for a major escalation of pressure on China, this time unleashing destabilization within Chinese territory, in the Tibet Autonomous Province.

This was an extremely sensitive time in US-China relations. United States financial markets were extremely dependent on China's investment of its trade surplus dollars into US Government debt, Treasury bonds, and also into its Freddie Mac and Fannie Mae real estate bonds. The Tibet unrest was timed for the run-up to the Beijing Olympics. Fanning the flames of violence in Tibet under these volatile conditions indicated that Washington had decided on an ultra-high risk geopolitical game with Beijing.

US meddling in Tibet had been initiated by the Bush Administration during previous months, coinciding with its interference in Sudan and Myanmar, and it included the special military entente with India directed against China. In late 2004 US Defense Secretary Rumsfeld proposed to India a comprehensive new level of military and strategic cooperation, updating the "Agreed Minute on Defense Relations of 1995." As US military and diplomatic sources later admitted, its strategic target was the growing economic role of China in Asia.[32]

The Tibet operation clearly got the green light in October 2007, when George Bush agreed to meet the Dalai Lama for the first time publicly in Washington. The President of the United States was well aware of the enormity of such an insult to China, its largest trading partner. Bush then deepened the affront to Beijing, by attending Washington's ceremony awarding the Dalai Lama the Congressional Gold Medal.

The decision by Bush, son of a former US Ambassador to Beijing, was deliberate. He would have been well aware that the presence of the President of the United States at an official US Government ceremony honoring the Dalai Lama would be seen as a signal of growing US backing for the Tibetan independence movement.

Immediately after Tibetan monks rioted in March 2008, the gush of pro-Tibet support from George Bush, Condoleezza Rice, France's Nicolas Sarkozy and Germany's Angela Merkel, took on dimensions of the absurd. While Chancellor Merkel announced she would not attend the Beijing Summer Olympics, she issued conflicting statements as to whether this was to protest Beijing's treatment of the Tibetan monks, or because of prior commitments. It did not matter; the publicity surrounding the "debate" sufficed to generate the impression of an international protest. In fact, Angela Merkel had not planned to attend the Olympics in the first place.

Merkel's announcement was followed by one from Poland's Prime Minister, the pro-Washington Donald Tusk, saying that he would also stay away, along with pro-US Czech President Vaclav Klaus. It was unclear whether they also had not planned to go in the first place, but their announcements created dramatic press headlines.

The wave of violent protests and attacks by Tibetan monks against Han Chinese residents in Tibet began on March 10 when several hundred monks marched on Lhasa demanding release of other monks allegedly detained for celebrating the Dalai Lama's receipt of the US Congressional Medal the previous October. The first group of monks were joined by other monks protesting Beijing rule and commemorating the 49th anniversary of an earlier Tibetan uprising against Chinese rule.

The Tibet Geopolitical Game

As the Chinese government itself was quick to point out, the sudden eruption of anti-Chinese violence in Tibet, a new phase in the movement led by the exiled Dalai Lama, was suspiciously timed. It was clearly an attempt to try to put the spotlight on Beijing's human rights record on the eve of the August 2008 Olympics, an event seen in China as a major affirmation of the arrival of a newly prosperous China on the world stage.

The background actors in Tibet's attempted 'Crimson Revolution' confirmed that Washington had been preparing another of its infamous Color Revolutions, this time fanning public protests designed to inflict maximum embarrassment on Beijing.

The actors on the ground in and outside Tibet were the usual agencies involved in US-sponsored regime destabilizations, including the

State Department's proxy, the National Endowment for Democracy (NED). In the case of Tibet, the CIA's Freedom House was also involved. Its chairman, Bette Bao Lord — wife of Winston Lord, former US Ambassador to China and President of the Council on Foreign Relations — played a role in the International Committee for Tibet.

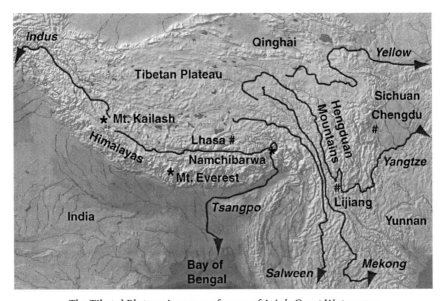

The Tibetal Plateau is source of seven of Asia's Great Waterways

Chinese Prime Minister Wen Jiabao accused the Dalai Lama of orchestrating the latest unrest to sabotage the Olympic Games "in order to achieve their unspeakable goal," a free Tibet. The stakes for China and for Washington were huge.

Bush telephoned his Chinese counterpart, President Hu Jintao, to pressure for talks between Beijing and the exiled Dalai Lama. The White House said that Bush "raised his concerns about the situation in Tibet and encouraged the Chinese government to engage in substantive dialogue with the Dalai Lama's representatives and to allow access for journalists and diplomats."[33]

Dalai Lama's Odd Friends

In the West the image of the Dalai Lama had been so carefully promoted that in many circles, particularly ones that considered themselves politically progressive, he was deemed almost a God. While the spiritual life of the Dalai Lama was another issue, it was relevant to note that the kinds of people swarming around the person of the 14th Dalai Lama were not of the best repute in terms of compassion or justice toward their fellow man.

The Dalai Lama traveled in rather extreme conservative political circles, as far back as the 1930's. At that time the German Nazis, including Gestapo chief Heinrich Himmler, and other top Nazi Party leaders, regarded Tibet as the holy site of the survivors of the lost Atlantis, and the origin of their 'Nordic pure race.'

Tenzin Gyatso, born in 1935, was the given name of the boy who, by age 11 was already designated as Dalai Lama. At that young age, he was befriended by Heinrich Harrer, a fanatic Nazi Party member and an officer in Heinrich Himmler's feared Schutzstaffel, the SS.

Far from the innocent image of Harrer portrayed in the popular Hollywood film, *Seven Years in Tibet*, by Brad Pitt, Harrer had willingly joined the SS, the Fuehrer's Praetorian Guard, and participated in burning the Jewish synagogues during the Kristallnacht terror of 1938. According to eyewitness accounts, Harrer remained a devoted Nazi to war's end. In 1944, Harrer escaped a British internment camp and fled to Tibet where he became the designated tutor of the young Dalai Lama for 'the world outside Tibet.'[34] The two remained friends until Harrer died in 2006 at age 93.[35]

That friendship was notable in the context of other friends of the Dalai Lama. In April 1999, backed by Margaret Thatcher and former US-China Ambassador, CIA Director and President, George H.W. Bush, the Dalai Lama demanded that the British government release Augusto Pinochet, the former fascist dictator of Chile and a longtime CIA client who had been put under house arrest while visiting England. The Dalai Lama urged that Pinochet not be extradited to Spain where he would stand trial for crimes against humanity. The Dalai Lama had also cultivated close ties to Miguel Serrano,[36] head of Chile's National Socialist Party, a proponent of something called 'esoteric Hitlerism.'[37]

Moreover, it had been revealed in official US Government documents that since 1959, the Dalai Lama had been surrounded and financed, in significant part, by various US and Western intelligence services and their gaggle of NGOs.[38]

It was the agenda of those Washington friends of the Dalai Lama that was relevant to the uprisings and riots in Tibet in March 2008.

The NED Again. . . .

Author Michael Parenti noted in his study, *Friendly Feudalism: The Tibet Myth*, that, "during the 1950s and 60s, the CIA actively backed the Tibetan cause with arms, military training, money, air support and all sorts of other help."[39]

According to Parenti, the US-based American Society for a Free Asia, a CIA front, publicized the cause of Tibetan resistance by enlisting the Dalai Lama's eldest brother, Thubtan Norbu, to play an active role in the group. The Dalai Lama's second-eldest brother, Gyalo Thondup, established an intelligence operation together with the CIA in 1951. It was later upgraded into a CIA-trained guerrilla unit whose recruits parachuted back into Tibet.[40]

Declassified US intelligence documents released in the late 1990s revealed that:

> *For much of the 1960s, the CIA provided the Tibetan exile movement with $1.7 million a year for operations against China, including an annual subsidy of $186,000 for the Dalai Lama.[41]*

In 1959, the CIA helped the Dalai Lama to flee to Dharamsala, India where he has lived ever since. He continued to receive millions of dollars in backing up to 2008, not from the CIA but from the more innocuous-sounding CIA front organization, the National Endowment for Democracy (NED) funded by the US Congress.[42]

The NED, as described above, had been instrumental in every US-backed Color Revolution destabilization from Serbia to Georgia to Ukraine to Myanmar. Its funds were used to back opposition media and global public relations campaigns to popularize their preferred opposition candidates.

The NED had been founded by the Reagan Administration in the early 1980s, on the recommendation of Bill Casey, Reagan's Director of the Central Intelligence Agency, following a series of high-publicity exposures of CIA assassinations and destabilizations of unfriendly regimes. The NED was designed to pose as an independent NGO, one step removed from the CIA and Government agencies, so as to be less conspicuous, presumably. The first acting President of the NED, Allen Weinstein, commented to the *Washington Post* that, "A lot of what we [the NED] do today was done covertly 25 years ago by the CIA."[43]

As historian of American intelligence activities, William Blum, stated:

The NED played an important role in the Iran-Contra affair of the 1980s, funding key components of Oliver North's shadowy and illegal 'Project Democracy.' That network privatized US foreign policy, waged war, ran arms and drugs, and engaged in other equally illegal activities. In 1987, a White House spokesman stated that those at NED 'run Project Democracy.'[44]

The most prominent pro-Dalai Lama Tibet independence organization in the destabilization attempt of 2008 was the International Campaign for Tibet (ICT), founded in Washington in 1988.

Since at least 1994 the ICT had been receiving funds from the NED. The ICT awarded their annual Light of Truth award in 2005 to Carl Gershman, founder of the NED. Other ICT award winners included the German Friedrich Naumann Foundation and Czech leader, Vaclav Havel. The ICT Board of Directors was populated with former US State Department officials, including Gare Smith and Julia Taft. [45]

Another very active anti-Beijing organization was the US-based Students for a Free Tibet (SFT), founded in 1994 in New York City as a project of the US Tibet Committee and the NED-financed ICT.

The SFT was best known for unfurling a 450 foot banner atop the Great Wall in China, calling for a free Tibet and accusing Beijing of wholly unsubstantiated claims of genocide against Tibet. Apparently it made good drama to rally naïve American and European students, most of whom had never been to Tibet.

'Tibetan People's Uprising' Made In USA

The SFT was among five organizations which on January 4, 2008 proclaimed the start of a 'Tibetan people's uprising' and set up a special temporary office in charge of coordinating and financing the uprising.

Harry Wu, a prominent Dalai Lama supporter in the agitation against Beijing, became notorious for his role in a controversial BBC documentary in which he alleged China was trafficking in human organs harvested from China's executed prisoners. The BBC documentary became the subject of controversy for its numerous inaccuracies.[46] Not content with this level of distortion, however, Wu augmented his allegations in a 1996 *Playboy* interview, claiming falsely that he had "videotaped a prisoner whose kidneys were surgically removed while he was alive, and then the prisoner was taken out and shot. The tape was broadcast by BBC."[47]

The BBC documentary showed nothing of the sort alleged by Wu, but the damage was done. How many people checked old BBC archives? Wu, a retired Berkeley professor who left China after imprisonment as a dissident, was head of the Laogai Research Foundation, a tax-exempt organization whose main funding was also from the NED.[48]

Among related projects, the US Government-financed NED also supported the *Tibet Times* newspaper, run out of the Dalai Lama's base in exile at Dharamsala, India. The NED also funded the Tibet Multimedia Center for what they described as, "information dissemination that addresses the struggle for human rights and democracy in Tibet." They were also based in Dharamsala. NED also financed the Tibetan Center for Human Rights and Democracy.[49]

In short, the fingerprints of the US State Department and US intelligence community were all over the upsurge around the 'Free Tibet' movement and the anti-Han Chinese attacks of March 2008. The question to be asked was why, and especially why at just that moment?

Tibet's Raw Minerals Treasure

Tibet was of strategic import to China not only for its geographical location astride the border with India — Washington's newest anti-China ally in Asia - but also because Tibet was a treasure of minerals and oil. Tibet contained some of the world's largest uranium and borax deposits, one half of the world's lithium, the largest copper deposits in Asia, enormous iron deposits, and over 80,000 gold mines. Tibet's forests contained the largest timber reserve at China's disposal. As of 1980, an estimated $54 billion worth of trees had been felled there. Tibet also contained some of the largest oil reserves in the region.[50]

Along the border between Tibet Autonomous Region and the Xinjiang Uygur Autonomous Region was also a vast oil and mineral region in the Qaidam Basin, known as a 'treasure basin.' The Basin had 57 different types of mineral resources with proven reserves including petroleum, natural gas, coal, crude salt, potassium, magnesium, lead, zinc and gold. These mineral resources had an estimated potential economic value of 15 trillion yuan or US $1.8 trillion. Proven reserves of potassium, lithium and crude salt in the basin were the largest in China.

Most strategically, Tibet was perhaps the world's most valuable water source. Situated as it was on the 'roof of the world,' Tibet was the source of seven of Asia's greatest rivers that provided water for 2 billion people. As Henry Kissinger might well have said, 'he who controls Tibet's water had a mighty powerful geopolitical lever over all Asia,' especially over China.

But Washington's primary interest in Tibet in the Spring of 2008 seemed to be its potential to act as a lever with which to destabilize and blackmail the Beijing Government.

'Nonviolence As A Form Of Warfare'

Events in Tibet after March 10, 2008 were covered by Western media with little regard to accuracy or independent cross-checking. Most of the pictures plastered across European and US newspapers and TV turned out not actually to be pictures or films of Chinese military oppression of Tibetan lamas or monks. They were proven in most cases to have been either Reuters or AFP pictures of Han Chinese being beaten by Tibetan monks operating in trained paramilitary organizations. In some instances some German TV stations ran video pictures of beatings that were not even from Tibet, but were of Nepalese police in Kathmandu.[51]

Western media complicity in this charade simply underscored the fact that the actions around Tibet were part of a well-orchestrated destabilization effort on the part of Washington. Repeating the same pattern as in earlier US-instigated and manipulated destabilizations, the mainstream media made no mention of the involvement of the ubiquitous NED, as well as

Gene Sharp's Albert Einstein Institution, which we met in Myanmar. As discussed earlier, the Albert Einstein Institution specialized in 'nonviolence as a form of warfare.'[52]

Interference in China by this Institution went back many years, through Colonel Robert Helvey, mentioned earlier, a 30-year veteran of the Defense Intelligence Agency, who had applied his techniques in encouraging the student protests at Tiananmen Square in June 1989. Colonel Helvey had been working with the Albert Einstein Institution and George Soros' Open Society Foundation at least since the mid-1980s. With respect to US operations in China, he was believed to be acting as an adviser to the Falun Gong in similar civil disobedience techniques. [53]

Among many threads connecting the Albert Einstein Institution to US military intelligence was also Major General Edward Atkeson who served on the Institution's original Board of Directors. It was Atkeson, former Deputy Chief of Intelligence for the US Army in Europe, who reportedly first "suggested the name 'civilian based defense' to Gene Sharp." [54]

As noted earlier, Sharp's Institution had developed the core tactics used by the US in its 'post-modern coups,' the new 'soft' destabilizations, non-violent regime changes, and what came to be called 'Color Revolutions' sweeping through countries coincidentally located in proximity to US rivals, China and Russia. Chief among these tactics was the application of electronic communications technologies. With the emergence of the Internet and widespread mobile telephone use, the US Pentagon refined an entirely new form of regime change and political destabilization. As Jonathan Mowat, a researcher of the phenomenon behind the wave of Color Revolutions, described it:

> ...*What we are seeing is civilian application of Secretary Donald Rumsfeld's 'Revolution in Military Affairs' doctrine, which depends on highly mobile small group deployments 'enabled' by 'real time' intelligence and communications. Squads of soldiers taking over city blocks with the aid of 'intelligence helmet' video screens that give them an instantaneous overview of their environment, constitute the military side. Bands of youth converging on targeted intersections in constant dialogue on cell phones constitute the doctrine's civilian application.*

> *This parallel should not be surprising since the US military and National Security Agency subsidized the development of the Internet, cellular phones, and software platforms. From their inception, these technologies were studied and experimented with in order to find the optimal use in a new kind of warfare.*

> *The 'revolution' in warfare that such new instruments permit has been pushed to the extreme by several specialists in psychological warfare. Although these military utopians have been working in high places (for example the RAND Corporation) for a very long time, to a large extent they only took over some of the most important command structures of the US military apparatus with the victory of the neoconservatives in the Pentagon of Donald Rumsfeld.*[55]

To Control The Chinese Giant

Washington operatives used and refined those techniques of 'revolutionary nonviolence,' organized through the NED, to instigate a series of 'democratic' or 'soft' political coups as part of the larger US strategy — one that would seek to cut China off from access to its vital external oil and gas reserves. Washington's attempt at destabilizing China by using Tibet was part of a clear pattern. In addition to their efforts at a 'Saffron Revolution' in Myanmar and the attempt to get NATO to seize China's oilfields in Darfur and block China's access to strategically vital oil resources there and elsewhere in Africa, it included attempts to foment problems in Uzbekistan and Kyrgyzstan, as well as to disrupt China's vital new energy pipeline to Kazakhstan.

The ancient Asian trade routes known as The Great Silk Road went through Tashkent in Uzbekistan and Almaty in Kazakhstan, for geographically obvious reasons. They were accessible in a region otherwise surrounded by major mountain ranges. Geopolitical control of Uzbekistan, Kyrgyzstan, and Kazakhstan would enable the United States to control any potential pipeline routes between China and Central Asia, just as the encirclement of Russia was aimed at controlling pipeline and other ties between Russia and Western Europe.

Moreover, China depended on uninterrupted oil flows from Iran, Saudi Arabia and other OPEC countries. The US militarization of Iraq and threats to attack Iran militarily jeopardized China's access to oil. By late 2007 it was becoming evident that China, along with Russia, loomed high on the list of strategic targets for hostile operations by the US Pentagon, State Department, and Intelligence agencies.

Behind The Strategy To Encircle China

In this context, Zbigniew Brzezinski's 1997 article in *Foreign Affairs,* the journal of the Council on Foreign Relations, was again relevant. Brzezinski's foreign policy 'pedigree,' it will be remembered, extended from having been a protégé of David Rockefeller in the 1970s, and a follower of British geostrategist, Sir Halford Mackinder, all the way to his role as a major foreign policy adviser to presidential candidate, Barack Obama. Brzezinski has long been one of the most influential figures in US intelligence and foreign policy circles. In 1997 he revealingly wrote:

Eurasia is home to most of the world's politically assertive and dynamic states. All the historical pretenders to global power originated in Eurasia. The world's most populous aspirants to regional hegemony, China and India, are in Eurasia, as are all the potential political or economic challengers to American primacy. After the United States, the next six largest economies and military spenders are there, as are all but one of the world's overt nuclear powers, and all but one of the covert ones. Eurasia accounts for 75 percent of the world's population; 60 percent of its GNP, and 75 percent of its energy resources. **Collectively, Eurasia's potential power overshadows even America's.**

Eurasia is the world's axial super-continent. A power that dominated Eurasia would exercise decisive influence over two of the world's three most economically productive regions, Western Europe and East Asia. A glance at the map also suggests **that a country dominant in Eurasia would almost automatically control the Middle East and Africa. With Eurasia now serving as the decisive geopolitical chessboard, it no longer suffices to fashion one policy for Europe and another for Asia. What happens with the distribution of power on the Eurasian landmass will be of decisive importance to America's global primacy....**[56] *(Emphasis added-w.e.).*

That statement, written well before the US-led bombing of former Yugoslavia and the US military occupations in Afghanistan and Iraq, revealed that US policy had never been about getting rid of tyranny. It was about global hegemony, not democracy.

Not surprisingly, China was not convinced that allowing Washington such overwhelming power was in China's national interest, any more than Russia thought that it would have enhanced peace to let NATO gobble up Ukraine and Georgia, or for the US to put its missiles on Russia's doorstep allegedly 'to defend against threat of Iranian nuclear attack on the United States.'

The US-led destabilization in Tibet was part of a strategic shift of great significance. It came at a time when the US economy and the US dollar, still the world's reserve currency, were in the worst crisis since the 1930s. It was significant that the US Administration sent Wall Street banker and former Goldman Sachs chairman, Henry Paulson to Beijing in the midst of its efforts to embarrass Beijing about Tibet. Washington was literally playing with fire. China long ago had surpassed Japan as the world's largest holder of foreign currency reserves. By July 2008, China's US dollar reserves were estimated to be well over $1.8 trillions, most of it invested in US Treasury debt instruments or bonds of Fannie Mae or Freddie Mac. Paulson knew well that Beijing could decide to bring the dollar to its knees by selling only a small portion of its US debt on the market.

By the end of 2008 the global superpower, the United States of America, was looking more and more like the British Empire of the late 1930s — a global imperium in terminal decline. The US empire, however, despite spiraling into its gravest financial crisis since the Great Depression of the 1930s, still seemed determined to impose its will on a world increasingly moving away from such absolutist control.

The world — or at least its major players outside Washington, from Russia to China to Venezuela to Bolivia and beyond — was beginning to think of better alternatives. To the Pentagon, such stirrings made the work of Full Spectrum Dominance more urgent than ever. The declining power of the American Century depended increasingly on direct military control, a control the Pentagon tried to establish through a worldwide network of its military bases.

Endnotes:

[1] Cited in William Blum, "The NED and 'Project Democracy'," January 2000 (www.friendsoftibet.org/databank/usdefence/usd5.html).

[2] F. William Engdahl, "The geopolitical stakes of 'Saffron Revolution," *Asia Times*, October 17, 2007 (http://www.atimes.com/atimes/Southeast_Asia/IJ17Ae01.html).

[3] US Department of State Bureau of East Asian and Pacific Affairs, *Report on Activities to Support Democracy Activists in Burma as Required by the Burmese Freedom and Democracy Act of 2003*, October 30, 2003 (http://www.state.gov/p/eap/rls/rpt/burma/26017.htm).

[4] Ibid.

[5] Ibid.

[6] Gene Sharp publicly claimed that his work was strictly independent of US Government involvement. However his activities over a period of years suggested the opposite. As one detailed account of his work reported: "Sharp's strategies of *civilian-based defense*—organized nonviolent non-cooperation and defiance—were dramatically applied during the Baltic states' secession from the Soviet Union. His book, *Civilian-Based Defense: A Post Military Weapons System*, helped shape the region's predominantly nonviolent liberation struggles. According to Sharp, in 1990 Audrius Butkvicius, then secretary of defense for Lithuania, obtained a smuggled copy of the book, which had yet to be published and was still in page-proof form. Butkvicius circulated 50 photocopied versions to states throughout the Soviet Union, including neighboring Latvia and Estonia. That year, Sharp and Bruce Jenkins, a research assistant at the Albert Einstein Institution, made several trips to the three Baltic capitals where *Civilian-Based Defense* was adapted as government policy." (cited in Claire Schaeffer-Duffy, "Honing nonviolence as a political weapon," *National Catholic Reporter*, Oct 21, 2005.

[7] Albert Einstein Institution website, *Burma* (http://www.aeinstein.org/organizationscf14.html).

[8] Amy Kazmin, "Defiance undeterred: Burmese activists seek ways to oust the junta," *Financial Times*, London, December 6 2007. Curiously, though Mr Sharp protested his organization's innocence from any involvement with the US Government in destabilizing the Burmese regime, he posted the *Financial Times* article on his own website.

[9] Ibid.

[10] Amitabh Pal, "Gene Sharp," *The Progressive*, March, 2007 (http://findarticles.com/p/articles/mi_m1295/is_3_71/ai_n19206283).

[11] Agence France Press, "Bush Urges Myanmar to free Suu Kyi," July 6, 2008.

[12] Juli A. Mac Donald, *Indo-US Military Relationship: Expectations And Perceptions*, Office of the Secretary of Defense – Net Assessment, October 2002.

[13] Condoleezza Rice, et al, *The National Security Strategy of the United States*, Washington, September 2002.

[14] US 7th Fleet Public Affairs, Navy News Stand, "Exercise Malabar 07-2 Kicks Off," Story Number: NNS070907-13, Navy News Stand, 9/7/2007.

[15] Deepal Jayasekara, "Indian prime minister's visit to China seeks to boost bilateral ties, but tensions persist," *WSWS News*, January 30, 2008 (http://www.wsws.org/articles/2008/jan2008/indi-j30.shtml).

[16] Keith Harmon Snow, "Merchants of Death: Exposing Corporate-Financed Holocaust in Africa: White Collar War Crimes; Black African Fall Guys," December 7, 2008 (http://www.globalresearch.ca/index.php?context=va&aid=11311).

[17] F. William Engdahl, "Darfur: Forget genocide, there's oil," *Asia Times*, May 25, 2007 (http://www.atimes.com/atimes/China).

[18] Quoted in Loro Horta, "China and Angola Strengthen Bilateral Relationship," PINR, 23 June, 2006.

[19] Jim Lehrer, *Powell Declares Killing in Darfur Genocide*, The News Hour with Jim Lehrer, Sep. 9, 2004 (http://www.pbs.org/newshour/updates/sudan).

[20] Mark Magnier, "China Stakes a Claim for Major Access to Oil Around the World," *The Los Angeles Times*, July 17, 2005 (http://articles.latimes.com/2005/jul/17/world/fg-chinaoil17).

[21] Jane Morse, "Assistant Secretary Sauerbrey Decries Genocide in Darfur," 17 November 2006, USINFO. (http://www.america.gov/st/washfile-english/2006/November/20061117175612ajesrom1.444209e-02.html#ixzz09dQe4AMz).

[22] *BBC News*, "UN 'rules out' genocide in Darfur," January 31, 2005. (http://news.bbc.co.uk/2/hi/africa/4222899.stm).

[23] Gary Pombeah, "Obituary: John Garang," *BBC News*, 3 August 2005. (http://news.bbc.co.uk/1/hi/world/africa/2134220.stm).

[24] Keith Harmon Snow, "Africom's Covert War in Sudan," *Dissident Voice*, March 6, 2009 (http://www.dissidentvoice.org/2009/03/africoms-covert-war-in-sudan/).

[25] Martin Plaut, "Who are Sudan's Darfur rebels?" *BBC News*, May 5, 2006 (http://news.bbc.co.uk/2/hi/africa/3702242.stm).

[26] International Crisis Group, "Darfur: Revitalizing the Peace Process," *Africa Report*, No. 125, April 30, 2007, p.1. On the role of Chad's Deby the report states: "Chad's role has complicated the conflict. The Zaghawa elements of the insurgency have enjoyed relatively consistent support from the Zaghawa-dominated government there. Though President Deby, himself a Zaghawa, initially cooperated with Khartoum against the rebellion, his government now gives the rebels open and sizeable support. In response, the NCP has been arming Chadian rebel groups, with the aim of overthrowing Deby and cutting off the SLA and JEM rear bases."

[27] Rob Crilly, "Sudan cuts ties with Chad after Darfur rebels reach Khartoum," *The Times* (London), May 12, 2008.

[28] *The World Bank, Report No. PID7288,* Cameroon-(Chad)Petroleum Development and Pipeline Project, *Implementation Agencies:Subsidiaries of Exxon, Shell and Elf, June 23, 1999.*

[29] Alexander's Oil & Gas, "Chad-China oil talks are going well," April 20, 2007 (http://www.gasandoil.com/goc/news/nta71983.htm).

[30] *BBC News*, "US naval base to protect Sao Tome oil," August 22, 2002 (http://news.bbc.co.uk/2/hi/business/2210571.stm).

[31] Walter Kansteiner, Assistant Secretary of State, cited in Ken Silverstein, "US Oil Politics in the 'Kuwait of Africa'," *The Nation*, April 4, 2002 (http://www.thenation.com/doc/20020422/silverstein).

[32] Kathleen T. Rehm, "Rumsfeld Discusses Defense Issues With Indian Officials,," *American Forces Press Service*, December 9, 2004 (http://www.defenselink.mil/news/newsarticle.aspx?id=24638).

[33] Dana Perino, "Bush raises concerns about Tibet with Chinese president," March 27th, 2008 accessed in, http://www.thaindian.com/newsportal/world-news/bush-raises-concerns-about-tibet-with-chinese-president_10031681.html.

[34] Rainer Amstaedter, "Der schmale Grat der Erinnerung: Zwischen Hitler und Himalaya," *DATUM - Seiten der Zeit*, January 2006 (http://www.datum.at/0106/stories/1476613/). Amstaedter conducted thorough research in the NSDA archives and interviews with former associates of Harrer to document the actual active Nazi past of Harrer who 'conveniently' forgot details of his SS days. The Wikipedia biography of Harrer omits any mention of the SS past, as well, preferring the Hollywood romanticized and sanitized version, evidently.

[35] Ex-Nazi, Dalai's tutor Harrer dies at 93," *The Times of India*, Jan 9, 2006 (http://timesofindia.indiatimes.com/articleshow/msid-1363946,prtpage-1.cms).

[36] *Nicholas Goodrick-Clarke*, Black Sun: Aryan Cults, Esoteric Nazism and the Politics of Identity *(New York: New York University Press, 2001), 177.*

[37] Goldner, Colin, *Mönchischer Terror auf dem Dach der Welt Teil 1: Die Begeisterung für den Dalai Lama und den tibetischen Buddhismus,* March 26, 2008, excerpted from *Dalai Lama: Fall eines Gottkönigs* (Alibri Verlag, April 2008) http://www.jungewelt.de/2008/03-27/006.php.

[38] Jim Mann, "CIA Gave Aid to Tibetan Exiles in '60s, Files Show," *Los Angeles Times*, September 15, 1998 (http://articles.latimes.com/1998/sep/15/news/mn-22993). Mann reported on the release of classified CIA documents that among other items stated: "For much of the 1960s, the CIA provided the Tibetan exile movement with $1.7 million a year for operations against China, including an annual subsidy of $180,000 for the Dalai Lama, according to newly released U.S. intelligence documents. The money for the Tibetans and the Dalai Lama was part of the CIA's worldwide effort during the height of the Cold War to undermine Communist governments, particularly in the Soviet Union and China. In fact, the U.S. government committee that approved the Tibetan operations also authorized the disastrous Bay of Pigs invasion of Cuba. The documents, published last month by the State Department, illustrate the historical background of the situation in Tibet today, in which China continues to accuse the Dalai Lama of being an agent of foreign forces seeking to separate Tibet from China. The CIA's program encompassed support of Tibetan guerrillas in Nepal, a covert military training site in Colorado, "Tibet Houses" established to promote Tibetan causes

in New York and Geneva, education for Tibetan operatives at Cornell University and supplies for reconnaissance teams.' Mann continued citing the declassified text of the CIA as released by the US State Department, 'The purpose of the program ... is to keep the political concept of an autonomous Tibet alive within Tibet and among foreign nations, principally India, and to build a capability for resistance against possible political developments inside Communist China,' explains one memo written by top U.S. intelligence officials."

[39] Michael Parenti, "Friendly Feudalism: he Tibet Myth," June 2007 (www.michaelparenti.org/Tibet.html).

[40] Ibid.

[41] Mann, Jim, "CIA funded covert Tibet exile campaign in 1960s," *The Age* (Australia), Sept. 16, 1998.

[42] Parenti, "Friendly Feudalism: The Tibet Myth."

[43] David Ignatius, "Innocence Abroad: The New World of Spyless Coups," *The Washington Post*, September 22, 1991.

[44] William Blum, "The NED and 'Project Democracy'," January 2000 (www.friendsoftibet.org/databank/usdefence/usd5.html).

[45] Michael Barker, "'Democratic Imperialism': Tibet, China and the National Endowment for Democracy," *Global Research*, August 13, 2007 (http://www.globalresearch.ca/index.php?context=va&aid=6530).

[46] Seth Faison, "China Says Detained American Rights Advocate Admits Falsifying Documentaries," *The New York Times*, July 28, 1995.

[47] Morgan Strong, "China Maverick Harry Wu," *Playboy*, February 1996.

[48] Ralph McGehee, *Ralph McGehee's Archive on JFK Place, CIA Operations in China Part III*, May 2, 1996 (www.acorn.net/jfkplace/03/RM/RM.china-for).

[49] Barker, Op. cit.

[50] US Tibet Committee, "Fifteen things you should know about Tibet and China," (http://ustibetcommittee.org/facts/facts.html).

[51] *Colin Goldner,* Mönchischer Terror auf dem Dach der Welt Teil 2: Krawalle im Vorfeld der Olympischen Spiele, *Op. cit.*

[52] Jonathan Mowat, "The new Gladio in action?," *Online Journal*, Mar 19, 2005 (http://onlinejournal.com/artman/publish/printer_308.shtml).

[53] Ibid.

[54] Ibid.

[55] Ibid.

[56] Zbigniew Brzezinski, "A Geostrategy for Eurasia," *Foreign Affairs*, 76:5, September/October 1997.

CHAPTER FIVE

The Empire of Bases— the Basis of Empire

If war aims are stated which seem to be solely concerned with Anglo-American imperialism, they will offer little to people in the rest of the world. The interests of other peoples should be stressed. This would have a better propaganda effect.

> — *Private memo from the Council on Foreign Relations to the US State Department, 1941, in CFR War & Peace Studies archives.*

US Bases Encircle Russia

The expansion of Washington's missile defense shield to Poland and the Czech Republic, as well as the decision to occupy Iraq and Afghanistan, could be better understood when viewed from the standpoint of the remarkable expansion of NATO since 1991.

As Russia's Putin noted in his February 2007 Munich remarks:

> *NATO has put its frontline forces on our borders...(I/we?) think it is obvious that NATO expansion does not have any relation with the modernisation of the Alliance itself or with ensuring security in Europe. On the contrary, it represents a serious provocation that reduces the level of mutual trust. And we have the right to ask: against whom is this expansion intended? And what happened to the assurances our western partners made after the dissolution of the Warsaw Pact?*[1]

Russian strategist and military expert, Yevgeny Primakov, former Prime Minister under Yeltsin and a close adviser to Vladimir Putin, noted that NATO had been "founded during the Cold War era as a regional organization to ensure the security of US allies in Europe." He added,

NATO today is acting on the basis of an entirely different philosophy and doctrine, moving outside the European continent and conducting military operations far beyond its bounds. NATO...is rapidly expanding in contravention to earlier accords. The admission of new members to NATO is leading to the expansion of bases that host the US military, air defense systems, as well as ABM components.[2]

By 2007, NATO member states included not only the Cold War core in Western Europe, commanded by an American, but also the former Warsaw Pact or Soviet Union states Poland, Latvia, the Czech Republic, Estonia, Lithuania, Romania, Bulgaria, Hungary, Slovakia and Slovenia, formerly of Yugoslavia. Candidates to join included the Republic of Georgia, Croatia, Albania and Macedonia. Ukraine's President, Victor Yushchenko, tried aggressively to bring Ukraine into NATO. This was all a clear message to Moscow which, not surprisingly, they didn't seem to welcome with open arms.

New NATO structures had been formed while old ones were abolished: The NATO Response Force (NRF) was launched at the 2002 Prague Summit. In 2003, just after the fall of Baghdad, a major restructuring of the NATO military commands began. The Headquarters of the Supreme Allied Commander, Atlantic was abolished. A new command, Allied Command Transformation (ACT), was established in Norfolk, Virginia. ACT was responsible for driving 'transformation' in NATO.

By 2007 Washington had signed an agreement with Japan to cooperate on missile defense development. Washington was deeply engaged in testing a missile defense system with Israel. The US had extended its European Missile Defense to the Czech Republic and to Poland, where the Minister of Defense, Radek Sikorski, was a close friend and ally of Pentagon neo-conservative warhawks.

NATO had also put the question of Ukraine's and Georgia's bids for NATO membership on a 'fast track.' On February 15, 2007 the US House of Representatives Foreign Affairs Committee approved a draft of the

Orwellian-named "NATO Freedom Consolidation Act of 2007," reaffirming US backing for the further enlargement of NATO, including support for Ukraine to join along with Georgia.

Meanwhile, the Middle East, despite the debacle in Iraq, was being militarized with a permanent network of US bases from Qatar to Iraq, Afghanistan and beyond.

From the Russian point of view, NATO's eastward expansion since the end of the cold war had been in clear breach of an agreement between former Soviet leader Mikhail Gorbachev and US President George H.W. Bush, which had opened the way for a peaceful unification of Germany in 1990. NATO's expansion policy was a continuation of a Cold War attempt to surround and isolate Russia. At least, that was how it most definitely appeared to those in Moscow looking west and south.

New US Bases To Guard 'Democracy'?

An almost unnoticed consequence of Washington's policy since the bombing of Serbia in 1999, had been establishment of an extraordinary network of new US military bases.

The bases were to be located in parts of the world where there was seemingly little to justify them as a US defensive precaution, given the absence of any conceivable threat. They had been built at huge taxpayer expense, above and beyond the vast costs of other US global military commitments.

The dominant trend from the end of the Second World War until the Korean War had been a *reduction* in the number of US overseas bases. Within two years of Victory-Japan Day, half the global US wartime basing structure was gone; half of what had been maintained until 1947 had been dismantled by 1949.

This postwar reduction in the number of overseas bases, however, ended with the Korean War in the early 1950's, when the number of bases increased once more, followed by further increases during the Vietnam War.

Camp Bondsteel in Kosovo is the largest Foreign US base since Vietnam
and a key launch point for control of the entire region

By 1988, US bases numbered slightly fewer than at the end of the Korean War, but reflected a very different global pattern than at the beginning of the post-Second World War period, with the sharpest declines in South Asia and Middle East/Africa.

In June 1999, the expansion of US bases around the world took on a qualitatively new dimension. Following the bombing of Yugoslavia, US forces began construction of Camp Bondsteel, on the border between Kosovo and Macedonia. It was the lynchpin in what was to be a new global network of US bases.

Bondsteel put US air power within easy striking distance of the oil-rich Middle East and Caspian Sea, as well as of Russia. Camp Bondsteel, at the time it was installed, was the largest US military base built since the Vietnam War. With nearly 7,000 troops, it had been built by the largest US military construction company, Halliburton's KBR. Halliburton's CEO at the time was Dick Cheney.

Before the start of the NATO bombing of Yugoslavia in 1999, the *Washington Post* matter-of-factly noted, "With the Middle-East increasingly fragile, we will need bases and fly-over rights in the Balkans to protect Caspian Sea oil."[3]

Camp Bondsteel was but the first in a vast chain of US bases that would be built during the decade. The US military went on to build military bases in Hungary, Bosnia-Herzegovina, Albania and Macedonia, in addition to Camp Bondsteel in Kosovo, then still legally part of Yugoslavia.

On August 16, 2004, President Bush announced what was described as the most comprehensive restructuring of US military forces overseas since the end of the Korean War. It was a program of sweeping changes to the numbers and locations of military basing facilities at overseas locations, now known as the Integrated Global Presence and Basing Strategy (IGPBS).

Roughly 70,000 personnel would return from overseas locations from Europe and Asia to bases in the continental United States. Other overseas forces would be redistributed within current host nations such as Germany and South Korea.

New bases would be established in Eastern Europe, Central Asia, and Africa. In the Pentagon's view, these locations would be closer to their targets, better able "to respond to potential trouble spots."[4] The new plan would require new facilities costing billions of dollars, some of the cost to be borne by the United States and some by other nations.

In a conflict—-and in Pentagon-speak there are now only 'conflicts,' no longer wars because wars require asking the US Congress to declare them officially, with justification and reasons—-the military would 'surge' men and materiel toward the front lines.

The provocative geopolitical nature of the global network of bases became clear because of their locations. One of the most important and least mentioned of the new US bases was in Bulgaria, a former Soviet satellite and now a NATO member. Understandably, Kremlin planners wondered if the new front lines included Russia.

But, alongside the encroachment and encirclement agenda of the Pentagon, another agenda appeared to be operating.

Defending The Opium Fields?

The US built bases in Afghanistan in the wake of its blitzkrieg war in late 2001, long after it had given up the charade of searching for Osama bin Laden in the caves of Tora Bora. Notably, along with the US occupation of Afghanistan, the cultivation of opium for heroin reached record high levels under the new US military presence.

This was reminiscent of the situation during the Vietnam War, when the CIA and special units of the US military worked with the Meo tribesmen in Laos to secure control over the heroin routes of South East Asia. The CIA then used the drug revenues, laundered through CIA bank proprietary front companies like the Nugan Hand Bank in Australia, to finance other covert operations and intelligence activities. Strong evidence emerged from Interpol and US surveys and reports that US forces in Afghanistan had more than a passing interest in the explosion of opium cultivation in Afghanistan after 2001. Along with the opium cultivation came an explosion in permanent US military bases as well.[5]

In December 2004, during a visit to Kabul, US Defense Secretary Donald Rumsfeld finalized plans to build nine new bases in Afghanistan in the provinces of Helmand, Herat, Nimrouz, Balkh, Khost and Paktia. The nine were in addition to the three major US military bases already installed in the wake of its occupation of Afghanistan in winter of 2001-2002, ostensibly to isolate and eliminate the terror threat of Osama bin Laden.

The Pentagon had built its first three bases at Bagram Air Field north of Kabul, the US' main military logistics center; Kandahar Air Field, in southern Afghanistan; and Shindand Air Field in the western province of Herat. Shindand, the largest US base in Afghanistan, was constructed a scant 100 kilometers from the border of Iran, and within striking distance of Russia as well as China.

Afghanistan had historically been the heartland for the British-Russia Great Game, the struggle for control of Central Asia during the 19th and early 20th Centuries. British strategy then was to prevent Russia at all costs from controlling Afghanistan and thereby threatening Britain's imperial crown jewel, India.

Afghanistan was similarly regarded by Pentagon planners as highly strategic. It was a platform from which US military power could directly threaten Russia and China, as well as Iran and other oil-rich Middle East lands. Little had changed geopolitically over more than a century of wars.

Afghanistan was in an extremely vital location, straddling South Asia, Central Asia, and the Middle East. Afghanistan also lay along a proposed oil pipeline route from the Caspian Sea oil fields to the Indian Ocean, where the US oil company, Unocal, along with Enron and Cheney's Halliburton, had been in negotiations for exclusive pipeline rights to bring natural gas from Turkmenistan across Afghanistan and Pakistan to Enron's huge natural gas power plant at Dabhol near Mumbai.

At that same time, the Pentagon came to an agreement with the government of Kyrgyzstan in Central Asia, to build a strategically important base there — Manas Air Base at Bishkek's international airport. Manas was not only close to Afghanistan; it was also within easy striking distance of Caspian Sea oil and gas, as well as the borders of both China and Russia.

As part of the price of accepting Pakistan's military dictator, General Pervez Musharraf as a US ally rather than a foe in the 'War on Terror,' Washington extracted an agreement from him: to allow the airport at Jacobabad, about 400km north of Karachi, to be used by the US Air Force and NATO to support their campaign in Afghanistan. Two additional US bases were built at Dalbandin and Pasni.

These 13 new US installations across Eurasia were merely a small part of the vast web of US-controlled military bases Washington constructed after 2001.

Yet, the alleged pretext for the military expansion evaporated almost instantly: within weeks of the attack on Afghanistan, the pursuit of Osama bin Laden somehow was lost in the shuffle, the arch-fiend left to roam in the caves of Tora Bora.

No sooner had Washington taken effective military control of Kabul, than the Pentagon turned its military sights on Saddam Hussein's Iraq, the fulcrum of Bush's 'Axis of Evil,' allegedly harboring nuclear, chemical and biological weapons of mass destruction aimed directly at America and its allies.

Within months of its occupation of Iraq, reports began leaking out indicating that the Pentagon was there to stay, as Defense Secretary Robert Gates put it, "for a very long time."[6]

In order to hide the staggering costs of the Iraq war and subsequent occupation from American taxpayers, the Bush Administration resorted to a practice of requesting Iraq funds in various 'supplemental funding bills' submitted separately after the main budget debate had ended. Buried in Bush's May 2005 Iraq 'supplemental funding' request was a provision for construction of US military bases, glibly described as "in some very limited cases, permanent facilities."

According to press reports, by 2006 the US had constructed no fewer than 14 permanent bases in Iraq— a country that is only twice the size of the state of Idaho, making a mockery of Presidential pledges to plan a US troop withdrawal. Fourteen bases built in Iraq by the US after March 2003 suggested that the US 'liberation' of Iraq from Saddam Hussein had a hardcore military content. The freedom seemed mainly to be freedom for Washington to build its military garrisons along Iraqi oil fields and on the Iraq border with Iran.[7]

By far the most significant Iraqi base was the combined Balad Air Base and Camp Anaconda, just north of Baghdad. It accommodated both Air Force fighters and transport aircraft. Camp Anaconda, adjacent to the air base, served as a main base and logistics center for US troops in central Iraq. Military analysts noted that Balad was perfectly positioned to project US power throughout the Middle East.[8]

The calculated positioning of new US military bases was by no means restricted to the Eurasian Continent, although Eurasia was clearly the strategic priority for US military planners; their geographic reach was global. As military analyst Zoltan Grossman noted:

> *The most direct US intervention after the Afghan invasion had been in the southern Philippines, against the Moro (Muslim) guerrilla militia Abu Sayyaf. The US claimed the tiny Abu Sayyaf group was inspired by Bin Laden, rather than a thuggish outgrowth of decades of Moro insurgency in Mindanao and the Sulu Archipelago.[9]*

US Special Forces 'trainers' were carrying out joint 'exercises' with Philippine troops in an active combat zone. Their goal was allegedly to achieve an easy Grenada-style victory over the 200 rebels, for the global propaganda effect against Bin Laden. But once in place, the counter-insurgency campaign could easily be redirected against other Moro or even Communist rebel groups in Mindanao. It could also help achieve the other major US goal in the Philippines: to fully re-establish US military basing rights, which had ended when the Philippine Senate terminated US control of Clark Air Base and Subic Naval Base after the Cold War ended, and after a volcanic eruption damaged both bases.

A US return to the Philippines, like Bush's threats against North Korea, was seen by many in the region as an effort to assert even greater US influence in East Asia, just when China was rising as a global power and other Asian economies were recovering from financial crises. A growing US military role throughout Asia could also raise fears in China of a US sphere of influence intruding on its borders. Additionally, the new US air base in the ex-Soviet republic of Kyrgyzstan was, for China, too close for comfort.

Meanwhile, other regions of the world were also being targeted in the US 'War on Terror,' notably South America. Just as Cold War propaganda had recast leftist rebels in South Vietnam and El Salvador as puppets of North Vietnam or Cuba, US 'War on Terror' propaganda recast Colombian rebels as allies of neighboring oil-rich Venezuela. The Venezuelan President, Hugo Chavez, was described as 'sympathetic' to Bin Laden and Fidel Castro, and as possibly turning OPEC against the US. Chavez could serve as an ideal new US enemy if Bin Laden were ever eliminated. The crisis in South America, though it could not be tied to Islamic militancy, was perhaps the next dangerous new war in the making.[10]

By 2007 it was becoming clear for much of the world that Washington was instigating wars or conflicts with nations all across the globe, and not merely to control oil — though strategic control of global oil flows had been at the heart of the American Century since the 1920's. The ultimate aim of the various conflicts and military actions was to control the economies of any and all of potential contenders for rival power, any nation or group of nations that might decide to challenge America's uncontested primary role as master in world affairs.

Beginning already in the 1980's, long-term Washington strategists and influential think-tanks realized that they had hollowed out US industrial capacities, and that soon other nations or regions, such as an emerging European Union or East Asian and Chinese economic powers, were developing the potential to one day challenge American supremacy.

By 2001, as George Bush and Dick Cheney came to Washington, the US establishment, the powerful old patricians of American power, had decided that drastic measures would be required to sustain American dominance well into the new century.

US Bases Expand After The Cold War

In the late 1980s, *Glasnost* and *Perestroika*, followed by the collapse of the Soviet-dominated regimes in Eastern Europe in 1989 and the demise of the Soviet Union itself in 1991, had generated expectations that there would be a rapid dismantling of the US basing system. Expectations were especially strong among those who had thought that US bases existed to contain the Soviet threat.

Yet, the Department of Defense insisted, in its 1989 *Report of the Secretary Defense*, that the "power projection" of the United States continued to necessitate such "forward deployments."[11]

On August 2, 1990 President George H.W. Bush had issued a statement indicating that although by 1995 US global security requirements might be met by an active force 25 percent smaller than in 1990, nonetheless the US overseas basing system should remain intact. On that same day Iraq invaded Kuwait.

The massive introduction of US troops into the Middle East during the Gulf War led to the proclamation of a New World Order rooted in US hegemony and US military power. "By God, we've kicked the Vietnam Syndrome once and for all," Bush jubilantly declared.[12] New military bases in the Middle East were soon established, most notably in Saudi Arabia, where thousands of US troops have been stationed ever since.

Although the Clinton administration was to insist more strongly than the Bush administration that preceded it on the need to diminish US foreign military commitments, no attempt was made to decrease the US 'forward presence' abroad represented by its far-flung military bases. The main shift was simply to reduce the number of troops permanently stationed overseas by deploying troops more frequently but for shorter stays.[13]

A 1999 Army War College study admitted, "While permanent overseas presence has decreased dramatically, operational deployments have increased exponentially." In earlier times, members of the armed forces were routinely 'stationed' overseas, usually for tours of several years and often accompanied by their families. Now they would be 'deployed,' with the length of tour more uncertain and dependents almost never allowed.

The deployments were frequent and lengthy, however. On any given day before September 11, 2001, according to the Defense Department, more than 60,000 military personnel were conducting temporary operations and exercises in about 100 countries. While the mammoth European installations had been cut back, Defense Department records showed that the new mode of operations called military personnel away from home about 135 days a year for the Army, 170 days for the Navy and 176 days for the Air Force. Each US Army soldier now averaged a deployment abroad every 14 weeks.

In addition to such frequent, periodic troop deployments, the bases were used for pre-positioning equipment for purposes of rapid deployment. For example, the United States pre-positioned equipment for a heavy brigade to be located in Kuwait, and for a second heavy brigade in Qatar, along with equipment for a tank battalion, also in Qatar.[14]

The 1990s ended with US military intervention in the Balkans and extensive US support for counterinsurgency operations in South America as part of 'Plan Colombia.' Conveniently, Colombia gave US troops a base next door to another potential US target: Venezuela.

Following the September 11, 2001 attacks on the World Trade Center and the onset of the 'Global War on Terrorism,' a rapid increase in the number and geographical spread of US military bases had begun.

According to the Defense Department's *Base Structure Report*, the United States at that time had overseas military installations in 38 countries and separate territories. If military bases in US territories/possessions outside the fifty states and the District of Columbia were added, it rose to 44. This number was extremely conservative, however, since it did not include strategically important forward bases, even some of those in which the United States maintains substantial numbers of troops, such as Saudi Arabia, Kosovo, and Bosnia-Herzegovina. Nor did it include some of the most recently acquired US bases.

Through 'Plan Colombia'—aimed principally, or nominally at least, against guerrilla forces in Colombia but also against the Chavez government of Venezuela and the massively popular movement opposing neoliberalism in Ecuador—the United States was also in the process of expanding its base presence in the Latin American and Caribbean region.

Puerto Rico replaced Panama as the hub for the region. Meanwhile the United States had been busy establishing four new military bases in Manta, Ecuador; Aruba; Curaçao; and Comalapa, El Salvador—all characterized as forward operating locations (FOLs). Since September 11, 2001 the United States had set up military bases housing 60,000 troops in Afghanistan, Pakistan, Kyrgyzstan, Uzbekistan, and Tajikistan, along with Kuwait, Qatar, Turkey, and Bulgaria. Crucial in the operation was a major US naval base at Diego Garcia in the Indian Ocean.

In some ways the official number of bases abroad was deceptively low. All issues of jurisdiction and authority with respect to bases in host countries were spelled out in what are called Status of Forces Agreements. During the Cold War years those were normally public documents. But now they were often classified as secret—for example, those with Kuwait, the United Arab Emirates, Oman, and in certain respects Saudi Arabia.

According to Pentagon records, the United States by 2007 had formal agreements of that kind with 93 countries.[15]

Apart from the Balkans and the former Soviet Republics of Central Asia, which were previously within the Soviet sphere of influence or part of the Soviet Union itself, the forward bases that were being acquired were in regions where the United States had previously experienced drastic reductions in the number of its bases. In 1990, prior to the Gulf War, the United States had no bases in South Asia, for example, and in the Middle East / Africa only 10 percent as many as in 1947. Similarly, in Latin America and the Caribbean, the number of US bases had declined by about two-thirds between 1947 and 1990.

From a geopolitical, geo-military standpoint, this was clearly a problem for a global economic and military hegemon such as the United States, even in the age of long-range cruise missiles. The appearance of new bases in the Middle East, South Asia, Latin America and the Caribbean since 1990— as a result of the Gulf War, the war in Afghanistan, and Plan Colombia—could therefore be seen as a reassertion of direct US military power in areas where it had eroded.

The build-up of bases in Afghanistan, Pakistan, and three of the former Soviet republics of Central Asia was inevitably seen by Russia and China as constituting additional and ongoing threats to their security.

Russia indicated its displeasure at the prospect of permanent US military bases in Central Asia. China was likewise displeased. As the *Guardian* of London noted on January 10, 2002, the base at Manas in Kyrgyzstan, where US planes were landing daily, was "250 miles from the western Chinese border. With US bases to the east in Japan, to the south in South Korea, and Washington's military support for Taiwan, China may feel encircled."[16] That was putting it mildly.

Decline Of An Empire?

Much as the old Roman Empire declined and ultimately vanished over the course of the fourth century AD, the American Empire, too, gave every sign of being in terminal decline as Bush and Cheney launched their bold military policies to extend its imperial life or, as George H.W.

Bush had more appropriately termed it at the end of the Cold War, the New World Order.[17]

Increasingly, American influence in the world could no longer be won by persuasion and Coca Cola or McDonalds 'Big Macs.' Raw military force was considered essential by the beginning of the new century. That itself was a *de facto* admission of the failure of the American Century.

This was merely a small part of the vast web of US-controlled military bases that Washington had been building globally since the so-called end of the Cold War.

'Leaner, Meaner' Nuclear Strike Force

During the early 1990s, at the end of the Cold War, the Yeltsin government had asked Washington for a series of mutual reductions in the size of each superpower's nuclear missile and weapons arsenal. Russian nuclear stockpiles were aging and Moscow saw little further need to remain armed to its nuclear teeth once the Cold War had ended.

Washington clearly viewed this as a golden opportunity to go for 'nuclear primacy,' the ability to launch a nuclear first strike against Russia for the first time since the 1950s, when Russia first developed Inter-Continental Ballistic Missile delivery capability for its growing nuclear weapons arsenal.

The Pentagon began replacing aging ballistic missiles on its submarines with far more accurate Trident II D-5 missiles with new, larger-yield nuclear warheads.

The Navy shifted more of its nuclear ballistic missile-launching SSBN submarines to the Pacific to patrol the blind spots of Russia's early warning radar net as well as to patrol near China's coast. The US Air Force completely refitted its B-52 bombers with nuclear-armed cruise missiles believed invisible to Russian air defense radar. New enhanced avionics on its B-2 stealth bombers gave them the ability to fly at extremely low altitudes, avoiding radar detection as well.

A vast number of stockpiled weapons were not necessary to the new global power projection. Little-publicized new technology has enabled the US to deploy a 'leaner and meaner' nuclear strike force. A case in point was the Navy's successful program to upgrade the fuse on the W-76 nuclear warheads sitting atop most US submarine-launched missiles, enabling them to hit very hard targets such as ICBM silos.

No one had ever presented credible evidence that Al Qaeda, Hamas, Hezbollah or any other organization on the US State Department's Terrorist Organization Black List possessed nuclear missiles in hardened underground silos. Aside from the US and perhaps Israel, only Russia and, to a far smaller degree, China had such nuclear missile arsenals in any significant number.

US Nuclear Bombers On Constant Alert

In 1991, at the presumed end of the Cold War, in a gesture to lower the danger of strategic nuclear miscalculation, the US Air Force was ordered to remove its fleet of nuclear bombers from Ready Alert status. After 2004 that order, too, was reversed.

CONPLAN 8022 again put US Air Force long-range B-52 and other bombers on 'Alert' status. The Commander of the 8th Air Force stated at the time, that his nuclear bombers were "essentially on alert to plan and execute Global Strikes" on behalf of the US Strategic Command or STRATCOM, based in Omaha, Nebraska.[18]

CONPLAN 8022 included not only long-range nuclear and conventional weapons launched from the US, but also nuclear and other bombs deployed in Europe, Japan and other sites. It gave the US what the Pentagon termed "Global Strike" — the ability to hit any point on the earth or sky with devastating force, nuclear as well as conventional. Since Rumsfeld's June 2004 readiness order, the US Strategic Command had boasted it was ready to execute an attack anywhere on earth "in half a day or less," from the moment the President gave the order.[19]

Interviewed by London's *Financial Times*, the US Ambassador to NATO, former Cheney advisor, Victoria Nuland, declared that the US wanted a ",globally deployable military force" that would operate everywhere – from Africa to the Middle East and beyond—"all across our planet."[20]

It would include Japan and Australia as well as the NATO nations. Nuland added, "It's a totally different animal."[21] NATO's ultimate role would be subject to US desires and adventures. Those were hardly calming words, given the record of Nuland's former boss, Vice President Dick Cheney, in faking intelligence to justify wars in Iraq and elsewhere.

Now, with the deployment of even a minimal missile defense, under CONPLAN 8022 the US would have what Pentagon planners called "Escalation Dominance"—the ability to win a war at any level of violence, including nuclear war.

As the authors of the *Foreign Affairs* article noted,

> *Washington's continued refusal to eschew a first strike and the country's development of a limited missile-defense capability take on a new, and possibly more menacing, look...a nuclear-war-fighting capability remains a key component of the United States' military doctrine and nuclear primacy remains a goal of the United States.* [22]

As some more sober minds argued, were Russia and China to respond to these US moves with even minimal self-protection measures, the risks of a global nuclear conflagration by miscalculation would climb to levels far beyond any seen even during the Cuban Missile Crisis or the most dangerous days of the Cold War.

However, for the hawks, the US military industrial machine, and the neo-conservatives surrounding the Bush-Cheney Administration, such fears of nuclear Armageddon were signs of cowardice and a lack of will. Here the curious history of what came to be known during the Reagan era as 'Star Wars' gave a better idea of what Washington's provocative missile defense strategy was about.

Endnotes:

[1] Vladimir Putin, *Rede des russischen Präsidenten Wladimir Putin auf der 43. Münchner, Sicherheitskonferenz,'* München, October 2, 2007.

[2] Yevgeny Primakov, "ABM sites on Russia's frontiers: Another Confrontation?," *Moscow News*, March 2, 2007.

[3] *Washington Post*, February 28, 1999.

[4] US Army Press Release, Integrated Global Presence and Basing Strategy, March 22, 2006 (http://lists.army.mil/pipermail/stand-to/2006-March/000037.html).

[5] Karen de Young, "Afghanistan Opium Crop Sets Record: U.S.-Backed Efforts At Eradication Fail," *Washington Post*, December 2, 2006.

[6] Sgt. Sara Wood, "Gates: Early Withdrawal Would Have Dire Consequences for US, US Department of Defense," *AFPS News Articles*, May 9, 2007 (http://www.defenselink.mil/news/newsarticle.aspx?id=45956).

[7] *Daniel Widome, "The Six Most Important US Military Bases," www.foreignpolicy.com* May 2006. Chalmers Johnson, *America's Empire of Bases*, in www.TomDispatch.com, January 15, 2004. Zoltan Grossman, *New US Military Bases: Side Effects or Causes of War?*, in www.counterpunch.org/zoltanbases.html, February 2, 2002. Ramtanu Maitra, *US Scatters Bases to Control Eurasia*, in Asia Times Online, March 30, 2005. William Clark, *Will US be asked to leave key military bases?*, www.csmonitor.com , July 5, 2005. Thom Shanker and Eric Smith, *'Pentagon Expects Long-Term Access to Four Key Bases in Iraq'*, New York Times, April 20, 2003. Christine Spolar, *'14 'Enduring Bases' Set for Iraq,'* Chicago Tribune, March 23, 2004. www.globemaster.de/cgi-bin/bases provides a profile of every listed US airbase.

[8] Ibid.

[9] Zoltan Grossman, "New US Military Bases: Side Effects or Causes of War?" (www.counterpunch.org/zoltanbases.html).

[10] Ibid.

[11] U.S. Dept. of Defense. Report of the Secretary of Defense to the Congress, *National Defense Authorization Act for Fiscal Year 1989*.

[12] Cited in George C. Herring, "America and Vietnam: The Unending War," *Foreign Affairs*, Winter 1991/1992.

[13] *Los Angeles Times*, January 6, 2002.

[14] Report of the Secretary of Defense, 1996, pp.13–4.

[15] Chalmers Johnson, Blowback*: The Costs and Consequences of American Empire* (New York: Henry Holt, 2001), 4.

[16] Ian Traynor, "Russia edgy at spread of US bases in its backyard," *The Guardian*, January 10, 2002.

[17] George H. W. Bush, *Toward a New World Order*, Address to Joint Session of Congress, September 11, 1990. The words of Bush are worth citing. He declared, referring to the imminent coalition war on Iraq in 1991: "The crisis in the Persian Gulf, as grave as it is, also offers a rare opportunity to move toward an historic period of cooperation. Out of these troubled times, our fifth objective — a new world order — can emerge: a new era — freer from the threat of terror, stronger in the pursuit of justice, and more secure in the quest for peace. An era in which the nations of the world, East and West, North and South, can prosper and live in harmony. A hundred generations have searched for this elusive path to peace, while a thousand wars raged across the span of human endeavor. Today that new world is struggling to be born, a world quite different from the one we've known..." Again in his State of the Union Address after the onset of military action against Iraq, Operation Desert Storm, Bush declared, on January 21, 1991, "We will succeed in the Gulf. And when we do, the world community will have sent an enduring warning to any dictator or despot, present or future, who contemplates outlaw aggression.

"The world can therefore seize this opportunity to fulfill the long-held promise of a new world order—where brutality will go unrewarded, and aggression will meet collective resistance. Yes, the United States bears a major share of leadership in this effort. Among the nations of the world, only the United States of America has had both the moral standing, and the means to back it up. We are the only nation on this earth that could assemble the forces of peace." It was clear that Bush's vision of the New World Order was a version of a Pax Americana, a vision which found little enthusiasm in much of the world, hence the term, New World Order was promptly dropped. The agenda of that New World Order, a Pax Americana was never dropped. The Cold War from the side of Washington never ended. It continued in covert form.

[18] Hans M. Kristensen, "Global Strike: A Chronology of the Pentagon's New Offensive Strike Plan," Federation of American Scientists, Washington, D.C., March 15, 2006. As Kristensen's analysis made clear: "CONPLAN 8022 is premised on the preservation and improvement of an assured destruction capability for nuclear weapons, not just in retaliation but in preemption."

[19] Ibid.

[20] Victoria Nuland, US NATO Ambassador, quoted in *London's Financial Times*, January 24, 2006.

[21] Ibid.

[22] Keir A. Lieber and Daryl G. Press, op. cit.

CHAPTER SIX

The Curious History Of Star Wars

The October 2006 White House announcement of a new national space policy, and subsequent statements by the State Department raise grave concerns about whether a new push to militarize space has begun.
  – Richard C. Cook [1]

The Origins Of The US Missile Defense

The US program to build a global network of 'defense' against possible enemy ballistic missile attacks began on March 23, 1983 when then-President Ronald Reagan proposed the program popularly known as 'Star Wars,' formally called the Strategic Defense Initiative.

In 1994 at a private dinner discussion with this author in Moscow, the former head of economic studies for the Soviet Union's Institute of World Economy & International Relations, IMEMO, declared that it had been the huge financial demands required by Russia to keep pace with the multi-billion dollar US 'Star Wars' effort that finally led to the economic collapse of the Warsaw Pact and, ironically, led to German reunification in 1990.[2]

Combined with losing a war in Afghanistan, and the collapse of oil revenues after the US flooded world markets with Saudi oil in 1986, the USSR's military economy was unable to keep pace, short of risking massive civilian unrest across the Warsaw Pact nations.

NASA And Military Secrecy

1986 witnessed the greatest disaster to hit America's NASA Space Program since it was launched. NASA was created as a civilian project by President Dwight Eisenhower. Authorized in 1958 by the National Aeronautics and Space Act, NASA was an attempt to show the world that American science could trump Russia's Sputnik triumph. The President deliberately decided to keep the military out of NASA in order to use the program as a broad civilian science booster to the overall economy. The Act declared, "The Congress hereby declares that it is the policy of the United States that activities in space should be devoted to peaceful purposes for the benefit of mankind."[3]

Then, on January 28, 1986, the Space Shuttle Challenger exploded in flight killing all seven people on board—six astronauts and one teacher. NASA's Shuttle program had begun in the 1970s to create reusable craft for transporting cargo into space. Previous spacecraft could only be used once, then had to be discarded. The first shuttle, Columbia, was launched in 1981. One year later, the Challenger rolled off as the second shuttle of the US fleet. They were followed by Discovery in 1983 and Atlantis in 1985. The Challenger had flown nine successful missions before that fateful disaster in 1986.[4]

The reasons for the explosion were complex. Dr. Richard C. Cook, a federal government analyst at NASA, had testified to Congress at the time about the faulty O-rings that were the initiating cause of the explosion. After retiring from government service, Cook explained the real cause of the Challenger tragedy:

> *The mixing of civilian and military priorities by NASA led to the Challenger disaster of January 31, 1986, an incident which showed how muddled motives and lack of candor in public programs can result in tragedy.[5]*

Cook, whose position at NASA was Resource Analyst for NASA's Comptrollers Office, including for the space shuttle solid rocket boosters, revealed the internal and external factors:

On February 9, 1986, almost two weeks after Challenger was lost, the New York Times published a series of explosive documents, including a memo I had written the previous July—and which I shared with Times science writer Phil Boffey— warning of a possible catastrophe from a flawed O-ring joint. Thus began a cascade of disclosures that included the account of how contractor engineers protested against launching in the cold weather and NASA's past knowledge of the deficient booster rocket seals.

But it was not until after the presidential commission which investigated the disaster completed its work that I learned why NASA kept flying shuttle missions after the worst damage to date had occurred on the seals during a January 1985 cold-weather flight, a full year before Challenger blew up. It was because a launch commit criterion for joint temperature could interfere with the military flights NASA planned to launch for the Air Force out of Vandenberg Air Force base in California, where the weather tended to be cooler than in Florida. Many of these flights were to carry 'Star Wars' experiments in preparation for possible future deployment of 'third-generation' nuclear weapons, such as the x-ray laser. [6]

The revelation by Cook of the militarization of NASA going back to the mid-1980's in connection with Reagan's Star Wars was ominous enough. It meant the US military had been secretly violating treaty commitments and had already started an arms race in space during the 1980s. There was no immediate or obvious target other than the nuclear arsenal of the Soviet Union.

However, the Challenger tragedy had resulted in a suspension of further weapons testing in space until 2006. Then, in a little-noted statement of October 2006, the Bush-Cheney-Rumsfeld administration changed all that, and the militarization of space that Putin had warned of in his February 2007 Munich speech developed an alarming new component.

As Richard Cook detailed:

To date, the principal beneficiary of the moon-Mars program is Lockheed Martin, to which NASA awarded a prime contract with a potential value stated at $8.15 billion. Already the world's largest defense contractor, Lockheed Martin's stock yielded an instant bonanza, rising more than seven percent in the five weeks following NASA's August 2006 announcement.

NASA is not paying the giant of the military-industrial complex $8.15 billion to have people hop around and hit golf balls on the moon. The aim of the moon-Mars program is US dominance, as suggested by NASA Administrator Michael Griffin's statements that 'my language'—i.e., English—and not those of 'another, bolder or more persistent culture will be passed down over the generations to future lunar colonies.'

The first step will be a colony at the moon's south pole, described by NASA in a December 2006 announcement. According to Bruce Gagnon of the Global Network Against Weapons and Nuclear Power in Space, 'In the end, NASA's plan to establish permanent bases on the moon will help the military control and dominate access on and off our planet Earth and determine who will extract valuable resources from the moon in the years ahead.'

NASA's plans appear to be a step backward to the Cold War perspective which the International Space Station (ISS) was supposed to transcend and is contrary to its original mission. NASA's 1958 authorization stated that '. . . activities in space should be devoted to peaceful purposes for the benefit of mankind.' Fostering a 21st century race to the outposts of the solar system, which Griffin has likened to the armed scramble by European nations for colonies, would not appear to further the visionary goals for which NASA was created.[7]

In private communication with this author, Cook was even more alarming:

I believe that the US Establishment is in fact planning a nuclear first strike on Russia. There is a profound split within the US military, however, in that the Army and Navy and elements of the Air Force still view their job as a defensive force to secure the safety of the United States. The element of the military which aims for world conquest, even through a [nuclear] first strike, includes higher echelons of the Air Force, the Missile Defense Agency, and that part of the civilian [Pentagon] leadership most aligned with the powerful financial forces that are the real overseers of the country. [8]

That was a pretty heavy allegation. Evidence uncovered unfortunately showed it was no exaggeration.

Rumsfeld Backs Missile Defense

In July 1998, a time when nuclear ballistic missile threats to the United States might have seemed remote, Donald Rumsfeld delivered a report of the Commission to Assess the Ballistic Missile Threat to the United States, The 'Rumsfeld Commission,' to President Bill Clinton.

The Rumsfeld Commission Report outlined what it viewed as the strategic danger to the United States:

*Concerted efforts by a number of overtly or potentially hostile nations to acquire ballistic missiles with biological or nuclear payloads pose a growing threat to the United States, its deployed forces and its friends and allies. These newer, developing threats in **North Korea, Iran and Iraq** are in addition to those still posed by the existing ballistic missile arsenals of Russia and China, nations with which we are not now in conflict but which remain in uncertain transitions. The newer ballistic missile-equipped nations' capabilities will not match those of US systems for accuracy or reliability. However, they would be able to inflict major destruction on the US within about five years of a decision to acquire such a capability (10 years in the case of Iraq). During several of those years, the US might not be aware that such a decision had been made.*

The threat to the US posed by these emerging capabilities is broader, more mature and evolving more rapidly than has been reported in estimates and reports by the Intelligence Community. [9]

What was notable was that this was 1998 — three years before the events of September 11, 2001, and Donald Rumsfeld and other senior US policy advisors had already targeted Iraq, Iran and North Korea, the trio later named by President Bush as his 'Axis of Evil.'

Also notable was the fact that Rumsfeld had been joined on the nine-member commission by two of the most vocal neo-conservative warhawks in Washington: Paul Wolfowitz, who would become Rumsfeld's Deputy Defense Secretary and prime architect of the US war on Iraq; and former CIA head, James Woolsey, who headed Freedom House, the murky NGO tied to the US intelligence community and active in the 'Color Revolutions' from Georgia to Ukraine.

Rumsfeld's choice for Staff Director of the Rumsfeld Commission was Dr. Stephen Cambone, a neo-conservative hawk who would draft key sections of the September 2000 Project for a New American Century report, *Rebuilding America's Defenses*. The PNAC report, in addition to calling for US intervention for regime change in Iraq a full year before the September 2001 attacks, also called for US development of ethnic and race-based biological warfare technologies. Many of the report's authors — including Dick Cheney, Wolfowitz, Cambone and Rumsfeld — went on to implement its recommendations within the Bush Administration after 9/11.

On May 8, 2003, Rumsfeld named Cambone Undersecretary of Defense for Intelligence, a new position which Deputy Secretary of Defense Paul Wolfowitz described thus: "The new office is in charge of all intelligence and intelligence-related oversight and policy guidance functions."[10]

In practice, this meant that Cambone controlled the Defense Intelligence Agency, the National Imagery and Mapping Agency, the National Reconnaissance Organization, the National Security Agency, the Defense Security Service and Pentagon's Counter-Intelligence Field Activity. Cambone met with the heads of these agencies, as well as top officials at the CIA and National Security Council twice a week to give them their marching orders.[11]

At the peak of his Pentagon career in 2005, according to knowledgeable Senate sources, Cambone had more effective power and influence over the shape of US intelligence estimates reaching the President than George Tenet or then-National Security Adviser to the President, Condoleezza Rice.[12]

Cambone's rise to power had been quiet, almost unnoticed until the Abu Ghraib scandal forced him briefly into the spotlight. Then his role in advancing the fraudulent intelligence used to persuade Congress to sanction war on Iraq — as well as his role in reportedly authorizing systematic torture of prisoners at Guantanamo, Cuba and Abu Ghraib prison in Iraq — put Cambone uncomfortably into the spotlight. His purging of any military opponents of his aggressive agenda, revealed more publicly what the true intent of the Rumsfeld missile defense was. It was aggressive and offensive in the extreme.[13]

Pentagon Strategy Report For Europe And NATO

In December 2000, just before Donald Rumsfeld became Secretary of Defense, the Pentagon released a Strategy Report for Europe and NATO. The report contained a section on 'Theater Missile Defense.' As an official US Defense Department policy paper it was worth careful study. It stated:

> *Theater Missile Defense: As part of broader efforts to enhance the security of the United States, Allied and coalition forces against ballistic missile strikes and to complement our counter-proliferation strategy, the United States is pursuing opportunities for TMD (Theater Missile Defense) cooperation with NATO Partners. The objectives of United States cooperative efforts are to provide effective missile defense for coalition forces...against short to medium range missiles. In its Strategic Concept, NATO reaffirmed the risk posed by the proliferation of NBC(Nuclear, Biological, Chemical) weapons and ballistic missiles, and the Alliance reached general agreement on the framework for addressing these threats. As part of NATO's DCI, Allies agreed to develop Alliance forces that can respond with active and passive defenses from NBC attack. Allies further agreed that TMD is necessary for NATO's deployed forces.*

*...The Alliance is undertaking a feasibility analysis for a lay-
ered defense architecture. As the ballistic missile threat to
Europe evolves in the direction of longer ranges, the Alliance
will need to consider further measures of defense incorporat-
ing upper-tier TMD and/or a defense against longer-range
missiles.[14]*

The Pentagon document then turned to Continental USA missile defense and declared:

*National Missile Defense: Iran, Iraq, Libya, and North Korea
do not need long-range missiles to intimidate their neighbors;
they already have shorter-range missiles to do so. Instead,
they want long-range missiles to coerce and threaten more
distant countries in North America and Europe. They presumably believe that even a small number of missiles, against
which we have no defense, could be enough to inhibit US actions in support of our Allies or coalition partners in a crisis.*

*Based on our assessment of these trends, the United States has
concluded that we must counter this threat before one of these
states attempts to blackmail the United States from protecting
its interests, including commitments to our Allies in Europe
and elsewhere. Thus, the United States is developing a NMD
(National Missile Defense) system that would protect all 50
states from a limited attack of a few to a few tens of warheads.[sic]*

*...Although Moscow argues to the contrary, the limited NMD
system the United States is developing would not threaten the
Russian strategic deterrent, which could overwhelm our defense even if Russian strategic forces were much lower than
levels foreseen under existing US-Russian strategic arms reduction agreements...*

Then the 2000 Pentagon policy document added a peculiar twist of
logic:

*The NMD we envisage would reinforce the credibility of US
security commitments and the credibility of NATO as a whole.*

Europe would not be more secure if the United States were less secure from a missile attack by a state of concern. An America that is less vulnerable to ballistic missile attack is more likely to defend Europe and common Western security interests than an America that is more vulnerable.

In September 2000, President Clinton announced that while NMD was sufficiently promising and affordable to justify continued development and testing, there was not sufficient information about the technical and operational effectiveness of the entire NMD system to move forward with deployment. In making this decision, he considered the threat, the cost, technical feasibility and the impact on our national security of proceeding with NMD. The President's decision will provide flexibility to a new administration and will preserve the option to deploy a national missile defense system in the 2006-2007 timeframe.[15]

The Clinton Administration had adopted the key recommendations of the 1998 Rumsfeld-Cambone report on ballistic missile defense.

In July of 2000, the heads of state of both Russia and China issued a common declaration on US plans to build its anti-missile defense. Their declaration stated in part,

...[T]he US programme to establish national missile defense, a system prohibited under the ABM Treaty, has aroused grave concern. China and Russia hold that this programme is, in essence, aimed at seeking unilateral military and security superiority. Such a programme, if implemented, will give rise to most serious negative consequences on the security of not only Russia, China and other countries, but the United States itself and global strategic stability as well. In this context, China and Russia have registered their unequivocal opposition to the above programme.[16]

In May 2001, in one of his first major policy statements as President, George W. Bush declared:

Today's Russia is not our enemy, but a country in transition with an opportunity to emerge as a great nation, democratic, at peace with itself and its neighbors.

The Iron Curtain no longer exists. Poland, Hungary and Czech Republic are free nations and they are now our allies in NATO, together with a reunited Germany. Yet, this is still a dangerous world; a less certain, a less predictable one.

More nations have nuclear weapons and still more have nuclear aspirations. Many have chemical and biological weapons. Some already have developed a ballistic missile technology that would allow them to deliver weapons of mass destruction at long distances and incredible speeds, and a number of these countries are spreading these technologies around the world.

Most troubling of all, the list of these countries includes some of the world's least-responsible states. Unlike the Cold War, today's most urgent threat stems not from thousands of ballistic missiles in the Soviet hands, but from a small number of missiles in the hands of these states — states for whom terror and blackmail are a way of life.

They seek weapons of mass destruction to intimidate their neighbors, and to keep the United States and other responsible nations from helping allies and friends in strategic parts of the world. When Saddam Hussein invaded Kuwait in 1990, the world joined forces to turn him back. But the international community would have faced a very different situation had Hussein been able to blackmail with nuclear weapons.

Like Saddam Hussein, some of today's tyrants are gripped by an implacable hatred of the United States of America. They hate our friends. They hate our values. They hate democracy and freedom, and individual liberty. Many care little for the lives of their own people. In such a world, Cold War deterrence is no longer enough to maintain peace, to protect our own citizens and our own allies and friends.[17]

Bush's remarks, delivered six months prior to September 11, 2001, were significant in many respects, particular in revealing Washington's complete lack of candor as to its reasons for aggressively pursuing Ballistic Missile Defense.

The President insisted that the purpose of his increased commitments to build a US missile shield was not aimed at Russia, but instead was aimed only at 'terrorists' or small so-called 'rogue' states such as North Korea or Iran or then Iraq, as well. Sometimes the tiny nation of Syria was added to the Axis list, though no reports of any such Syrian missile plans existed. In fact, as military experts from Moscow to Beijing to Berlin were quick to point out, no 'terrorists' or small rogue state had any such nuclear missile delivery capability.

The details of official US military policy reports demonstrated, beyond doubt, that it had been the deliberate and unflinching policy of Washington since the collapse of the Soviet Union to systematically and relentlessly — throughout the administrations of three US Presidents — to pursue nuclear primacy (unilateral assured destruction) and the capacity for absolute, global military dominance, what the Pentagon called Full Spectrum Dominance.

Why Missile Defense Now?

It became increasingly clear, at least in Moscow and Beijing, that Washington had a far more ominous grand strategy behind its seemingly irrational and arbitrary unilateral military moves. The US Government tried, incessantly although rather poorly, to cultivate the impression that its interest in missile defense had been motivated by the new threat of terrorism after September 2001.

However, for the Pentagon and the US policy establishment, regardless of political party, the Cold War with Russia had never really ended. It merely continued in disguised form. This had been the case with Presidents G.H.W. Bush, William Clinton, and George W. Bush. Pentagon strategists had no fear of a nuclear strike on the territory of the United States from Iran. The US Navy and Air Force bomber fleet stood in full preparation to bomb Iran, even with nuclear weapons, 'back to the stone age' over mere suspicions that Iran was trying to develop independent nuclear weapon technology. States like Iran had no capability to attack America — much less render it defenseless — without risking its own nuclear annihilation many times over. Iran was well aware of this, one could be sure.

'Missile defense' projects emerged in the 1980's when Ronald Reagan proposed developing systems of satellites in space, as well as radar bases listening stations, and interceptor missiles around the globe, all designed to monitor and shoot down nuclear missiles before they hit their intended targets.

It was dubbed 'Star Wars' by its critics, but the Pentagon officially had spent more than $130 billion on developing the system since 1983. George W. Bush, beginning in 2002, increased that amount significantly to $11 billion a year. That was double the amount allocated during the Clinton years. And another $53 billion for the following five years was budgeted, excluding the untold billions which were being diverted to missile defense under secret and unaccountable Pentagon 'black box' budgets.

The Star Wars target of the Pentagon was not Iran or even North Korea. It was the only other nuclear power on the face of the earth standing in the way of total US military domination of the planet—Russia. That was the clear message that Russia's President Putin delivered to a shocked world press from Munich in February 2007. [18]

Endnotes:

[1] Richard C. Cook, "Militarization and The Moon-Mars Program: Another Wrong Turn in Space?," *Global Research*, January 22, 2007. www.globalresearch.ca.

[2] Conversation in Moscow in May 1994 between author and the Director of Economic Research of the Russian Institute for International Strategic Studies (IISS).

[3] The National Aeronautics and Space Act of 1958 (Space Act) (P.L. 85-568, 72 Stat. 426)

[4] Nick Greene, "Space Shuttle Challenger Disaster - A NASA Tragedy." www.space.about.com/cs/challenger/a/challenger.htm.

[5] Richard C. Cook, Op. Cit.

[6] Ibid.

[7] Ibid.

[8] Richard C. Cook, in private correspondence with the author, March 24, 2007.

[9] Donald Rumsfeld, et al, *Report of the Commission to Assess the Ballistic Missile Threat to the United States*, July 15, 1998. Washington D.C.

[10] Bill Gertz, "Cambone's Empire," *Inside the Ring*, May 23, 2003 (http://www.gertzfile.com/gertzfile/ring052303.html).

[11] Ibid.

[12] Jeffrey St. Clair, "The Secret World of Stephen Cambone, Rumsfeld's Enforcer," Counterpunch, February 7, 2006 (http://www.counterpunch.org/stclair02072006.html).

[13] Ibid.

[14] United States Department of Defense, *Strategy Report for Europe and NATO Excerpt on Ballistic Missile Defenses*, December 1, 2000. Washington, D.C.

[15] Ibid.

[16] Joint Statement by the Presidents of the People's Republic of China and the Russian Federation on Anti-Missile Defense, July 18, 2000. www.nuclearfiles.org.

[17] George W. Bush, *Speech on Missile Defense*, May 1, 2001. www.nuclearfiles.org.

[18] Vladimir Putin, Rede des russischen Präsidenten Wladimir Putin auf der 4, *Münchner, Sicherheitskonferenz*, München, October 2, 2007.

CHAPTER SEVEN

Washington's Nuclear Obsession

'Missile defense is the missing link to a First Strike.'
- *Lt. Colonel Robert Bowman, former Director, US Missile Defense Program*[1]

The Secret Quest For Nuclear Primacy

What Washington did not say, but Putin alluded to in his February 2007 speech in Munich, was that the US missile defense was not at all defensive. It was offensive in the extreme.

If the United States were able to shield itself effectively from a potential Russian retaliation for a US nuclear First Strike, then the US would be able to dictate its terms to the entire world, not just to Russia. That would be Nuclear Primacy. That was the real meaning of Putin's unusual speech. He wasn't paranoid. He was being starkly realistic.

It was now becoming clear that even after the end of the Cold War in 1989, the US Government had never for a moment stopped its pursuit of Nuclear Primacy. For Washington and its financial and political elites, the Cold War never ended. They just forgot to tell the rest of the world.

The US attempt to take control of oil and energy pipelines worldwide, its installation of military bases across Eurasia, its modernization and upgrades of nuclear submarine fleets and Strategic B -52 bomber commands only made sense when seen through the perspective of the relentless pursuit of US Nuclear Primacy.

In December 2001, the Bush Administration announced its decision to unilaterally withdraw from the US-Russian Anti-Ballistic Missile Treaty. This was a critical step in Washington's race to complete its global network of 'missile defense' capability as the key to US Nuclear Primacy.

In its pursuit of Nuclear Primacy, Washington simply ripped up its international treaty obligations because such missile build-ups were explicitly banned by them. In abrogating the ABM Treaty by Executive Order, the President also usurped powers granted by the United States Constitution to the US Congress. Ominously, in the national hysteria after September 11, there was hardly a peep of protest from Congress

According to *The New York Times,* the use of space for weaponry directed back at earth or weaponry guided from space was already a reality by 2001: "War planners have conceived scores of new and exciting weapons," the article enthused.

> *Talking about them is not a conversation the military wants to have in public, given the gnarly debate over the missile shield, but it is one they have been having in private for some time.*[2]

Evidence of uninterrupted global ambitions on the part of the US military could be found in a "future study" commissioned in 1995-96, by the US Air Force Chief of Staff. The report, *Air Force 2025,* was a massive 4-volume elaboration of hundreds of technologically advanced, super-sophisticated space-based weapons systems intended to provide the United State with global combat support capabilities in space. These were considered the systems necessary for the US "to remain the dominant air and space force in the future,"[3] an integral part of the Pentagon's Full Spectrum Dominance strategy.

One weapon, for example, was a "laser cannon" in space, described chillingly, as follows:

> *[It would] successfully attack ground or airborne targets by melting or cracking cockpit canopies, burning through control cables, exploding fuel tanks, melting or burning sensor assemblies and antenna arrays, exploding or melting munitions pods, destroying ground communications and power grids, and melting or burning a large variety of strategic targets*

(e.g., dams, industrial and defense facilities and munitions factories) — all in a fraction of a second.[4]

Another section of *Air Force 2025* described small metal projectiles fired at the earth from space. Those "flechettes" could penetrate the earth to a depth of a half mile, destroying targets like underground bunkers.[5]

Despite caveats and disclaimers to the effect that the Report did not represent the views of the United State or its Department of Defense, or even the Air Force, it had been authorized at the highest ranks of the Pentagon.

Dr. Robert Bowman, a retired Lieutenant Colonel of the US Air Force who directed the US Government's early anti-missile defense effort when it was still top secret, noted:

[They] mirror the results of studies we performed in the 1970s and early 80s. The difference is that then we considered the results sufficient reason to continue our national policy of keeping weapons out of space, while now they entice the hawks into discarding treaty constraints and pursuing a still more total form of absolute military superiority. Bush's first budget quadrupled the spending on laser battle stations. In his new budget, he gives the space warriors an essentially blank check. Now he has once again renamed and reorganized the Pentagon office doing 'Star Wars.'

Under Reagan and Bush I, it was the Strategic Defense Initiative Organization (SDIO). Under Clinton, it became the Ballistic Missile Defense Organization (BMDO). Now Bush II has made it the Missile Defense Agency (MDA) and given it the freedom from oversight and audit previously enjoyed only by the black programs. If Congress doesn't act soon, this new independent agency may take their essentially unlimited budget and spend it outside of public and Congressional scrutiny on weapons that we won't know anything about until they're in space. In theory, then, the space warriors would rule the world, able to destroy any target on earth without warning.

Will these new super weapons bring the American people security? Hardly.[6]

Nmd— 'The Missing Link To A First Strike'

With even a primitive missile defense shield, the US could attack Russian missile silos and submarine fleets with less fear of effective retaliation; the few remaining Russian nuclear missiles would be unable to launch a response sufficiently destructive.

During the Cold War, the ability of both sides—the Warsaw Pact and NATO—to mutually annihilate one another, had led to a nuclear stalemate dubbed by military strategists, MAD—Mutually Assured Destruction. It was scary but, in a bizarre sense, more stable than what would come later with a unilateral US pursuit of nuclear primacy. MAD was based on the prospect of mutual nuclear annihilation with no decisive advantage for either side; it led to a world in which nuclear war had been 'unthinkable.'

Now, the US was pursuing the possibility of nuclear war as 'thinkable.' That was really and truly 'mad.'

The first nation with a nuclear missile 'defense' shield (NMD) would *de facto* have 'first strike ability.' Quite correctly, Lt. Colonel Bowman, who had been Director of the US Air Force Missile Defense Program during the Reagan era, called missile defense, "the missing link to a First Strike."[7]

The US nuclear missile defense shield, which had been under top secret development by the Pentagon since the 1970s involved a ground-based system that could respond to a limited missile attack. There were five parts to the NMD system, including phased array radar installations that could detect a launch of enemy missiles and track them. In theory once the detected missiles had been launched and were confirmed to be targeting the United States or any other specific target, the next phase was to trigger one or more of the one-hundred interceptor missiles to destroy the enemy ballistic missile before it reached US air space.

The American media and its usual political commentators were virtually silent on the implications of Washington's pursuit of missile 'defense' in Poland and the Czech Republic, or its overall drive for Nuclear Primacy.

The history of the often-secret negotiations with the governments of Poland and the Czech Republic to place US-controlled missiles in those two former Warsaw Pact countries revealed the hypocrisy of US policy regarding its true goals.

The US missile talks with Warsaw and Prague began at the end of 2003, only a few months after the fall of Baghdad, according to sources inside the Polish government.

On July 13, 2004 the *Guardian* newspaper reported that senior officials in Prague had confirmed the US-Poland/Czech negotiations. It revealed that talks were under way over the establishment of American advanced radar stations in the Czech Republic as part of the missile shield project. "We're very interested in becoming a concrete part of the arrangement," Boguslaw Majewski, the Polish Foreign Ministry spokesman told the paper. "We have been debating this with the Americans since the end of last year."[8]

Other sources in Warsaw told the *Guardian* that Pentagon officers had been scouting the mountains of southern Poland, pinpointing suitable sites for two or three radar stations connected to the so-called 'Son of Star War' program.

As well as radar sites, the Poles said they wanted to host a missile interceptor site, a large reinforced underground silo from which long-range missiles could be launched to intercept and destroy incoming rockets.

Under Bush administration plans, two missile interceptor sites were being built in the US—one in California, the other in Alaska. The site in Poland would be the first such installation outside America and the only one in Europe. This remarkable and unprecedented extension of US nuclear capability went virtually unnoticed in the American media.

"An interceptor site would be more attractive. It wouldn't be a hard sell in Poland," commented Janusz Onyszkiewicz, a former Polish defense minister. But others expressed more concern. "I knew about possible radar sites, but I was surprised to hear talk about missile silos," another Warsaw observer noted.[9]

Significantly, the Polish Defense Minister most involved—at least until February 2007— in negotiating the placement of the provocative

American missiles in Poland was Radek Sikorski. Soon after, Sikorski became Foreign Minister. The 44 year-old Sikorski attended Oxford's Pembroke College in England and in 1984 had become a naturalized British citizen. He was also a full-blown Polish neo-conservative who had returned to Poland to advance the agenda of Washington's neo-conservative hawks.

Sikorski's Anglo-American career then took off in 1990 after the collapse of communism. He had then been taken under the wing of neo-conservative financial backer, Rupert Murdoch, the powerful billionaire owner of the London *Times*, the tabloid *Sun*, and the aggressively neo-conservative *Fox TV* network in the USA. Sikorski advised Murdoch on 'investments' in Poland.

Despite his British citizenship, Sikorski was appointed to several junior posts in the Polish government, including Deputy Defense Minister, and in 2002, he crossed the Atlantic for a job in Washington— working with neo-conservative 'Prince of Darkness' Richard Perle. Sikorski became a Resident Fellow at Perle's American Enterprise Institute (AEI) where Perle secured Sikorsi's promotion to Executive Director of the New Atlantic Initiative. From there, Sikorski returned to Poland as Minister of National Defense in 2005.[10]

The notable thing about Sikorski's stellar career, was that as Executive Director at the AEI's New Atlantic Initiative, he had prepared policy papers on NATO and anti-missile defense, i.e. NMD. The Pentagon's missile defense installations on Russia's perimeters in 2006 implemented the project that Sikorski's friends in Washington had formulated a few years earlier. [11]

The US missile infrastructure in East Europe was far and away the most reckless enterprise of a cabal that had already demonstrated its bent for dangerous and foolish brinkmanship.

The US construction of missile 'defenses' in Poland and the Czech Republic would include missile silos within minutes of potential Russian targets. No one would be able to say whether they contained US nuclear missiles or not. That, in effect, would put the world on a hair-trigger to possible nuclear war, by design or miscalculation, far more dangerous than NATO's 1980 decision to deploy Pershing (nuclear) missiles in Western Europe.

It called to mind the document that became the strategic blueprint for defense and foreign policy after George W. Bush entered the White House in January 2001: *Rebuilding America's Defenses,* the September 2000 report of the neo-conservative stronghold, the Project for the New American Century.

The PNAC strategy paper declared:

> *The United States must develop and deploy global missile defenses to defend the American homeland and American allies, and to provide a secure basis for US power projection around the world.*[12]

Before becoming Bush's Defense Secretary in January 2001, Rumsfeld had also headed a Presidential Commission advocating the development of missile defense for the United States, in addition to participating in the PNAC project.[13]

So eager was the Bush-Cheney Administration to advance its missile defense plans, that the President and Defense Secretary Rumsfeld had waived the usual operational testing requirements needed to determine whether the highly complex systems were even effective.

The Rumsfeld missile defense program was strongly opposed within the military command. On March 26, 2004 no fewer than 49 US generals and admirals, including Admiral William J. Crowe, former Chairman of the Joint Chiefs of Staff of the Armed Forces, signed an Open Letter to the President, appealing for missile defense postponement. In it, they explicitly pointed out:

> *US technology, already deployed, can pinpoint the source of a ballistic missile launch. It is, therefore, highly unlikely that any state would dare to attack the US or allow a terrorist to do so from its territory with a missile armed with a weapon of mass destruction, thereby risking annihilation from a devastating US retaliatory strike.*

As you have said, Mr. President, our highest priority is to pre-
vent terrorists from acquiring and employing weapons of
mass destruction. We agree. We therefore recommend, as the
militarily responsible course of action, that you postpone op-
erational deployment of the expensive and untested GMD
(Ground-based Missile Defense) system and transfer the asso-
ciated funding to accelerated programs to secure the multi-
tude of facilities containing nuclear weapons and materials,
and to protect our ports and borders against terrorists who
may attempt to smuggle weapons of mass destruction into the
United States.[14]

Preparing Nuclear First Strike

What the seasoned military officers did not say was that Rumsfeld, Cheney, Bush and company had quite a different agenda in mind other than rogue terror threats. They were after Full Spectrum Dominance, the New World Order, and the elimination of Russia, once and for all, as a potential rival for power.

The US rush to deploy a missile defense shield was clearly not aimed at North Korea or Middle East terror attacks. It was aimed at Russia. It was aimed also, if less so, at the far smaller nuclear capacities of China. As the 49 generals and admirals noted in their letter to the President in 2004, the US already had more than enough nuclear warheads to hit a thousand bunkers or caves of any potential rogue state or an Osama bin Laden.

Two US military analysts came to the same ominous conclusion. Writing in *Foreign Affairs*, journal of the Council on Foreign Relations in March 2006, they noted:

If the United States' nuclear modernization were really aimed
at rogue states or terrorists, the country's nuclear force would
not need the additional thousand ground-burst warheads it
will gain from the W-76 modernization program. The current
and future US nuclear force, in other words, seems designed to
carry out a pre-emptive disarming strike against Russia or
China.

The two strategic analysts continued with their argument:

. . . .Today, for the first time in almost 50 years, the United States stands on the verge of attaining nuclear primacy. It will probably soon be possible for the United States to destroy the long-range nuclear arsenals of Russia or China with a first strike. This dramatic shift in the nuclear balance of power stems from a series of improvements in the United States' nuclear systems, the precipitous decline of Russia's arsenal, and the glacial pace of modernization of China's nuclear forces. Unless Washington's policies change or Moscow and Beijing take steps to increase the size and readiness of their forces, Russia and China — and the rest of the world — will live in the shadow of US nuclear primacy for many years to come.

Referring to the aggressive new Pentagon deployment plans for missile defense, Lieber and Press concluded:

. . .[T]he sort of missile defenses that the United States might plausibly deploy would be valuable primarily in an offensive context, not a defensive one—as an adjunct to a US First Strike capability, not as a stand-alone shield. If the United States launched a nuclear attack against Russia (or China), the targeted country would be left with only a tiny surviving arsenal—if any at all. At that point, even a relatively modest or inefficient missile defense system might well be enough to protect against any retaliatory strikes. . . .[15]

This was the real agenda in Washington's Eurasian Great Game.

The Bush Administration's provocative missile defense shield for Poland and the Czech Republic had caused enormous friction in US-Russian relations, both within the NATO alliance and directly with Russia. The world watched to find a clue as to whether President Barack Obama might move to de-escalate the growing tensions by offering to reopen negotiations on the missile placement with Moscow.

Barack Obama's decision to retain Republican Defense Secretary Robert Gates, an outspoken advocate of the Bush missile defense plan, and to bring in General James Jones, a military man, as his National Security Adviser did not bode well for any such policy reversal. By early

2009 the world was on a collision course with potential nuclear dimensions, almost two decades after the nominal end of the Cold War.

Full Spectrum Dominance

To better understand the enormity of the US military power projection since the Cold War, it was necessary to view the provocative Missile Defense plans for eastern Europe in the overall context of dramatic changes in US military force posture and US establishment of military bases since the 1990s.

Official US military strategy had been defined by the Pentagon doctrine of Full Spectrum Dominance, of which 'ballistic-missile defense' was a defining component. According to official Pentagon statements, Full Spectrum Dominance, or FSD, was:

> *The overarching concept for applying force today, and provides a vision for future joint operations. Achieving FSD requires the Armed Forces to focus transformation efforts on key capability areas that enhance the ability of the joint force to achieve success across the range of military operations. FSD requires joint military capabilities, operating concepts, functional concepts and critical enablers adaptable to diverse conditions and objectives.*
>
> *FSD recognizes the need to integrate military activities with those of other government agencies, the importance of interoperability with allies and other partners.*[16]

Full Spectrum included the entirety of land and space, even cyberspace. As the Pentagon stated, among its eight priorities was "Operating from the Commons: Space, International Waters and Airspace, and Cyberspace."[17]

The development of an operational US missile defense system as a high priority during the Bush Administration was alarming enough. Few realized the added dimension of instability, in that it was coupled with the Top Secret order by the Secretary of Defense for the Armed Forces of the United States to implement something called Conplan 8022, "which provides the President a prompt, global strike capability."[18]

That meant that the United States establishment had decided to make nuclear war an 'option.' It was a dangerous road to follow to put it mildly.

Endnotes:

[1] Robert Bowman, Lt. Colonel, USAir Force (Ret.), Statement made during a telephone interview with the author, March 15, 2009. Bowman was Director of Advanced Space Programs Development for the Air Force Space Division until 1978. In that capacity, he controlled about half a billion dollars worth of space programs, including the "Star Wars" programs, the existence of which was (at that time) secret.

[2] Jack Hitt, "Battlefield: Space," The New York Times, August 5, 2001, Section 6, 30.

[3] Jamie G. G. Varni, et al, "Space Operations: Through the Looking Glass (Global Area Strike System)," Air War College, Maxwell AFB, August, 1996.

[4] Air Force 2025, Vol. 13, Ch. 3, "The Integrated Systems-of-Systems," 21.

[5] Ibid.

[6] Robert M. Bowman, Lt. Colonel, US Air Force (Ret.), The ABM Treaty: Dead or Alive? (March 2002) www.rmbowman.com/ssn/ABMTreaty2.htm

[7] Robert Bowman, Lt. Colonel, US Air Force (Ret.), Statement made during a telephone interview with the author, March 15, 2009.

[8] Ian Traynor, "US in talks over biggest missile defence site in Europe," Warsaw, July 13, 2004, The Guardian.

[9] Ibid.

[10] American Enterprise Institute for Public Policy, Washington D.C. website, Radek Sikorski, on their official website, http://www.aei.org/scholars/scholarID.64/scholar.asp.

[11] For a former Soviet official's view of the dangers of the Pershin missile deployment, see Yevgeny Primakov, "ABM sites on Russia's frontiers: Another Confrontation?" Moscow News, March 2, 2007.

[12] Thomas Donnelly, Donald Kagan, et al., Rebuilding America's Defenses: Strategy, Forces and Resources for a New Century, The Project for a New American Century, Washington, D. C., September, 2000. (http://www.newamericancentury.org/RebuildingAmericasDefenses.pdf).

[13] Donald H. Rumsfeld, et al, ""Report of the Commission to Assess the Ballistic Missile Threat to the United States," Washington, D.C., July 15, 1998, accessed in http://www.fas.org/lrp/threat/missile/rumsfeld. See also Lt. Gen. Robert G. Gard and Kingston Reif, Time To Rethink Missile Defense, Defense News, October 20, 2008.

[14] Reprinted in Center for Arms Control and Non-Proliferation, Briefing Book on Ballistic Missile Defense, Washington, D.C., May 2004, in http://www.armscontrolcenter.org/resources/20040501_bb_nmd.pdf.

[15] Keir A. Lieber and Daryl G. Press, "The Rise of US Nuclear Primacy," Foreign Affairs, March/April 2006, p. 51.Ibid, p.52.

[16] US Joint Chiefs of Staff, The National Military Strategy of the United States of America, 2004. Washington, D.C.

[17] Ibid.

[18] Hans M Kristensen, Global Strike: A Chronology of the Pentagon's New Offensive Strike Plan, Federation of American Scientists, Washington, D.C., March 2006, accessed in http://www.fas.org/ssp/docs/GlobalStrikeReport.pdf.

CHAPTER EIGHT

Dr. Strangelove Lives!

Well, boys, I reckon this is it. Nookular combat, toe-to-toe with the Rooskies.
 — *Major T. J. 'King' Kong in Stanley Kubrick's film, Dr. Strangelove (1964)*

Bombs Away...

The entire US program of missile defense and nuclear First Strike modernization was hair-raising enough as an idea. Under the Bush Administration, it was made operational and airborne, hearkening back to the dangerous days of the Cold War with fleets of nuclear-armed B-52 bombers and Trident nuclear missile submarines on ready alert around the clock — a nuclear horror scenario.

In 1964, US film director, Stanley Kubrick, made film history with a scathing political satire, *Dr. Strangelove, or How I learned to stop worrying and love the bomb.* Dr. Strangelove was Kubrick's provocative black comedy regarding nuclear doomsday. It featured Cold War politics that culminated in an accidental, inadvertent, pre-emptive US nuclear attack on the Soviet Union.

The landmark film, a political satire about nuclear war, dramatizes a world in which technology has gone haywire and has come to dominate humanity. In the film, the lead character, Dr. Strangelove, is an eccentric, wheelchair bound German scientist, a Presidential adviser who has an uncontrollable mechanical hand that involuntarily makes Nazi salutes and threatens homicide.

In the closing scene of *Dr. Strangelove*, a siren is heard in the background, signalling that the base is on alert. The special code is transmitted to a fleet of nuclear-armed B-52's. The narrator makes a final statement regarding Strategic Air Command readiness, later dubbed 'Operation Dropkick.'

> *In order to guard against surprise nuclear attack, America's Strategic Air Command maintains a large force of B-52 bombers airborne 24 hours a day. Each B-52 can deliver a nuclear bomb-load of 50 megatons, equal to 16 times the total explosive force of all the bombs and shells used by all the armies in World War Two. Based in America, the Airborne alert force is deployed from the Persian Gulf to the Arctic Ocean, but they have one geographical factor in common - they are all two hours from their targets inside Russia.*

In the claustrophobic interior of one of the B-52 bombers at its fail-safe point – the point beyond which the pilots must have follow-up orders to proceed — a dim-witted crew is engaged in mundane pursuits. The plane's crew is commanded by Major T. J. 'King' Kong, a simple-minded, ape-like, thick-accented Texas cowboy who is flipping through a *Playboy* Magazine. Another crew member amuses himself practicing shuffling tricks with a deck of cards. Radio operator Lieutenant B. "Goldie" Goldberg is munching on some food when he receives a loud radio transmission that clicks into view on his dial. The letters and numbers are decoded in his Top Secret Aircraft Communications Codes manual as 'Wing attack Plan R.'[1]

Irritated when informed of the orders for Wing attack Plan R (R for Romeo), Major Kong questions whether his crew is playing a practical joke and dismisses the order: "How many times have I told you guys that I don't want no horsin' around on the airplane?...Well I've been to one World Fair, a picnic, and a rodeo and that's the stupidest thing I ever heard come over a set of earphones." Kong insists that the message and code be confirmed, muttering to himself: "there's just gotta be somethin' wrong." The bombadier suspects that the top secret order may be "some kind of loyalty test." After Goldberg examines the code book, decodes the message, and receives legitimate confirmation from the base, Kong declares that they have indeed received Plan R:

Ain't nobody ever got the 'Go' code yet. And old Ripper wouldn't be giving us Plan R unless them Russkies had already clobbered Washington and a lot of other towns with a sneak attack.

The soundtrack plays the theme song, 'When Johnny Comes Marching Home,' accentuated with snare drum. Major Kong dons his ten-gallon hat and solemnly announces to his crew, "*Well, boys, I reckon this is it. Nuclear* (pronounced 'nookular') *combat, toe-to-toe with the Rooskies.*" [2]

The parallels between Kubrick's fictionalized rendition of nuclear conflagration by miscalculation *circa* 1964, and the reality more than four decades later — including a President from Texas who was fond of playing cowboy on his Crawford ranch, and who insisted on pronouncing the word nuclear as 'nookular' — were too uncanny to miss. Unfortunately, Washington's nuclear politics in 2007 was no Hollywood film. It was reality.

The march towards possible nuclear catastrophe by intent or by miscalculation, as a consequence of the bold new Washington policy, took on significant new gravity in June 2004. A few weeks earlier, 49 generals and admirals had taken the highly unusual step of writing an Open Letter to their President appealing for postponement of the missile defense system installation.[3]

Rumsfeld's Conplan 8022

In June 2004, Defense Secretary Rumsfeld approved a Top Secret order for the Armed Forces of the United States to implement something called Conplan 8022, 'which provides the President a prompt, global strike capability.'[3]

The term 'Conplan' was Pentagon shorthand for Contingency Plan. What 'contingencies' were Pentagon planners preparing for? A pre-emptive conventional strike against tiny North Korea or even Iran ? Or a full-force pre-emptive nuclear assault on the last formidable nuclear

power not under the thumb of the US' Full Spectrum Dominance—
Russia?

The two words, 'global strike,' were notable. It was Pentagon-speak
for a specific pre-emptive US military attack that, for the first time since
the earliest Cold War days, included a nuclear option. This was directly
counter to the traditional US military notion of nuclear weapons being
used only in defense, to deter attack.

Conplan 8022 was unlike traditional Pentagon war plans that had
been essentially defensive responses to invasion or attack.[4]

Like the aggressive pre-emptive 2002 Bush Doctrine, Bush's new
Conplan 8022 was offensive. It could be triggered by the mere 'percep-
tion' of an imminent threat, and carried out by Presidential order,
without consulting Congress or obtaining its Constitutionally required
authorization. The Constitutional 'checks and balances' which the US
Founding Fathers had taken such care to embed into the Constitution
were gone. The President, on his own, could detonate nuclear war, pre-
emptively.

Given the callous disregard of both Bush and Vice President Cheney
for the Constitutional system of checks and balances between the powers
of the three branches of Government—executive, legislative and judi-
cial—in favor of what the Bush Administration called a 'unitary executive,' a phrase which took on a meaning akin to Papal infallibility for the
President, Conplan 8022 was alarming, to put it mildly. [5]

Given the details about false or faked 'perceptions' in the Pentagon,
the CIA, and the Office of the Vice President about Iraq's threat of
weapons of mass destruction in 2003, the new Conplan 8022 suggested a
US President might order the missiles against any and every perceived
threat or even a potential, unproven threat.

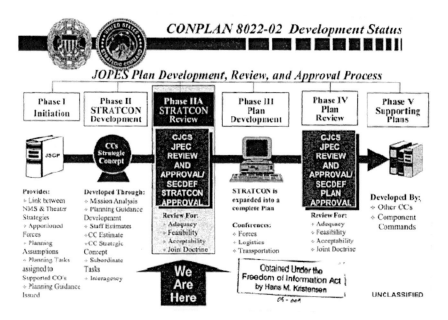

According to the FAS, Conplan 8022-1 went into effect in 2004 (Source: FAS)

In response to Rumsfeld's June 2004 order, General Richard Myers, then Chairman of the Joint Chiefs of Staff, signed the order to make Conplan 8022 operational. Selected nuclear-capable bombers, ICBMs, SSBNs, and 'information warfare' (sic) units were deployed against unnamed high-value targets in 'adversary' countries.[6]

Was Iran an adversary country, even though it had never attacked the United States or anyone else? Was North Korea, even though it had never in five decades launched a direct attack on South Korea, let alone anyone else? Was China an 'adversary' because it was simply becoming economically too influential?

Was Russia now an adversary because she refused to lay back and accept being made what Brzezinski termed a 'vassal' state[7] of the American Empire?

There were no clear answers, but the world was beginning to get a little apprehensive about the manifest deterioration in the foundations of American power, its legal framework, its decision making procedures, not to mention its motives.

Because there was no open debate inside the United States about such profoundly important issues as Conplan 8022, there was no discussion of any of these potentially nuclear-loaded questions among the broader population. Most Americans lived in a state of ignorant bliss, preoccupied with the growing stresses of merely surviving in an economic collapse.

What made the June 2004 Rumsfeld order particularly unsettling was that the rest of the world – including, no doubt, most Americans — truly had hoped nuclear mushroom clouds had become a threat of the past. But Conplan 8022 contained a significant nuclear attack component.

It was true that the overall number of nuclear weapons in the US military stockpile had been declining since the end of the Cold War. But this was not, it seemed, because the US was pulling the world back from the brink of nuclear war by miscalculation.

Some more serious minds were beginning to ask how the policies of the United States of America, once the beacon of liberty and freedom, had come so fully under the sway of its military. The answer to that had a longer history as well.

Endnotes:

[1] Tim Dirks review of "Dr. Strangelove: or, How I Learned to Stop Worrying and Love the Bomb, in http://www.filmsite.org/drst.html.

[2] Dialogue from "Dr. Strangelove" quoted in Tim Dirks, http://www.filmsite.org/drst.html.

[3] F. William Engdahl, "When Cowboys Don't Shoot Straight," *Asia Times*, March 1, 2007.

[3] Hans M Kristensen, *Global Strike: A Chronology of the Pentagon's New Offensive Strike Plan*, Federation of American Scientists, Washington, D.C., March 2006, accessed in http://www.fas.org/ssp/docs/GlobalStrikeReport.pdf.

[4] William Arkin, *Not Just A Last Resort? A Global Strike Plan, With a Nuclear Option*, The Washington Post, May 15, 2005.

[5] During the Bush Presidency, Cheney and his assistant, David Addington , promoted the bizarre and de facto unconstitutional theory, the so-called unitary executive theory. As award-winning journalist Robert Parry noted, the unitary executive idea of Cheney, "asserts that all executive authority must be in the President's hands, without exception." President George W. Bush asserted from the outset of his presidency that presidential

power must be unilateral, and unchecked. In an analysis of Bush's invocation of a Unitary Executive, legal writer Jennifer van Bergen noted, 'the President does not have unlimited executive authority, not even as Commander-in-Chief of the military. Our government was purposely created with power split between three branches, not concentrated in one...Separation of powers, then, is not simply a talisman: It is the foundation of our system.' (Jennifer van Bergan, *The Unitary Executive: Is The Doctrine Behind the Bush Presidency Consistent with a Democratic State?* , FindLaw's Writ, January 9, 2006, accessed in http://writ.news.findlaw.com/commentary/20060109_bergen.html#bio.

[6] William Arkin, Op. Cit.

[7] Zbigniew Brzezinski, *The Grand Chessboard: American Primacy and Its Geostrategic Imperatives*, New York, Basic Books, 1998.

CHAPTER NINE

The Permanent War State Lobby

In the councils of government, we must guard against the acquisition of unwarranted influence, whether sought or unsought, by the military-industrial complex. The potential for the disastrous rise of misplaced power exists and will persist...We must never let the weight of this combination endanger our liberties or democratic processes...

— *Farewell Address to Nation by President Dwight D. Eisenhower, January 17, 1961*

The Military-Industrial Complex Goes To Washington

The United States hegemony or dominance in the decades since its victory in World War II had depended on two main pillars. The first was the role of the US dollar as world reserve currency. Here the axiomatic pricing of oil and most other hard commodities played a significant role in preserving the dominance of American capital after 1971 when the gold backing of the dollar was unilaterally dropped by Washington.

That oil and commodity dollar dominance was further buttressed by the paramount role of Wall Street banks in world financial markets, especially their overwhelming domination of financial derivatives trading — a dollar-denominated business worth today hundreds of trillions of nominal dollars annually.

The second pillar of US supremacy, notably since the end of the 1980s, had been the overwhelming dominance of US military power. This domination was intimately connected to a tightly linked network of political think-tanks in and around Washington D.C., together with a handful of giant global defense contractors whose financing of US political parties made their voice disproportionately large.

This was the modern incarnation of the military-industrial complex which then-President Dwight D. Eisenhower warned of in his last public speech before leaving office in January 1961.

In his farewell speech, the former military commander of US forces in Europe warned his fellow citizens:

> *In the councils of government, we must guard against the acquisition of unwarranted influence, whether sought or unsought, by the military-industrial complex. The potential for the disastrous rise of misplaced power exists and will persist.*
>
> *We must never let the weight of this combination endanger our liberties or democratic processes. Only an alert and knowledgeable citizenry can compel the proper meshing of the huge industrial and military machinery of defense with our peaceful methods and goals, so that security and liberty may prosper together.[1]*

The American Security Council

One of the least-known and most influential organizations to formulate policy initiatives for this military-industrial complex was the American Security Council (ASC), based in Washington D.C. It had been founded in 1956, although its origins dated back to1938. The non-profit ASC had a profound impact on the history of the United States and its global leadership role, yet it remained almost completely shielded from public view. It played a prominent role in almost every important foreign policy or national security program since World War II. On its website it boasted:

> *The ASC's outstanding record of accomplishment should make all Americans proud. It is the story of prominent representatives of business, labor, academia and government who worked together well before they formed the organization known as ASC in 1956. These were the statesmen who were either at the center of the action, or at least on the fringes of power....*

The origins of ASC date back to 1938. The inner circle which would form the Council was originally composed of the most influential names in the American establishment of the day.[2]

Interestingly enough, 1938 was around the time when the same leading circles in and around the Council on Foreign Relations and with funding from the Rockefeller Foundation, launched their groundbreaking and monumental War & Peace Studies project.

The War & Peace Studies project developed the blueprint for establishing a postwar American imperium that would disguise its real intent with misleading rhetoric about 'anti-colonialism,' 'free enterprise' and promotion of 'democratic ideals' around the world. Many of the people who were involved in the American Security Council and its militarist agenda, were also prominent in the CFR's War & Peace Studies. These were the architects of the new American Empire, dubbed 'The American Century' by one of its most influential advocates, *Time* and *Life* magazine's founder, Henry Luce.[3]

The original board of the ASC included Henry Luce and his politically influential wife, Clare Boothe Luce. After World War II and during the Cold War, Henry Luce, a close friend of spy chief Allen Dulles, was considered one of the CIA's most valuable assets in the media. Jay Lovestone was another board member of the influential ASC. Lovestone was director of the AFL-CIO's International Affairs Department, which covertly channelled millions of CIA dollars to anti-communist activities internationally, particularly in Latin America. Two hugely influential and financially powerful American entrepreneurs who helped establish the ASC were Hughston McBain, reactionary chairman of the giant Chicago department stores, Marshall Field, and Theodore V. Houser, chairman of the even larger Sears & Roebuck stores.

Other ASC founding members included some of the most prominent military hawks of the postwar era. One such hawk was senior CIA officer, Ray S. Cline, author of an infamous CIA report[4] that manipulated American public perceptions and led to the 3-year US military action called the Korean War that, in turn, was crucial to justifying a permanent American war economy.

Other names on the ASC list included: Hollywood media mogul, Walt Disney; former Soviet Ambassador and Roosevelt's wartime liaison to Churchill, Averell Harriman; Senator Thomas J. Dodd (D-CT)(father of current US Senator Chris Dodd, prominent in the current Wall Street bailout); hawkish Senator Henry M. Scoop Jackson (D-WA); General Douglas MacArthur; former US House Speaker Sam Rayburn (D-TX); Nelson A. Rockefeller, scion of Standard Oil, wartime head of the CIA in Latin America, later National Security Adviser to President Eisenhower, and Vice President under Gerald Ford; Kennedy adviser, Eugene V. Rostow; Senator John G. Tower, later Secretary of Defense under Reagan; General Nathan Twining, US Air Force; and Admiral Elmo Zumwalt, US Navy.

According to one knowledgeable source:

> *[ASC worked with] officials from the Pentagon, National Security Council, and organizations linked to the CIA, discussed cold war strategy with leaders of many large corporations, such as United Fruit, Standard Oil, Honeywell, US Steel, and Sears Roebuck. CIA-linked Foreign Policy Research Institute... Aircraft Industries Association... National Association of Manufacturers, Chambers of Commerce...*[5]

The ASC during the Cold War was an umbrella organization that served, among other things, as a lobbying group for the armaments industry, for the biggest defense contractors. It included some of the most aggressive military organizations in the United States:

- **Coalition for Peace Through Strength**. Described as "an ASC spin-off," the key outreach arm of the ASC was the Coalition for Peace Through Strength, a high powered lobbying group. It produced the propaganda film, "The SALT Syndrome" in the 1970s, "to oppose Senate ratification of the SALT treaty and to suggest that Jimmy Carter was unilaterally disarming the US."[6] The film was so inaccurate and biased that even the Pentagon refuted its contents.[7]

- **America First Committee**. General Robert E. Wood, Chairman of Sears, Roebuck & Co., was also chairman of AFC. Wood "opposed all efforts to aid Allies besieged by Nazi Germany. Within weeks of Germany's declaration of War on the US, the AFC met in New York to plan for what they assumed would be the Axis victory in Europe and the Far East..."[8]

- **American Coalition of Patriotic Societies**. This still exists as a member of the Coalition for peace Through Strength. It sponsored various racist and eugenics causes including the 1924 Immigration Restriction Act. Harry Laughlin, notorious eugenicist, was a member, as was AFC's General Wood who helped found the John Birch Society's *Human Events* magazine.

- **Rev. Sun Myung Moon**, founder of Unification Church and owner of *Washington Times* newspaper with close ties to the South Korean intelligence agency, KCIA.

- **National Republican Heritage Groups Council**. An umbrella organization for various ethnic Republican clubs, operating under the auspices of the Republican National Committee (RNC). In the 1950s, it became the strategy of the Eisenhower/Nixon Administration to paint the Democrats as 'soft on communism.' Liberating Eastern Europe became part of the GOP message. In order to create a political base for these views, the RNC formed an Ethnic Division to bring former Nazi sympathizers into the US and organize them politically; some have cited this as a precursor for right wing extremism in the United States.[9]

During the entirety of the Cold War the ASC was at the heart of propaganda and lobbying initiatives which supported the military-industrial complex and the establishment of America's permanent Security State and war economy. This grandiose program was euphemistically called, 'defense of the free enterprise system.' It was crucial to the creation of the permanent USA National Security State after 1945.

The New Military-Industrial Complex

As times changed, and especially as the Soviet Union dissolved into chaos, new structures were needed to advance and perpetuate the ongoing, uninterrupted global agenda of US hegemony, the American Century. In 1999, according to *Foreign Policy in Focus*:

> [T]he military-industrial complex did not fade away with the end of the cold war. It simply reorganized itself....
>
> As a result of a rash of military-industry mergers encouraged and subsidized by the Clinton Administration, the Big Three weapons makers—Lockheed Martin Corporation, Boeing Corporation, and Raytheon Corporation—now receive among themselves over $30 billion per year in Pentagon contracts. This represents more than one out of every four dollars that the Defense Department doles out for everything from rifles to rockets.
>
> In 1999, the Clinton Administration's five-year budget plan for the Pentagon called for a 50% increase in weapons procurement, which would be an increase from $44 billion per year to over $63 billion per year by 2003. Additionally, the arms industry launched a concerted lobbying campaign aimed at increasing military spending and arms exports. These initiatives are driven by profit and pork barrel politics, not by an objective assessment of how best to defend the United States in the post-cold war period.[10]

Writing for the March 2003 issue of *Business2.0*, Ian Mount, David H. Freedman, and Matthew Maier addressed what was by then being called the "New Military-Industrial Complex," where, as they put it, "the nature of the battle was unlike anything the world has ever known."[11] Afghanistan in 2001-2002, they wrote:

> [P]rovided a glimpse of the latest generation of high-tech weaponry, but it was only a glimpse. A major assault by combined American forces will provide a full demonstration of the military's new doctrine of faster, lighter, smarter warfare —

*combat in which cutting-edge technology becomes U.S.
troops' deadliest weapon. The Pentagon calls this new doctrine RMA, for Revolution in Military Affairs, and it's made
possible not just by fresh thinking in the Pentagon but also by
a subtle shift in the ranks of US defense contractors. In building its new high-tech arsenal, the United States has also created a new military-industrial complex.*

*When it comes to military spending, the tradition of the iron
triangle—Congress, the Pentagon, and defense industries—
joining to push costly weaponry is nothing new.* [12]

The Pentagon's Revolution in Military Affairs however, was anything
but a clever new term for the same military strategy. It was a strategy to
enable total control over every nation, every potential competitor on the
face of the earth. It was the blueprint for America's Full Spectrum
Dominance, the New American Century of the new millennium.

The strategy was guided by a reclusive long-range war policy planner
at the Pentagon who had reached his mid-80s and was considered
untouchable, having endured through every post World War II Administration. He had earned within the Pentagon the nickname of 'Yoda,'
from the Hollywood *Star Wars* films. His 'Jedi Knights' numbered some
of the most powerful people ever to have come to Washington, including
Donald Rumsfeld and Dick Cheney.

Endnotes:

[1] Dwight D. Eisenhower, *Farewell Speech*, 17 January 1961 in Public Papers of the
Presidents, Dwight D. Eisenhower, p. 1035- 1040.

[2] www.americanssecuritycouncil.org

[3] Henry R. Luce, "The American Century" reprinted in *The Ambiguous Legacy*, M. J.
Hogan, ed. (Cambridge, UK: Cambridge University Press, 1999).

[4] Richard L. Russell, "Tug of War: The CIA's Uneasy Relationship with the Military," *SAIS
Review* - Volume 22, Number 2, Summer-Fall 2002, 1-18.

[5] Russ Bellant, *Old Nazis, the New Right, and the Republican Party: The American Security
Council – 'The Cold War Campus: The Heart of the Military-Industrial Complex,'* cited in
www.sourcewatch.org.

[6] Ibid.

[7] Ruth McDonough Fitzpatrick, "A Review of Contemporary Media," *Jump Cut*, no. 26, December 1981, p. 24.

[8] Bellant, Op. Cit.

[9] Ibid.

[10] *Military-Industrial Complex* Revisited, in www.fpif.org/papers/micr/introduction_body.html.

[11] Ian Mount, Mathew Maier, and David H. Freedman, *The New Military-Industrial Complex*, March 1, 2003 (http://money.cnn.com/magazines/business2/business2_archive/2003/03/01/338099/index.htm)

[12] Ibid.

CHAPTER TEN

Yoda's 'Revolution in Military Affairs'

'Since the 1980s Mr Marshall has been a promoter of an idea first posited in 1982 by Marshal Nikolai Ogarkov, then chief of the Soviet general staff, called RMA, or 'Revolution in Military Affairs.'
   – Pentagon colleague of Andrew Marshall[1]

Covertly Ending The Era Of MAD

The 'Revolution in Military Affairs' that was implemented in Afghanistan and then Iraq after 2001 was an outgrowth of seeds that were planted decades earlier during the tumultuous Nixon era. As powerful US financial elites and their small circle of strategic planners began to assess the debacle of the Vietnam War, they focused on developing alternative methods to secure the American Century well into the future.

By the early 1970s, US policy regarding the possibility of using a nuclear First Strike capability against the Soviet Union had changed considerably. Nixon, backed by hawkish National Security Adviser, Henry Kissinger, a protégé of the Rockefeller family, initiated the transition away from the Cold War balance of terror, Mutual Assured Destruction or MAD. Nixon was determined to go for global nuclear supremacy.

The Cuban Missile Crisis of October 1962, during the Kennedy Administration, had brought the world to within a hair's breadth of nuclear annihilation. It was by all serious accounts one of the most dangerous periods in world history. The Russians were delivering nuclear warheads to Cuba by sea; the Russian ship captain had orders to use his own judgment whether to launch his nuclear payload in the event of interdiction by US forces. At the moment of interdiction, he decided not to launch. For several years following that grave nuclear showdown the world seemed to pull back from what US Secretary of State John Foster Dulles had termed nuclear Brinksmanship.

However, within the most powerful US political and military circles, the US march to Nuclear Primacy — an impregnable first strike nuclear capability against the USSR — had begun well before George W. Bush became President.

On June 11, 1962, Defense Secretary Robert S. McNamara declared that the ". . . principal military objectives, in the event of nuclear war...should be the destruction of the enemy's military forces." [2] As one former McNamara aide bluntly explained, "there could be no such thing as primary retaliation against military targets after an enemy attack. If you're going to shoot at missiles, *you're talking about first strike.*" [3]

'Counterforce,' as it was dubbed in the Pentagon, meant the destruction of all the adversary's nuclear missiles before they had even been launched. Ballistic Missile Defense (BMD) grew out of that period of Pentagon planning. BMD would be the system that could 'clean up' the few remaining un-hit Soviet missiles. The BMD was seen as essential to make the US plans for First Strike credible, as well as feasible. First Strike capability was essential to assure the role of the United States as the sole hegemon, the only global superpower with absolute power and authority over other nations.[4]

From 1962 to 1974, most of the world was under the mistaken illusion that the USA was still operating under the rules of Mutually Assured Destruction and that both the USSR and the United States had decided, after the Cuban Missile Crisis, that nuclear war was 'unthinkable' because it would destroy both countries and was, therefore, un-winnable. However, during the 1970s, this changed. For Richard Nixon and his National Security Adviser, Henry Kissinger, as well as many leaders of the US military-industrial complex, nuclear war was not only 'thinkable,' it was do-able. They were that determined to secure US Nuclear Primacy.

In January 1974 President Nixon, amid the Watergate scandals that would ultimately destroy his Presidency, signed National Security Decision Memorandum 242 (NSDM-242) drafted by Defense Secretary and former RAND associate and CIA director, James R. Schlesinger.[5] The USA was going for it all.[6]

It was Kissinger who had recommended to Nixon the appointment of James Schlesinger as Secretary of Defense. Schlesinger, then briefly and controversially CIA Director, had been a weapons analyst at the RAND Corporation where he was considered "the war-fighter's war-fighter," [7] a super hawk among hawks. It was Schlesinger, with Kissinger's backing, who had undertaken development of weapons programs specifically for the purpose of taking out Soviet ICBMs with First Strike systems that would leave no retaliatory capacity.[8]

The technological problems to First Strike, however, were enormous, as were the costs. Until the 1970s, the state of nuclear technology had precluded a first strike without the guaranteed mutual annihilation that had been the basis of the 'balance' of MAD.[9] During the 1970s, under Schlesinger's direction, new weapons technologies were developed that changed this. First was the miniaturization of nuclear warheads that made it possible to pack up to seventeen warheads into one missile nose cone. The second, made possible by advances in atomic physics and computerized navigational devices, was the NAVSTAR satellite system in deep space that enabled an enormous increase in warhead accuracy (to within 50 feet of its target).[10]

These two technological advances allowed the US for the first time to deploy a Counterforce knock-out hit against widely dispersed Soviet missiles in hardened silos, submarines and aircraft.

The final, essential element to make the entire program workable and operational remained the most difficult: a Ballistic Missile Defense (BMD) system to take out any Soviet missiles that would somehow survive and could be launched at US targets.[10]

Rumsfeld's 'Marshall Plan': 'Bleeding-Edge' Technology

During the Nixon era, the Pentagon hired a RAND think-tank specialist who was to become the most powerful man in US military policy in the nation's history, despite the fact he remained unknown to the world outside, almost never gave interviews, and defied attempts by his rivals to oust him. That man was Dr. Andrew W. Marshall, Director of the

Office of Net Assessment, US Department of Defense, who created
something called the 'Revolution in Military Affairs.'

The best definition of Revolution in Military Affairs, or RMA, as it
soon was dubbed within Pentagon and Washington think-tank circles,
was the one provided by Marshall himself:

> *A Revolution in Military Affairs (RMA) is a major change in
> the nature of warfare brought about by the innovative appli-
> cation of new technologies which, combined with dramatic
> changes in military doctrine and operational and organiza-
> tional concepts, fundamentally alters the character and con-
> duct of military operations.*[11]

Marshall was a remarkable man in many respects. By 2008, at the
ripe age of 86 years, he had retained his unique status as a US Government civil servant exempt from the usual federal retirement conditions.
Andrew Marshall was known in defense circles as 'Yoda,' a reference to
the fictional character from the *Star Wars* movies, the mysterious and
whimsical little critter who was Grand Master of the Jedi Order.

A RAND Corporation nuclear expert, Marshall was brought by Henry
Kissinger onto the National Security Council that Kissinger headed.
Marshall was then appointed by President Nixon in 1973, on Kissinger's
and Defense Secretary James R. Schlesinger's recommendation, to direct
the Office of Net Assessment, a secretive internal Pentagon think tank.[12]

Marshall was reappointed by every president thereafter, a feat surpassed only by the late FBI Director, J. Edgar Hoover. Andrew Marshall
was the only official in the Rumsfeld Pentagon who had participated in
strategic war planning throughout virtually the entire Cold War, beginning in 1949 as a nuclear strategist for RAND Corporation, then moving
to the Pentagon in 1973.

> *He has been there ever since, despite efforts by some defense
> secretaries to get rid of him. His innocuous-sounding office
> comes with a big brief: to assess regional and global military
> balances and to determine long-term trends and threats.*[13]

The 'Missing Link'

The development of Nuclear First Strike systems did not die with the end of the Nixon Presidency. Between August 1977 and July 1980, President Jimmy Carter issued a series of Presidential Directives — PD 18 through PD 59 — calling for 1) the development of Anti-Satellite weapons (ASAT) to knock out the Soviet warning system; 2) decapitation of the Soviet leadership via highly accurate Pershing II missiles; and 3) deployment of Counterforce Nuclear First Strike that would destroy almost all Soviet nuclear weapons. By the end of his Presidency, Carter "had authorized the greatest commitment to war-fighting of any President in history."[14]

Andrew Marshall the 87-year-old head of the Pentagon future war planning, known as the Defense Department's "Yoda"— is behind the Iraq war strategy, the Revolution in Military Affairs and the Missile Defense plans of the Pentagon

In 1972 the Anti-Ballistic Missile Treaty (ABM Treaty) between Moscow and Washington had placed severe limits on development or deployment of Ballistic Missile Defense, although it did not prevent intense research on such systems. That is what President Ronald Reagan proclaimed to the world in March 1983 when he proposed the Strategic Defense Initiative (SDI), which the press quickly dubbed, 'Star Wars.'

According to Lt. Col. Robert Bowman, former head of President Carter's then-top secret SDI research, anti-missile defense remained in 2009, "the missing link to a First Strike" capability.[15]

The United States military and political establishment did not relinquish that Nuclear First Strike goal for one minute despite the end of the Cold War in 1990 with the dissolution of the Soviet Union and the independence of the former Warsaw Pact countries. Washington's power elites were more determined than ever to secure the grand prize: global domination through Nuclear Primacy.[16]

The *Times* noted that Andrew Marshall was behind some of the key strategic decisions of the Reagan years:

His strategy for a protracted nuclear war — based on weapons modernization, protection of governmental leaders from a first strike and an early version of Star Wars — effectively beggared the Soviet war machine. He advocated providing Afghan resistance fighters with the highly effective Stinger missiles.

Supporters call Mr. Marshall iconoclastic and Delphic. His detractors prefer paranoiac or worse. No one has ever called him prolix. At a future-war seminar that he sponsored, Mr. Marshall mumbled a few introductory words and then sat in silence, eyebrows arched, arms folded, for the remaining two days. His only intervention came at the end. He suggested that when it came to the future, it would be better to err on the side of being unimaginative. After that experience, I better understood why he has been called the Pentagon's Yoda.[17]

Andrew Marshall was part of a group formed nearly 50 years earlier at the Air Force's RAND Corporation, a think tank in Santa Monica, California. With a graduate degree in economics from the University of Chicago in 1949, he joined a group of future-war strategists whose job was, in the words of RAND nuclear specialist, Herman Kahn, to 'think the unthinkable'. In other words, they played nuclear war games and imagined horrifying scenarios.

At RAND, Marshall worked not only with Herman Kahn – a model for Stanley Kubrick's *Dr. Strangelove*[18] — but also with Albert Wohlstetter, one of the early guiding lights of the neo-conservative hawks of the Bush Administration.

While at RAND, Marshall and several colleagues played an important if hidden role in the 1960 presidential election when they served as advisers to John F. Kennedy and devised the bogus 'missile gap,' which JFK used to defeat Richard Nixon.[19]

Later examination of Presidential archives and other material confirmed that Kennedy had genuinely been convinced of reports coming out of the Pentagon, particularly the Air Force, which was close to RAND people, that the Soviets would have an overwhelming intercontinental ballistic missile capability over the United States by the early 1960's.

When he, as President, realized he had been deceived, it clearly fostered his deep distrust of the Pentagon and CIA.[20]

In the late 1960's Andrew Marshall replaced James Schlesinger as director of strategic studies at RAND. Marshall's quest for a framework for structuring and giving direction to RAND's program of strategic war studies led to his report, *Long Term Competition with the Soviets: A Framework for Strategic Analysis*, published in 1972.

As one analyst put it:

> *Since the 1980s Mr Marshall has been a promoter of an idea... called RMA, or 'Revolution in Military Affairs.' The RMA, in general terms, opines that technological advances have changed the very nature of conventional war. Rather than conflict conducted by ground troops, the new conventional war will be conducted almost like a nuclear war, managed by strategic defense and computers at remote locations targeting missiles at enemies.*

The battlefield, as it once was known, would no longer exist. War, in the RMA lexicon, would be conducted by spy satellites and long-range missiles, by computer viruses that would disable the enemies' offensive and defensive systems, and by a 'layered' defense system that would make the US impenetrable.[21]

For most of the 1990s under the Clinton administration, Marshall and his protégés languished in bureaucratic obscurity in various places. Neither the technological advances nor the political climate existed to make the RMA feasible.

Then, during the 2000 presidential campaign, Bush promised an "immediate, comprehensive review of our military." Just weeks into the new administration, the new Defense Secretary, Donald Rumsfeld, ordered that review, to be carried out. It was done by Rumsfeld's old crony, Andrew Marshall.

Marshall had known both Rumsfeld and Dick Cheney when each had served as Defense Secretary in the 1980s and early 1990s respectively. Marshall had immense influence over – indeed had shaped — their views of modern warfare and military force deployment.

Marshall's 'Jedi Knights'

Some in Washington considered Marshall a neo-conservative. It was more the case that Marshall represented the consensus of the US establishment's military and intelligence community that had helped support and shape neo-conservative war hawks into a powerful voice in US foreign policy.

The entire Bush military strategy flowed from a close-knit network of Marshall protégés. A closer look at the main protégés who worked under him at the Pentagon over the years was revealing. It included all the architects of 'Operation Shock and Awe,' the Bush Administration's disastrous war strategy in Iraq.

Among Marshall's protégés were Donald Rumsfeld. Rumsfeld was Andrew Marshall's boss, both in 1977 when Rumsfeld served as President Gerald Ford's Defense Secretary, and again from 2001 until his forced resignation in 2006 as the 'fall guy' for President Bush's debacle in Iraq.

Since 1974 Rumsfeld had been Ford's White House Chief of Staff until 1975 when he was named Secretary of Defense, during George H. W. Bush's tenure as CIA Director. The Rumsfeld and Bush, Sr. collaboration was to be long-standing, though at the time Bush, Sr. was suspicious that Rumsfeld had appointed him CIA chief in order to kill his chances of becoming President.[22]

Rumsfeld And Bush's Team B Fakery

During his tenure as Defense chief after 1975, Rumsfeld fought to greatly increase the defense budget and to build up US strategic and conventional forces. He asserted, along with CIA Director Bush's 'Team B,' that trends in comparative US-Soviet military strength had gone against the United States for 15 to 20 years and that, if continued, they would have the effect of injecting a fundamental instability in the world.

Team B had been set up, with the approval of President Gerald Ford in 1976 by then-CIA Director Bush, Sr. Its mission was to come up with an alternative assessment of the Soviet military threat to that of the CIA under its previous Director, William Colby.

When Colby had been approached in 1975 by the President's Foreign Intelligence Advisory Board to set up an outside panel of experts to challenge the CIA estimate, Colby had refused, claiming it was unnecessary. Notably, Colby was fired during Gerald Ford's infamous 'Halloween Massacre' and was replaced by Bush, Sr. as CIA Director in 1976. The man orchestrating the massacre was the President's Chief of Staff, Donald Rumsfeld.

Team B came to the conclusion that the Soviets had developed several new weapons, featuring a nuclear-armed submarine fleet that used a sonar system that didn't depend on sound and was, thus, undetectable by existing technology.

The analysis that Team B produced was later determined to be false. According to Dr. Anne Cahn of the Arms Control and Disarmament Agency, 1977-1980:

> *I would say that all of it was fantasy... if you go through most of Team B's specific allegations about weapons systems, and you just examine them one by one, they were all wrong.* [23]

Team B— (Team A had produced the original CIA analysis indicating there was no major new Soviet threat) —was headed by Harvard history professor Richard Pipes whose son, Daniel Pipes joined the later George W. Bush Administration as a strident neo-conservative. Among the team's members was Air Force retired General Daniel Graham, considered by some in Washington as the innovator of Reagan's 'Star Wars' anti-missile concept.

Another Team B consultant was neo-conservative hawk, Paul Wolfowitz who would serve under Defense Secretary Rumsfeld after 2001. Wolfowitz oversaw the application of Andrew Marshall's Revolution in Military Affairs in Iraq, and also the revival of 'Star Wars' aimed at Russia.

As critics pointed out, Team B members all shared a similar bias towards exaggerating the Soviet threat in order to justify US military buildup.[24]

Bush Sr.'s Team B was an utter fraud, an exercise in faked intelligence estimates not unlike those that Rumsfeld and Wolfowitz would generate for Bush, Jr. during the buildup to the 2003 Iraq War. Team B's efforts not only undermined the incoming Carter Administration's disarmament efforts but also laid the foundation for the unnecessary explosion of the US defense budget during the Reagan Administration. It was during those years that virtually all of Rumsfeld's compatriots were elevated to positions of power in the executive branch.

Before he joined the George W. Bush Administration in 2001 Rumsfeld had been a member of the Project on the New American Century (PNAC), the Washington think-tank that formulated the policy of regime change against Saddam Hussein in 1998 in an Open Letter to President Clinton, three years before September 11, 2001.

When he was forced to resign over the debacle in Iraq in November 2006, Rumsfeld was cited by military analysts as the worst Defense Secretary in US history. He was replaced by a Bush family loyalist, Robert Gates, former CIA head under President George H. W. Bush.

The Marshall War Cabal

The protégés of Andrew Marshall going back to the 1980s formed the hard core defense and intelligence team, the nefarious neoconservatives, in the Administration of President George W. Bush after 2001.

One prominent member of Bush, Jr.'s war cabal spawned by Marshall was Dick Cheney who had previously worked with Marshall in 1989 when Cheney became Bush Sr.'s Defense Secretary — just prior to the first Iraq-US war of 1991.

Among Cheney's first recommendations as head of George W. Bush's Transition Team in 2000 was the appointment of his former mentor, Donald Rumsfeld, as Defense Secretary, and the appointment of Paul

Wolfowitz as Rumsfeld's Deputy. Cheney then insisted on making John Bolton, serving as vice-president of the neo-conservative American Enterprise Institute (AEI), the new Undersecretary of State for Arms Control and International Security.[25]

Cheney repeatedly visited CIA headquarters in the run-up to the war in Iraq, pressuring CIA analysts to take a darker view of Saddam Hussein's alleged ties to al Qaeda and weapons of mass destruction. [26] It seemed strikingly similar to the kind of pressures that had been applied in previous administrations to come up with "intelligence" to bolster a military agenda and buildup.

Cheney also backed the creation of the Pentagon's Office of Special Plans (OSP) and the appointment of Under Secretary of Defense Douglas Feith as its director. [27]

Feith, a former Harvard student of Team B's Richard Pipes, before joining the Pentagon had been a Washington lobbyist for defense corporations Lockheed Martin and Northrop Grumman. He then headed the controversial Office of Special Plans from September 2002 to June 2003, during the run up to the invasion of Iraq.

The now defunct unit was accused of manipulating intelligence to bolster support for the illegal invasion. According to the *Guardian*, "This rightwing intelligence network was set up in Washington to second-guess the CIA and deliver a justification for toppling Saddam Hussein by force." [28] It recalled almost exactly father Bush's set up of Team B to fake intelligence estimates more than a quarter century earlier.

According to Feith's former deputy, Lieutenant Colonel Karen Kwiatkowski – who was in a position to observe its operations personally — the Office of Special Plans was "a propaganda shop."

> *[I] witnessed neoconservative agenda bearers within OSP usurp measured and carefully considered assessments, and through suppression and distortion of intelligence analysis promulgate what were in fact falsehoods to both Congress and the executive office of the president.[29]*

Senator Carl Levin, in an official report on Feith's Office of Special Plans singled Feith out as providing to the White House a large amount of Iraq-Al Qaeda allegations which, post-invasion, turned out to be false.[30] Then Secretary of State Colin Powell called Feith's operation at the Pentagon the "Gestapo" office, alleging that it amounted to a separate, unchecked governing authority within the Pentagon.[31]

Feith, like Cheney, Rumsfeld and other Andrew Marshall protégés, was a founding member of the PNAC and advocated Iraqi regime change well before becoming Deputy Defense Secretary under Rumsfeld.[32]

Another key figure in the post-2001 Bush Administration from the Andrew Marshal stable was Zalmay Khalilzad. An Afghan-born naturalized American, Khalilzad became an advisor to Secretary of Defense Rumsfeld. He was also a member of the Project for the New American Century (PNAC).

Khalilzad was key in making Hamid Karzai, a long-time CIA asset, the President of Afghanistan. In September 2004, Khalilzad was charged with trying to influence the upcoming Afghan presidential elections. According to the *Los Angeles Times*:

Several Afghan presidential candidates ... maintain that the US ambassador and his aides are pushing behind the scenes to ensure a convincing victory by the pro-American incumbent, President Hamid Karzai.[33]

Khalilzad, a protégé of Dick Cheney and Paul Wolfowitz, also served as US Ambassador to Iraq, placing him at the center of two major US war disasters since 2003. Khalilzad's rise to power began in 1984 when he joined the Reagan Administration as an advisor on the arming of Afghan Mujahadeen against the Soviet Union in Afghanistan. Khalilzad was a RAND military analyst and also a special consultant to Unocal Oil Co. where he served as liaison with the Taliban in Afghanistan. Khalilzad initially recommended that the Bush administration support the Taliban.

Wolfowitz Doctrine: Mach I

Rumsefeld's Deputy Secretary of Defense Paul D. Wolfowitz had worked with Andrew Marshall in the Pentagon from 1989 to 1992 when Cheney was Defense Secretary. One of the most hawkish neo-conservatives, he was the principal author of the September 2002 Bush Doctrine, officially known as the National Security Strategy of the United States, sometimes known as the 'Wolfowitz doctrine' — the policy of pre-emptive military strikes against perceived or 'anticipated' enemies or rivals.

As a student at the University of Chicago in 1964, Wolfowitz had come under the influence of a former RAND colleague of Andrew Marshall, Albert Wohlstetter – another nuclear strategist who is said to have inspired Stanley Kubrick's *Dr. Strangelove*.[34]

During the Clinton administration, Wolfowitz formulated a new foreign policy with regard to Iraq and other 'potential aggressor states,' dismissing containment in favor of 'pre-emption'— strike first to eliminate threats, a version of the old 'shoot first and ask questions later.'

Together, Wolfowitz and Secretary of Defense Rumsfeld in early 2002 formulated and defined the Bush Doctrine of unilateral, pre-emptive aggression.

Wolfowitz had been the author of an earlier version of pre-emptive war. In March 1992, the *Washington Post* printed a sensational story based on a leaked Pentagon document:

> *In a classified blueprint intended to help 'set the nation's direction for the next century,' the Defense Department calls for concerted efforts to preserve American global military supremacy and to thwart the emergence of a rival superpower in Europe, Asia or the former Soviet Union...[T]he document argues not only for preserving but expanding the most demanding American commitments and for resisting efforts by key allies to provide their own security.*

> *In particular, the document raises the prospects of 'a unilateral US defense guarantee' to Eastern Europe, 'preferably in cooperation with other NATO states,' and contemplates use of American military power to pre-empt or punish use of nuclear, biological or chemical weapons, 'even in conflicts that otherwise do not directly engage US interests'*

Wolfowitz was the architect of that proposed 1992 policy. The Post noted,

> *The memo was drafted under supervision of Paul Wolfowitz,*
> *Undersecretary for Policy...The central strategy of the Penta-*
> *gon framework is to 'establish and protect a new order' that*
> *accounts 'sufficiently for the interests of **the advanced indus-***
> ***trial nations to discourage them from challenging our***
> ***leadership,'** while at the same time **maintaining a military***
> ***dominance capable of 'deterring potential competitors***
> ***from even aspiring to a larger regional or global role.'***[35]
> *(Emphasis added, w.e.)*

The leaked document, called *Defense Planning Guidance (DPG)*, was an outline of US grand strategy through the end of the 20th Century. Written in the aftermath of the Gulf War of 1991, the draft called for US military pre-eminence over the world, but particularly over Eurasia, including the former Soviet Union and China, by preventing the rise of any potentially hostile or rival power. It called for pre-emption against states even suspected of developing weapons of mass destruction. The *DPG* envisioned a world in which US military intervention overseas would become "a constant feature." It failed even to mention the United Nations.

The *DPG* articulated the essence of the 2002 Bush Doctrine, well before his administration. Known as the 'Wolfowitz Doctrine,' it was particularly revealing of the intentions of the US military-industrial complex, having been written during the months immediately following the collapse of the Soviet Union and the presumed end of the Cold War.[36]

Although softened in its final form at the insistence of then National Security Adviser Brent Scowcroft and Secretary of State James Baker, the draft *DPG* occupied a central place in the minds of its two authors, Paul Wolfowitz and Lewis 'Scooter' Libby, as well as their boss at that time, Defense Secretary Dick Cheney.

A decade later, theory was transformed into practice following the attacks of September 11, 2001. By then, Dick Cheney had become the most powerful vice president in US history, and the *DPG*'s authors, Paul Wolfowitz and Lewis Libby, had moved to the center of foreign policy-making in the Bush administration.[37]

Another notable protégé of Andrew Marshall, Dennis Ross, had been key in US Middle East policy under the Clinton Administration and would re-emerge as Special Adviser for the Persian Gulf and Southwest Asia, including Iran, to President Obama's Secretary of State Hillary Clinton. After leaving the Clinton Administration in 2000 Ross had gone to the Washington Institute for Near East Policy, a prominent neo-conservative think-tank. Earlier Ross had served as Deputy Director of the Pentagon's Office of Net Assessment under Andrew Marshall from 1982-1984.

Dennis Ross was a member of the PNAC and also was Executive Director of AIPAC, the powerful unregistered Washington lobby for Israel's rightwing Likud Party.

As a group, Andrew Marshall's protégés formed the most powerful military lobby in the US policy establishment in the first years of the 21st Century. They advocated radical force transformation, deployment of anti-missile defense, unilateral pre-emptive aggression, and militarization of space in order to use the US military to achieve for the United States and its closest allies, total domination of the planet as well as outer space. It was perhaps the most dangerous group of ideologues in United States history.

Marshall's Vision Of Hi-Tech Warfare

Among Marshall's pet military projects were various precision weapons, including robotic devices, unmanned vehicles for sky, land and undersea, as well as smaller devices that could change urban warfare by being able to crawl through buildings.

Marshall was also intrigued by pharmaceutical companies that were experimenting with neurological manipulation and nerve and mind-altering drugs. In 2003, just before the invasion of Iraq, Marshall told a journalist in a rare and chilling interview:

> *People who are connected with neural pharmacology tell me that new classes of drugs will be available relatively shortly, certainly within the decade. These drugs are just like natural*

chemicals inside people, only with behavior-modifying and performance-enhancing characteristics. [38]

Weaponizing new technologies was a core element of Marshall's RMA. Afghanistan and then Iraq became huge, gruesome testing grounds for many of Marshall's RMA pet projects.

According to the January/February 2003 *Multinational Monitor*, each major element of the Bush administration's national security strategy — from the doctrines of pre-emptive strikes and 'regime change' in Iraq, to its aggressive nuclear posture and commitment to deploying a Star Wars-style missile defense system – had been developed and refined before Bush took office.

The new policies and programs had been designed at corporate-backed conservative think tanks like the Center for Security Policy, the National Institute for Public Policy and the Project for a New American Century.[39]

Unilateralist ideologues and neo-conservative hawks, almost all con-nected with the Pentagon's Andrew Marshall, along with major admini-stration appointees who had ties to top Defense contractors, designed and implemented US foreign and military policy in the Bush Administra-tion. The appointments of Barack Obama gave little reason to believe there would be any change in that despite the new President's campaign for 'change.'

The Real Meaning Of 'Pre-Emption'

Exploiting the fears following 9/11, and impervious to budgetary con-straints imposed on virtually every other form of federal spending, the military-industrial complex drove the United States to war in Iraq and into a permanently aggressive war-fighting posture.[40]

The theory behind Bush's war drive against Iraq could be found in the administration's September 2002 *National Security Strategy*:

> *While the United States will constantly strive to enlist the sup-port of the international community, we will not hesitate to*

act alone, if necessary, to exercise our right of self-defense by acting pre-emptively against such terrorists, to prevent them from doing harm against our people and our country.[41]

This doctrine of pre-emptive warfare as official US policy opened the Pandora's Box to unilateral wars across the globe. Moreover, as military analysts Hartung and Ciarrocca pointed out:

The pre-emption doctrine is actually misnamed. Pre-emption suggests striking first against a nation that is poised to attack. The Bush doctrine is much more open-ended, implying that a U.S. attack is justified if a nation or organization might pose a threat at some unknown future date.[42]

That, combined with changes in US military doctrine, including Nuclear Primacy, made the US military position one of utmost alarm to seasoned military strategists and those aware of the dangers of a new nuclear war by miscalculation.

The Pentagon's 2003 Nuclear Posture Review already made clear that nuclear weapons were here to stay. The declared purpose of US nuclear weapons under the hawkish Bush-Cheney era was changing from deterrence and weapons of last resort to a central, usable component of the US military arsenal. This was the real reason for the alarm sounded by Russia's Putin at Munich in February 2007.

One of the primary sources of this dramatic shift in US nuclear policy—from threat-based deterrence to pre-emption without provocation—could be traced to corporate-financed think tanks like the National Institute for Public Policy (NIPP).

NIPP's January 2001 report, *"Rationale and Requirements for US Nuclear Forces and Arms Control,"* served as a model for Bush's 2003 report. Both the Bush report and the NIPP report recommended developing a new generation of 'usable' lower-yield nuclear weapons, expanding the US nuclear 'hit list' of potential targets and expanding the set of scenarios in which nuclear weapons may be used.

False Flags And The Achille Lauro

At the conclusion of its recommendations about 'Rebuilding America's Defenses, the PNAC group included a shocking statement. — shocking only in the aftermath of the dramatic events of September 11, 2001, one full year after the PNAC report was released. Initially, President Bush had referred to September 11 as "a new Pearl Harbor." He quickly dropped the reference. The following excerpt from the PNAC report may reveal why:

> *The United States cannot simply declare a 'strategic pause' while experimenting with new technologies and operational concepts. Nor can it choose to pursue a transformation strategy that would decouple American and allied interests. A transformation strategy that solely pursued capabilities for projecting force from the United States, for example, and sacrificed forward basing and presence, would be at odds with larger American policy goals and would trouble American allies. Further, **the process of transformation, even if it brings revolutionary change, is likely to be a long one, absent some catastrophic and catalyzing event – like a new Pearl Harbor.**[43] (Emphasis added—w.e.)*

American and other intelligence services had long ago perfected the technique of "false flag" operations. These were acts of horror which were made to appear the work of some opponent or enemy—in intelligence jargon, a "false flag." Ideally the perpetrators would not be aware on whose behalf they acted.

"False Flag" operations, in the jargon of secret intelligence services, were covert operations conducted by governments, corporations, or other organizations, which are designed to appear as if they are being carried out by other entities. The name was derived from the military concept of flying false colors—that is, flying the flag of a country other than one's own, in order to deceive.

False Flag terrorism meant that the terrorists believed that they were following orders "to help their cause," without realizing that their leadership had long since been taken over by their enemy.

A successful false flag terrorist attack that discredited the cause of the Palestinians was the case of the hijacking of the Italian cruise ship, "Achille Lauro" in 1985. The operation was ordered by Mossad, the Israeli secret services and carried by their agents inside Palestinian organizations. The details of the preparations were related by an insider of the Israeli secret services, Ari Ben-Menashe, former special intelligence advisor to Israeli Prime Minister Yitzhak Shamir, in his book, *"Profits of War."* According to Ben-Menashe, the attack on the Achille Lauro was "an Israeli 'black' propaganda operation to show what a deadly, cut-throat bunch the Palestinians were."[44] He said Mossad paid millions of dollars, via agents posing as "Sicilian dons," to a man named Abu'l Abbas to follow orders "to make an attack and do something cruel."

> *Abbas then gathered a team to attack the cruise ship. The team was told to make it bad, to show the world what lay in store for other unsuspecting citizens if Palestinian demands were not met. The group picked on an elderly American Jewish man, Leon Klinghoffer, in a wheelchair, killed him, and threw his body overboard. They made their point. But for Israel it was the best kind of anti-Palestinian propaganda.* [45]

September 11, 2001

The call by Deputy Defense Secretary Wolfowitz, Donald Rumsfeld and others immediately after September 11, 2001 to launch a military assault on Iraq, rather than go after the alleged mastermind, Osama bin Laden, led many astute investigators to ask whether the attacks of September 11, 2001 were in fact the "new Pearl Harbor" the authors of the PNAC report had been praying for.

A growing number of critical citizens began to question the accusations against an elusive Osama bin Laden as mastermind of 19 Arabic-speaking terrorists. The idea that they could commandeer, with only primitive boxcutters, four sophisticated Boeing commercial jets and redirect three of them, successfully, as apparently poorly-trained amateur pilots in air maneuvers which seasoned pilots claimed were near impossible, was creating growing disbelief among ordinary Americans in the official US Government version of the events.

What became clearer in the months after 9-11 was that the attack was clearly used immediately by the Bush Administration, at the very least, as the pretext to launch a war on Islam under the name of a 'War on Terror,' the 'Clash of Civilizations,' which Harvard Professor Samuel Huntington outlined in the early 1990's.

Many senior international intelligence experts began to put forward the possibility that the attacks of September 11, 2001 had been a "False Flag" operation.

Eckehardt Werthebach, former president of Germany's domestic intelligence service, *BundesVerfassungsschutz*, told the press just after 9/11 that, "the deathly precision and the magnitude of planning behind the attacks would have needed years of planning."

Such a sophisticated operation, Werthebach said, would require the "fixed frame" of a state intelligence organization, something not found in a "loose group" of terrorists like the one allegedly led by Mohammed Atta while he studied in Hamburg.

Many people would have been involved in the planning of such an operation and Werthebach pointed to the absence of leaks as further indication that the attacks were "state organized actions." [46]

Andreas von Bülow served on a German Parliamentary Commission which oversaw the three branches of the German secret service while a member of the *Bundestag* or German parliament from 1969 to 1994. Von Bülow told American Free Press he believed that the Israeli intelligence service, Mossad, and the CIA were behind the 9/11 terror attacks. [47]

He believed the planners used corrupt "guns for hire" such as Abu Nidal, the Palestinian terrorist who von Bülow called "an instrument of Mossad," high-ranking *Stasi* (former East German secret service) operatives, or Libyan agents who organize terror attacks using dedicated people, for example Palestinian and Arab "freedom fighters." [48]

Both Werthebach and von Bülow said the lack of an open and official investigation, like Congressional hearings, into the events of September 11 was incomprehensible. US Vice President Cheney dismissed calls for such an independent inquiry, insisting it would 'detract' from the War on Terror.

Only in 2002, a full year later, did Congress, and not the White House, establish an official inquiry to investigate the events surrounding September 11, 2001. The two co-chairmen of the "joint oversight hearings," however were Florida Senator Bob Graham, and Florida Congressman Porter Goss, a former CIA agent who was later to become George W. Bush's handpicked choice to head CIA. Graham and Goss, chairmen of the Senate and House Intelligence Committees, respectively, chose to conduct their inquiry "behind closed doors." [49]

There was little reason to expect anything approaching a neutral or honest investigation from an inquiry headed by Graham and Goss. As one Canadian researcher noted, its final report, issued in July 2003, omitted crucial links between the alleged Al Qaeda hijackers and the Pakistan ISI secret intelligence services, which enjoyed intimate ties to both Taliban and Al Qaeda forces. According to the *Washington Post*:

> *On the morning of September 11, Goss and Graham were having breakfast with a Pakistani general named Mahmud Ahmed — the soon-to-be-sacked head of Pakistan's intelligence service. Ahmed ran a spy agency notoriously close to Osama bin Laden and the Taliban.*[50] *(Washington Post, 18 May 2002).*

Canadian award-winning researcher, Michel Chossudovsky observed:

> *While the Joint inquiry has collected mountains of intelligence material, through careful omission, the numerous press and intelligence reports in the public domain (mainstream media, alternative media, etc), which confirm that key members of the Bush Administration were involved in acts of political camouflage, have been carefully removed from the Joint inquiry's hearings.*[51]

German Minister of Justice, Horst Ehmke, PhD had coordinated the German secret services directly under Prime Minister Willy Brandt in the

1970s. When Ehmke saw the televised images from September 11, he said it looked like a "Hollywood production...Terrorists could not have carried out such an operation with four hijacked planes without the support of a secret service."[52] Ehmke did not want to point to any particular agency.

Even starker in his assessment of the events of September 11 in the United States was one of the most senior of Russian military figures, a veteran of Cold War methods, General Leonid Ivashov. In a speech delivered in an international conference in Brussels in early 2006, Ivashov declared:

> ...[T]errorism is not something independent of world politics but simply an instrument, a means to install a unipolar world with a sole world headquarters, a pretext to erase national borders and to establish the rule of a new world elite. It is precisely this elite that constitutes the key element of world terrorism, its ideologist and its "godfather". The main target of the world elite is the historical, cultural, traditional and natural reality; the existing system of relations among states; the world national and state order of human civilization and national identity....
>
> Terrorism is the weapon used in a new type of war. At the same time, international terrorism, in complicity with the media, becomes the manager of global processes. It is precisely the symbiosis between media and terror, which allows modifying international politics and the exiting reality.

The Russian terrorism expert went on to look at the details of 9/11:

> In this context, if we analyze what happened on September 11, 2001, in the United States, we can arrive at the following conclusions: 1. The organizers of those attacks were the political and business circles interested in destabilizing the world order and who had the means necessary to finance the operation. The political conception of this action matured there where tensions emerged in the administration of financial and other types of resources. We have to look for the reasons of the attacks in the coincidence of interests of the big capital at

global and transnational levels, in the circles that were not satisfied with the rhythm of the globalization process or its direction. Unlike traditional wars, whose conception is determined by generals and politicians, the oligarchs and politicians submitted to the former were the ones who did it this time.

2. Only secret services and their current chiefs - or those retired but still having influence inside the state organizations - have the ability to plan, organize and conduct an operation of such magnitude... Planning and carrying out an operation on this scale is extremely complex....

3. Osama bin Laden and "Al Qaeda" cannot be the organizers nor the performers of the September 11 attacks. They do not have the necessary organization, resources or leaders. Thus, a team of professionals had to be created and the Arab kamikazes are just extras to mask the operation.

The September 11 operation modified the course of events in the world in the direction chosen by transnational mafias and international oligarchs; that is, those who hope to control the planet's natural resources, the world information network and the financial flows. This operation also favored the US economic and political elite that also seeks world dominance.[53]

In Ivashov's view, the use of the term 'international terrorism' had the following goals:

Hiding the real objectives of the forces deployed all over the world in the struggle for dominance and control; Turning the people to a struggle of undefined goals against an invisible enemy;

Destroying basic international norms and changing concepts such as: aggression, state terror, dictatorship or movement of national liberation;

Depriving peoples of their legitimate right to fight against aggressions and to reject the work of foreign intelligence services;

> *Solving economic problems through a tough military rule us-*
> *ing the war on terror as a pretext.*[54]

Some held George W. Bush, Cheney and Rumsfeld directly responsible for September 11. Stanley Hilton, the former Chief of Staff of Senator Bob Dole, a Washington attorney, represented families of victims of September 11. He sued President George Bush for involvement in 9/11. In a September 10, 2004 radio interview on the Alex Jones Radio Show, Hilton stated:

> *...[W]e are suing Bush, Condoleezza Rice, Cheney, Rumsfeld,*
> *(FBI chief) Mueller for complicity in personally not only al-*
> *lowing 9/11 to happen, but in ordering it...more evidence that*
> *I have been adducing over a year and a half has made it so*
> *obvious to me that this is now without any doubt a govern-*
> *ment operation and that it amounts to the biggest act of trea-*
> *son and mass murder in American history.*

Hilton was convinced that the four attack planes were "controlled by remote control." He explained further:

> *As I stated previously a year and a half ago, there's a system*
> *called Cyclops. There is a computer chip in the nose of the*
> *plane and it enables the ground control to disable the pilot's*
> *control of the plane and to control it and to fly it directly into*
> *those towers.*[55]

Attorney Hilton would never win his case, and the world would likely never obtain the necessary evidence — especially since the Bush Administration vehemently refused to name a truly independent commission of inquiry into 9/11 and had allowed most of the vital evidence, including especially the steel pillars of the World Trade Center towers, to be immediately shipped overseas for scrap. Bush's ally, the media-anointed "Hero of 9/11," New York Mayor Rudy Giuliani, even issued orders prohibiting New York Firefighters from attempting to recover the remains of their dead colleagues from the rubble, arresting several firemen who defied the order.

A 'New Pearl Harbor'?

Hours after the attacks on the New York World Trade Center on September 11, 2001 President George W. Bush told the world, "We have been attacked like we haven't since Pearl Harbor." The White House quickly dropped further reference to Pearl Harbor. In the context of the World Trade Center attacks, Bush's comment provoked serious journalists to go back to the September, 2000 Project for a New American Century report, "Rebuilding America's Defenses." In that report, the authors — including Dick Cheney and Donald Rumsfeld — had argued for a major transformation of America's defense posture. Such a "transformation," they wrote, "is likely to be a long one, **absent some catastrophic and catalyzing event—like a new Pearl Harbor.**" [Emphasis added, w.e.].

The reference to Pearl Harbor was a poor use of words by the President that led to too many embarrassing questions about how much the Bush Administration knew prior to September 11.

Whoever ultimately was responsible for the September 11, 2001 attacks, the undeniable result was a military hysteria and defense mobilization not seen in the United States since the Pearl Harbor attack in December 1941 that brought the United States into World War II against Germany, Japan and Italy.

That original bombing attack by Japan at Pearl Harbor, as 1946 classified US Congressional Hearings established, was known well in advance by President Roosevelt and a handful of top US military officials, days before the US fleet was bombed. It could have been avoided, and thousands of American lives saved. Roosevelt cold-bloodedly decided to "let it happen" to bring the United States into a war that he and his top planners had calculated they would win. It was the beginning shot in a war to establish what Henry Luce immediately termed "The American Century."

In 1946, at the end of the War, a Joint Committee on the Investigation of the Pearl Harbor Attack of the US Congress, chaired by Senator Alben Barkley of Kentucky, heard a report from the US Army's Pearl Harbor Board. It was classified "Top Secret" and only declassified decades later. [56]

The report was a bombshell indictment of the Roosevelt Administration, Roosevelt himself and General MacArthur, the great Army "hero" of the Pacific war. The attacks on Pearl Harbor and on the US Army Air Force bomber fleet by Japan in 1941 cost 2,403 American dead, 1,178 wounded, as well as the loss of 18 battleships and 188 airplanes. As early as November 26, two weeks before the attack, Roosevelt had been urgently and personally alerted to an imminent attack on Pearl Harbor by British Prime Minister Winston Churchill. Roosevelt responded by stripping the fleet at Pearl Harbor of air defenses, to insure Japanese success. Churchill's November 26 message to Roosevelt was the only document in their correspondence which has to this day never been made public on grounds of "national security."

The devastating attack on Pearl Harbor gave Roosevelt the cause to wage the war he so urgently sought. It was a war to create a new American Empire. The American military machine lost no time in responding to the attack of September 11, 2001 as a "new Pearl Harbor." It was as if a dream came true for the American military industrial complex and its backers within the Administration and Congress.[57]

The attacks of September 11, 2001 laid the ground for what the Bush Administration solemnly declared would be a Global War on Terror, an amorphous, undefined war against potential "enemies" in every land, every village, every area of potential combat from cyberspace to sea lanes. It was a made-to-order argument or pretext for a massive scale-up of military spending and a global projection of the Pentagon's Full Spectrum Dominance.

Whatever the ultimate truth about the events of 9/11, the American power elite clearly intended to use its global military dominance to extend the bounds of its power and influence to the entire planet after September 2001, much as the blueprint of the PNAC's September 2000 report, *Rebuilding America's Defenses*, had demanded. It was to be an increasingly desperate bid to prop up a crumbling empire that, like ancient Rome, the Ottoman Empire, Czarist Russia and the British Empire before it, had already rotted far too deeply from within.

Endnotes:

[1] Elaine Lafferty, "Missile defence is about money and it's here to stay," *Irish Times*, July 25, 2001 (http://www.globalsecurity.org/org/news/2001/010725-bmd.htm)

[2] *Robert McNamara*, Speech at the University of Michigan commencement, *Ann Arbor, June 22, 1962, quoted in Michio Kaku and Daniel Axelrod*, To Win A Nuclear War: The Pentagon's Secret War Plans *(Boston: South End Press, 1987), 138.*

[3] Henry I. Trewitt, *McNamara: His Ordeal in the Pentagon,* (New York: Harper and Row, 1971), 115.

[4] David R. Morgan, *Ballistic Missile Defense in the context of the evolution of US nuclear weapons policy during the past fifty years,* Testimony to Standing Committee on National Defense, House of Commons, Ottawa, March 19, 1999, in cndyorks.gn.apc.org.

[5] Michio Kaku, Op. Cit.

[6] David R. Morgan, Op. Cit. See also National Security Council Institutional Files, *Policy for Planning the Employment of Nuclear Weapons,*, 17 Jan 1974, NSDM 242, in http://64.233.183.104/search?q=cache:xHvc_74xiroJ:nixon.archives.gov/find/textual/pre sidential/nsc/institutional/finding_aid.pdf+NSDM-242+henry+kissinger+role+in&hl=en&ct=clnk&cd=3&gl=de&client=firefox-a.

[7] Michio Kaku, Op. Cit., 76.

[8] Herbert Scoville, MX: *Prescription for Disaster,* (Boston: MIT Press, 1981), 54.

[9] Kaku, Op. Cit., 179.

[10] Ibid, 207.

[10] Morgan, Op. Cit.

[11] "The Battlefield of the Future" - 21st Century Warfare Issues", Air University, (http://www.cdsar.af.mil/battle.bfoc.html) Chapter 3, p. 1, Jeffrey McKitrick, James Blackwell, Fred Littlepage, Georges Kraus, Richard Blanchfield and Dale Hill

[12] Nicholas Lehman, "Dreaming About War," *The New Yorker,* July 16, 2001.

[13] James Der Derian, "The Illusion of a Grand Strategy," *The New York Times,* May 25, 2001.

[14] Kaku, Op. Cit., 186.

[15] Lt. Col. Robert Bowman, *Arming the Heavens,* radio documentary for the National Radio Satellite System, WBAI-FM, NewYork, 1985.

[16] Morgan, Op. Cit.

[17] Derian, Op. Cit.

[18] Elaine Lafferty, "Missile Defense Is About Money And It's Here To Stay," *Irish Times,* July 25, 2001.

[19] Ken Silverstein, "The Man From ONA," *The Nation,* October 25, 1999. After his election, when President Kennedy discovered that he had been deceived by senior Pentagon and

RAND analysts, he became distrustful of the military leadership. This mutual distrust was a prominent factor during JFK's reaction to the Cuban missile crisis.

[20] Christopher A. Preble, "Who Ever Believed in the 'Missile Gap?: John F. Kennedy and the Politics of National Security," *Presidential Studies Quarterly*, Vol. 33, 2003.

[21] Lafferty, Op. Cit.

[22] Bob Woodward, *Bush At War* (New York: Simon and Schuster, 2002) 21-22.

[23] Melvin A. Goodman, "Righting the CIA (About Team B)", *The Baltimore Sun*, November 19, 2004, p.21. Goodman notes he resigned from the CIA in 1990 because of the 'politicization of intelligence on the Soviet Union by CIA Director William Casey, and his Deputy for Intelligence, Robert Gates.' Gates by 2006 repaced Rumsfeld as US Secretary of Defense, a post he remained in under President Barack Obama.

[24] Sam Tanenhaus, "The Mind Of The Administration: A Continuing Series On The Thinkers Who Have Shaped The Bush Administration's View Of The World," *The Boston Globe*, November 2, 2003. Tanenhaus notes, "At times, Team B performed logical somersaults that eerily foreshadowed Bush administration statements on Iraq and weapons of mass destruction. Just because super-weapons like a "non-acoustic anti-submarine system" couldn't be found, Pipes's report argued, that didn't mean the Soviets couldn't build one, "even if they appeared to lack the technical know-how."

[25] Jim Lobe, "Cheney's Mask is Slipping," *Asia Times*, October 1, 2003.

[26] Ibid.

[27] Julian Borger, "The Spies Who Pushed for War," *The Guardian* (London), July 17, 2003.

[28] Ibid.

[29] Ibid.

[30] Ibid.

[31] William Hamilton, "Bush Began to Plan War Three Months After 9/11," *Washington Post*, April 17, 2004.

[32] Gary Kamiya, "The Road to Hell," *Salon.com*, October 2, 2005, accessed in http://dir.salon.com/story/books/review/2005/10/07/packer/index.html.

[33] Paul Watson, "US Hand Seen in Afghanistan Election," *Los Angeles Times*, September 23, 2004

[34] Laura Rosen, "Inside AEI's Bunker," *Mother Jones*, January 7, 2009.

[35] Barton Gellman, "Keeping the U.S. First; Pentagon Would Preclude a Rival Superpower," *Washington Post*, March 11, 1992.

[36] David Armstrong, "Dick Cheney's Song of America: Drafting a Plan for Global Dominance," *Harpers Magazine*, October 2002.

[37] Tom Barry and Jim Lobe, "The Men Who Stole The Show," October 2002, in *Foreign Policy in Focus*, http://www.fpif.org/papers/02men/index.html.

[38] Douglas McGray, "The Marshall Plan," *WIRED*, issue 11.02, February 2003.

[39] William Hartung and Michelle Ciarrocca, "The Military-Industrial Think Tank Complex: Corporate Think Tanks And The Doctrine Of Aggressive Militarism. (The Business of War)," *Multinational Monitor*, Jan-Feb. 2003, in www.allbusiness.com/specialty-businesses/473260-1.html.

[40] Ibid.

[41] Ibid.

[42] Ibid.

[43] Project for the New American Century, *Rebuilding America's Defenses*, Washington D.C., September 2000 (http://www.newamericancentury.org/defensenationalsecurity.htm).

[44] Ari Ben-Menashe, *Profits of War: Inside the Secret U.S.-Israeli Arms Network* (New York: Sheridan Square Press, 1992) 122.

[45] Ibid. In a curious footnote to the Achille Lauro case, it was notable that the UN Naval officer who led the successful capture of the Achille Lauro hijackers in October 1985, was Admiral David Jeremiah, who on retiring became an active member of JINSA and other neo-conservative organizations close to the Likud Israeli right-wing. See Stephen Green, Op.Cit.

[46] Christopher Bollyn, Intel Expert Says 9-11 Looks Like A Hollywood Show, 22 March 2004, accessed in www.globalresearch.ca/articles/BOL403A.html.

[47] Christopher Bollyn, "Euro Intel Experts Dismiss 'War on Terrorism' as Deception," *American Free Press*, December 4, 2001 (http://www.ratical.org/ratville/CAH/911deception.html)

[48] Ibid.

[49] James Risen, "Trace of Terror: The Congressional Hearings; Rifts Plentiful as 9/11 Inquiry Begins Today," *The New York Times*, June 4, 2002.

[50] Richard Leiby, "A Cloak But No Dagger," *Washington Post*, May 18, 2002.

[51] Michel Chossudovsky, *The 9/11 Joint Inquiry chairmen are in "conflict of interest: Mysterious September 11 Breakfast Meeting on Capitol Hill*, August 4, 2003, accessed in http://www.globalresearch.ca/articles/CHO308C.html.

[52] Christopher Bollyn, "The German Secret Service Speaks of 9/11," *OpEdNews*, June 15, 2007 (http://www.opednews.com/articles/ genera_christop_070612_the_german_secret_se.htm)

[53] Leonid Ivashov (General, ret.), *International Terrorism does not exist*, Axis for Peace Conference, Brussels, January17, 2006, in physics911.net/ivashov.

[54] Ibid.

[55] Stanley Hilton, *Transcript: Alex Jones Interviews Stanley Hilton*, The Alex Jones Show, September 13 2004, in
http://www.prisonplanet.com/articles/september2004/130904hiltontranscript.htm.

[56] Alben W. Barkley, Senator, et al, *Investigation of the Pearl Harbor Attack*, Report of the Joint Committee on the Investigation of the Pearl Harbor Attack, 79th Congress, 2nd Session, US Senate, Document No. 244, US Government Printing Office, July, 1946.

[57] Mark E. Willey, *Pearl Harbor: Mother of All Conspiracies* (Philadelphia: ELibris Press 2001).

CHAPTER ELEVEN

Full Spectrum Dominance or Fully Mad?

'Potentially the most dangerous scenario would be a grand coalition of China, Russia and perhaps Iran, an 'anti-hegemonic' coalition united not by ideology but by complementary grievances...Averting this contingency...will require a display of US geostrategic skill on the western, eastern and southern perimeters of Eurasia simultaneously.'
    — *Zbigniew Brzezinski, adviser to candidate Obama[1]*

Eurasian Geopolitics

During the eight years of the Bush presidency, the scale of America's military expenditure underwent a radical transformation. The annual official Pentagon budget, including the Iraq and Afghanistan wars and their bloody aftermath, had exploded beyond all precedent. In Fiscal Year 2001, before the declaration of the War on Terror influenced spending, the Pentagon spent $333 billion on arms and manpower around the world to 'defend democracy,' above all what was defined as America's 'national security interests.' By 2009 that annual sum had more than doubled, when Iraq and Afghan costs were included, to $711 billion.[2]

In comparison with the rest of the world's military spending, the sums spent by Washington were even more impressive. The United States was far and away the global leader in military spending: in 2008 it spent more than the next 45 highest spending countries in the world combined. Its Pentagon and related budget accounted for 48 percent of the world's total military spending, almost one half of every military dollar. Compared with potential rivals, the US spent on its military almost six times more than China, ten times more than Russia, and nearly one hundred times more than Iran. China, with the world's second largest defense budget, spent $122 billion or approximately one-sixth of the US spending.

When the combined military budgets of the United States and all its NATO allies as well as key Pacific allies Japan, South Korea and Australia were totaled, the US-dominated alliance spent annually $1.1 trillion on their combined militaries, representing 72 percent of the world's total military spending.[3] If sheer dollars and hardware were the sole criteria, the world would long ago have been a helpless vassal colony under US Full Spectrum Dominance.

The extent of permanent US military bases over that eight-year period had expanded enormously from the Middle East to Central Asia to Afghanistan and Pakistan and across Africa. The Pentagon had deployed every weapon in its arsenal: raw military conquest in Iraq; 'soft power' regime change to pro-US dictatorships in former Soviet Republics, Ukraine and Georgia; and support of 'failed states' like Kosovo.

The strategic focus of that overwhelming US military buildup was the control of potential rivals on the Eurasian Continent, most directly, Russia and China.

Kosovo: Washington's Mafia State In The Balkans

Washington's bizarre diplomatic recognition of the tiny breakaway province of Kosovo in the Balkans was indicative of their determination to use any and all means to extend their military reach into vital strategic areas of the globe after 2001.

In early 2008 the tiny region of Kosovo adjacent to Serbia declared its 'independence.' President Bush, then visiting Tanzania, lost no time in declaring, "The Kosovars are now independent." Washington formally recognized Kosovo as an independent country soon afterward, despite the objections of several European Union governments. It didn't seem to bother the US State Department that Kosovo independence and its recognition openly violated UN resolutions for Kosovo, making a farce of the UN, as well as violating international law.[4]

US NATO control over Kosovo was a major step in control of Central Europe

The new Kosovo regime was headed by Prime Minister Hashim Thaci, a 39 year-old man identified by Interpol as well as German BND intelligence reports as a criminal, a boss of Kosovo organized crime in charge of drug running, extortion and prostitution. These facts were well known in Washington. It didn't seem to matter. In fact, quite the opposite.

Hashim Thaci had been a personal protégé of President Clinton's Secretary of State Madeleine Albright during the 1990s, when he was a mere 30 year-old gangster. According to various intelligence sources, the apparently intimate relation between Albright, then in her sixties and the handsome young Thaci, was not only about fine points of diplomacy.[5] Thaci, whose *nom de guerre* was Snake, was alleged to have ordered the killing of his KLA rivals.[6] He also allegedly financed his arms purchases for the Kosovo Liberation Army by drug dealing—specifically the heroin trade—across the Balkans.[7]

The so-called Kosovo Liberation Army (KLA) was supported from the outset by the US Defense Intelligence Agency and British MI6 and reportedly also by the German BND.[8] During the 1999 NATO war against Serbia, the KLA was directly supported by NATO.

Kosovo, formerly part of Yugoslavia and then Serbia, was being made into a *de facto* NATO client state run by an internationally known drug dealer in order to provide the US military with unfettered control over the entire Middle East and the Balkans.[9]

The question then became, why were Washington, NATO, the EU and the German Government so eager to legitimize the breakaway Kosovo?

The answer was not hard to find. A Kosovo run internally by organized criminal networks was easy for NATO to control. It insured a weak state that was far easier to bring under NATO domination. And, it was a prime piece of real estate in a strategically critical location.

Immediately after the bombing of Serbia in 1999, the Pentagon had seized a 1000-acre parcel of land in Kosovo at Uresevic near the border of Macedonia, and awarded a contract to Halliburton (when Dick Cheney was CEO) to build one of the largest US overseas military bases in the world, Camp Bondsteel. Camp Bondsteel was later revealed to be a site of illegal CIA torture prisons.[10]

Thaci's dependence on the US and NATO's good graces ensured that Thaci's government would do what it was told in matters of key foreign policy. This assured the US a major military gain, consolidating its permanent presence in the strategically vital southeast Europe. It was a major step in consolidating NATO's control of Eurasia, especially of Russia, and it gave the US a large boost in its favor in the European balance of power.

Little wonder Moscow did not welcome this development. Kosovo was part of a far larger and more dangerous Pentagon project to militarize the entire region, the 'Greater Middle East' as the Pentagon called it. Russia had observed the instrumental role of the US in shaping the policies of nearby Georgia and its hand-picked President, Mikhail

Saakashvili, not just regarding NATO membership, but in provoking the military strike in August 2008 that had threatened to restart the Cold War, or worse.

Georgia's Mad Military Play

In August 2008, after months of increasing tensions, Georgia's President Mikhail Saakashvili ordered an invasion of the breakaway province South Ossetia. His decision was no solo act. He had met with former Bush strategist Karl Rove in Ukraine three weeks prior to the invasion, and during this time period had had frequent phone contact with Republican Presidential candidate John McCain, whom he reportedly knew well.[11] Saakashvili had also met with Secretary of State Condoleezza Rice in Tbilisi on July 10, one day after Rice had signed an agreement with the Czech Republic allowing the US to station advanced ballistic missile defense radar there. Rice, a Russian expert by background, reportedly backed Saakashvili's plan to launch the attack while publicly claiming distance.[12]

Days after the war began, Saakashvili and his Defense Minister, David Kezerashvili, a dual citizen with an Israeli passport and fluent in Hebrew, told the press that Georgia's military owed a debt to Israel for arming and training its forces. Moreover, Georgia's Minister for Reintegration, Temur Yakobashvili, also fluent in Hebrew, added to the embarrassment of Tel Aviv officials by stating to Israel's Army Radio: "Israel should be proud of its military, which trained Georgian soldiers."[13]

These public statement, delivered in Hebrew shortly after the fighting erupted, raised more than a few eyebrows in European diplomatic circles. Israel had reportedly sold Georgia some 200 million dollars worth of equipment since 2000, including remotely piloted drones, rockets, night-vision equipment, sophisticated electronic systems, and training by former senior Israeli officers.[14]

Russian Deputy Chief of General Staff, Colonel-General Anatoly Nogovitsyn, accused Israel of supplying arms to Georgia and delivering weapons systems, including eight types of unmanned aircraft and about

100 anti-tank mines. The Israeli presence in Georgia consisted of IDF special forces, Israeli Air Force personnel, detachments of Mossad and other Israeli groups, including mercenaries—all working in complete cooperation with American forces—to train and equip the new Georgian armed forces.

At the same time, Israel was preparing to move some of its attack aircraft into Georgia, base them on Israeli-controlled airfields in southern Georgia, and arm and equip them for a strike on Tehran, Nogovitsyn charged. It should be noted that the distance from Tel Aviv to Tehran is 1,600 km, and the distance from Southern Georgia to Teheran is 1,149 km. Slip tanks add 600-800 miles to the overall range.

According to a report by Brian Harring in *TBRNews.org*, the Israeli air strike was to be aimed at Iranian government buildings with one Israeli group striking where top Iranian officials were known to be working, another at housing for the top leadership, and others at any identified laboratory where nuclear work was being carried on. A second flight was to strike at Iranian oil wells, pipelines and Persian Gulf oil terminals. Once the dual strike was completed, the aircraft would head towards Israel and then be refuelled in mid-air by an American tanker aircraft.[15]

After the Russian invasion of Georgia and the disintegration of the Georgian army, a Russian spy satellite spotted a convoy of US Humvees heading down the highway towards the Georgian port of Poti, then occupied by Russian troops, Harring reported. The convoy, filled with a group of Georgian special troops, was captured. The vehicles were loaded with plastic explosives, silenced firearms and, to the pleasant surprise of Russian military intelligence, a large trove of top-secret NATO documents concerning their highly secret satellite technology.

It appears that the Georgians commandeered the US vehicles to flee the Russians, totally unaware of their contents.

The remarkable security leaks from both US and Israeli sources were sent to Moscow for evaluation. Putin then saw an excellent chance to wreak havoc on his Georgian enemies, crush their military, capture the vast stocks of American military equipment stored in Georgia, and force both the Americans and the Israelis out of the country under humiliating circumstances. Russian units also took over a part of the vital trans-

Caucasus pipeline, secured the former Russian breakaway provinces and drew a strong line in the sand.

According to Harring, a Russian GRU report, dated September 3, 2008, concerned one aspect of the huge trove of American and Israeli intelligence documents found abandoned in Georgia by both American intelligence units as well as Israeli. The documents disclosed that the U.S. electronic equipment captured at Poti by Russian *spesnatz* units was partially manufactured at Odessa in the Ukraine, under US license. The Ukraine was not a member of NATO, but NATO-compatible sensitive military equipment was being manufactured in a non-NATO country. The Russian report went on to state that the Georgian military not only abandoned "significant amounts of" valuable equipment, but also had totally compromised both the American and Israeli intelligence networks set up in Georgia for the purpose of electronic spying on Iran, Russia and Turkey.[16]

Israel claimed it was not a major supplier of arms to Georgia, insisting that the US and France had supplied Tbilisi with most of its weapons. *Debka*, an Israeli news service with reportedly close ties to Mossad, Israel's CIA equivalent, reported:

> *Israel's interest in the conflict from its[Debka] exclusive military sources: Jerusalem owns a strong interest in Caspian oil and gas pipelines reach the Turkish terminal port of Ceyhan, rather than the Russian network. Intense negotiations are afoot between Israel Turkey, Georgia, Turkmenistan and Azerbaijan for pipelines to reach Turkey and thence to Israel's oil terminal at Ashkelon and on to its Red Sea port of Eilat. From there, supertankers can carry the gas and oil to the Far East through the Indian Ocean. [17]*

In any event, Israel promptly announced suspension of all arms sales to Georgia. Israel, according to diplomatic sources, feared that Russia would retaliate by selling advanced anti-missile missiles to Iran.[18]

Months later, a special Ukrainian Parliamentary Commission of Inquiry investigated allegations of illegal arms sales to Georgia by Ukraine's pro-NATO President, Viktor Yushchenko. The commission found that the President was personally implicated in an illegal arms sale and fraudulent under-reporting of its value to Ukraine's tax authorities.[19]

Ukraine had supplied weapons to Georgia even after the war with Russia had broken out. Valery Konovaliuk, head of the Ukrainian Parliamentary Ad Hoc Investigation Commission, stated to the press that the Commission held documents confirming that Ukraine continued to supply arms to Georgia even after the conflict with Russia ended. He claimed certain documents indicated that ammunition and artillery guns, disguised as humanitarian aid, were shipped to Batumi September 22, 2008, long after the end of the conflict.

At the time he was evidently arming his neighbor and fellow NATO candidate, Saakashvili's Georgia, to the teeth, Ukraine's President Viktor Yushchenko was also asking to join NATO, fully backed by Washington. Not surprisingly, Germany and France were less than eager to admit two such unstable candidates into NATO where 'an attack against one is an attack against all,' meaning they might face a future war against Russia over tiny Georgia.

The Ukraine Commission also found that there had been embezzlement of revenues from the arms sales, with large sums not reaching the state treasury and defense ministry accounts. According to calculations, Ukraine sold $2 billion worth of arms over three years, while $840 million were officially declared. The rest presumably lined the pockets of Yushchenko and friends.[20]

Washington's *de facto* client regimes in Ukraine and Georgia after 2004 were being exposed as ill-disguised gangster dictatorships posing as 'democracies.' Both states were, in fact, forms of totalitarian 'democracy' in which laws were irrelevant when they hindered the goals of the US-backed Yushchenko in Ukraine or Saakashvili in the Republic of Georgia.

As Washington was engaged in heating up the Balkans and Ukraine against Russia, it was simultaneously also upping the stakes against China in the war over oil and strategic raw materials then developing in Africa.

Africom, China And Resource Wars

Just weeks after President George W. Bush signed the Order creating AFRICOM, the new US military command dedicated to Africa, several ominous events erupted on the mineral-rich continent. These events suggested that a major agenda of the Obama Presidency would be to focus US resources—military and other—on dealing with four key areas of Africa: the Republic of Congo; the oil-rich Gulf of Guinea; the oil-rich Darfur region of southern Sudan; and increasingly, the Somali 'pirate threat' to sea lanes in the Red Sea and Indian Ocean.[21]

The African Continent contains what most geologists believe to be the planet's most abundant mineral riches. With China, Russia, India and other potential US 'rivals' beginning to develop ties to various African nations and their raw materials, the Washington response was clear—military.

Africa's Great Rift Valley holds the world's greatest concentration of raw materials and hence the cause of wars for control

The Democratic Republic of Congo had been renamed from the Republic of Zaire in 1997 when the forces of Laurent Désiré Kabila (father of President Joseph Kabila) had brought Mobutu's thirty two year reign-of-terror to an end. Locals continued to call the country Congo-Kinshasa.

The Kivu region of the Congo was the geological repository of some of the world's greatest strategic minerals. The eastern border straddling Rwanda and Uganda runs on the eastern edge of the Great African Rift Valley, believed by geologists to be one of the richest repositories of minerals on the face of the earth. The Great Rift was the largest rupture

on the earth's land surface, extending more than 4,000 miles from
Lebanon to the Mozambique Channel in the southern part of the Continent, containing perhaps the most fertile volcanic soil and greatest
mineral concentration on the planet. Quite literally for whoever controlled it, this region was a goldmine.[22]

The Democratic Republic of Congo contained more than half the
world's cobalt. It held one-third of its diamonds, and, extremely significantly, fully three-quarters of the world resources of columbite-tantalite
or "coltan" — a primary component of computer microchips and printed
circuit boards, essential for mobile telephones, laptops and other
modern electronic devices.[23]

America Mineral Fields, Inc., a company heavily involved in promoting the 1996 accession to power of Laurent Kabila, was, at the time of its
involvement in the Congo's civil war, headquartered in Hope, Arkansas,
hometown of then-President Bill Clinton. Major stockholders included
long-time associates of Clinton going back to his days as Governor of
Arkansas.

Several months before the downfall of Zaire's French-backed dictator
Mobutu Sese Seko, Laurent Kabila had renegotiated the mining contracts
with several US and British mining companies, including American
Mineral Fields. Mobutu's corrupt rule was brought to a bloody end with
the help of the US-directed International Monetary Fund, which cut
funding at a critical time.[24]

Washington was not entirely comfortable with Laurent Kabila, who
was finally assassinated in 2001 under murky circumstances. In a study
released in April 1997 barely a month before President Mobutu fled the
country, the IMF had recommended "halting currency issue completely
and abruptly" as part of an economic "recovery" program. That had the
effect of ending Mobutu's control of money in the country.

Kabila, as Mobutu's successor, had upset his US backers by reneging
on deals to sell off mining concessions as well as by refusing to accept
IMF proposals to pay off the country's huge debts incurred under Mobutu. The elder Kabila had developed ties to China soon after taking office,
traveling to Beijing where he was warmly greeted by Chinese officials.[25]

The IMF-mandated privatizations of state mining assets would have opened the door for US or related mining companies to grab control of the country's prize mineral assets. A few months after assuming power in Kinshasa, the new government of Laurent Kabila was also ordered by the IMF to freeze civil service wages with a view to "restoring macro-economic stability," a move that would have made him a captive of foreign 'protectors' from his own government. Eroded by hyperinflation, the average public sector wage had fallen to the equivalent of one US dollar a month. The attraction of China's 'no-strings-attached' economic aid, in contrast to the IMF demands, was clear.

According to Canadian researcher Michel Chossudovsky, the IMF's demands were tantamount to maintaining the entire population in abysmal poverty. They precluded from the outset a meaningful post-war economic reconstruction, thereby fuelling the continuation of the Congolese civil war in which close to two million people died. Laurent Kabila was succeeded by his son, Joseph Kabila who went on to become the Congo's first democratically elected President, and who appeared to have kept a closer eye on the welfare of his countrymen than did his father.

No sooner had AFRICOM become operational on October 1, 2008 than major new crises broke out in Kivu Province in Kabila's Democratic Republic of Congo. [26] The common thread linking Kivu with Darfur in southern Sudan was that both regions were strategically vital for China's future raw materials flow.

Washington policy was simple: attempt to get into a position of 'strategic denial,' the military term for the ability to cut off vital mineral and oil flows to a potential rival such as China.

According to the International Rescue Committee, more than 5,400,000 Congolese civilians had died over the course of an ongoing war in the Congo since 1996, making the wars in the DR Congo the deadliest conflict in the world since World War II.[27] Curiously enough, unlike the case of Darfur, no Washington outcry of genocide was heard over this staggering number of deaths in the Republic of the Congo—orders of magnitude larger than those cited as proof of genocide in Darfur.

Most of the deaths had occurred in the eastern part of the Democratic Republic of Congo (DRC) where rebel leader Laurent Nkunda continued to wage a resource war against the democratically elected and internationally recognized government of President Joseph Kabila. Laurent Nkunda alleged that he was protecting the minority Tutsi ethnic group in the DR Congo against remnants of the Rwandan Hutu army that fled to the Democratic Republic of the Congo after the Rwandan genocide in 1994.[28]

The most intense fighting in the eastern part of the DRC had broken out in late August 2008 when Tutsi militiamen from Nkunda's CNDP forced loyalist DRC troops to retreat from their positions near Lake Kivu, sending hundreds of thousands of displaced civilians fleeing and prompting the French foreign minister, Bernard Kouchner, to warn of the imminent risk of huge massacres.

Laurent Nkunda was an ethnic Tutsi, as was his patron, Rwanda's US-backed dictator Paul Kagame. UN peacekeepers reported no atrocities against the minority Tutsi in the northeastern, mineral rich Kivu region. Congolese sources reported that attacks against Congolese of all ethnic groups were a daily occurrence in the region and that Laurent Nkunda's troops were responsible for most of these attacks.[29]

Strange Resignations

The political chaos in DR Congo intensified in September 2008 when the Democratic Republic of Congo's 83 year old Prime Minister, Antoine Gizenga, resigned. Then in October, unexpectedly, the commander of the United Nations peacekeeping operation in Congo, Spanish Lieutenant General Vicente Diaz de Villegas, resigned after less than seven weeks on the job. He cited lack of confidence in the leadership of UN Under-Secretary General, Alan Doss. He told the Spanish paper, *El Pais*, "I felt that resigning was my duty in order to attract the attention and not to assume the responsibility of the potential consequences [of applying the Plan of Separation.]" [30] That UN Plan of Separation was, in effect, to split Kivu Province from the DR Congo, a move that would severely weaken the DRC and have consequences for China, among others.[31]

Joseph Kabila, the Democratic Republic of Congo's first democratically elected President, had been negotiating a major $9 billion trade agreement between the DRC and China, something that Washington was clearly not happy about. In April 2008 Kabila had given an interview to a Belgian newspaper, *Le Soir*, where he declared that China was now Congo's most important trade and development partner, promising that its influence would expand further at the expense of Europe. The interview took place after a Belgian government delegation raised human rights and corruption concerns during an official visit to Congo, which President Kabila considered arrogant and provocative. Belgium's colonial record for human rights abuses in the Congo was hardly exemplary.[32]

Kabila was quoted as saying that Congo had made an "irreversible choice" to pick China as its preferred partner instead of Europe and Belgium, Congo's former colonial master. [33]

Not long after Kabila's interview in *Le Soir*, Nkunda launched his new offensive. Nkunda was a long-standing henchman of Rwanda's President Kagame who had been trained at Fort Leavenworth, Kansas. All signs pointed to a heavy, if covert, USA role in the Congo killings by Nkunda's men. Nkunda himself was a former Congolese Army officer, a teacher and Seventh Day Adventist pastor. But, thanks to his training at Fort Leavenworth, he became best known for killing.

Nkunda's well-equipped and relatively disciplined forces were primarily from the neighboring country of Rwanda, where US military trainers had been active. A portion had been recruited from the minority Tutsi population of the Congolese province of North Kivu. Supplies, funding and political support for his Congolese rebel army came from Rwanda. According to the *American Spectator* magazine, "President Paul Kagame of Rwanda has long been a supporter of Nkunda, who originally was an intelligence officer in the Rwanda leader's overthrow of the Hutu despotic rule in his country."[34]

The *Congo News Agency* charged that it was not to protect his native Tutsi brothers that Nkunda was fighting, but instead:

[H]is true motives. . .are to occupy the mineral-rich North-Kivu province, pillage its resources, and act as a proxy army in eastern Congo for the Tutsi-led Rwandan government in Kigali. Kagame wants a foothold in eastern Congo so his country can continue to benefit from the pillaging and exporting of minerals such as Columbite-Tantalite (Coltan). Many experts on the region agree today that resources are the true reason why Laurent Nkunda continues to create chaos in the region with the help of Paul Kagame.[35]

Coltan provided a vital metal that controlled the flow of electricity in every mobile phone in the world, meaning its strategic importance over the previous decade had exploded. One Danish church mission organization stated that control over the profits from the eastern DR Congo Coltan mines were a driving cause of the ongoing bloody conflicts there. The region held the world's largest reserves of the important mineral. [36]

Hutu And Tutsi Genocide: The US Role

A French court in 2006 ruled that Kagame had organized the shooting down of the plane carrying Hutu President of Rwanda, Juvénal Habyarimana, in April 1994, the event that set off the indiscriminate, rampaging slaughter of hundreds of thousands of people, both Hutu and Tutsi, across the region.[37]

The end result of the Rwandan genocide, in which perhaps as many as a million Africans perished, was that US and UK backed Paul Kagame—a ruthless military strongman trained at the US Army Command and General Staff College at Fort Leavenworth Kansas—was firmly in control as the US-backed dictator of Rwanda. The Clinton Administration had done nothing to intervene to halt the killing. On the contrary—the US had actively blocked UN Security Council action. At the time, according to a later declassified Pentagon memo, the Pentagon had predicted a "massive bloodbath" and announced that it would not intervene "until peace is restored."[38]

Beginning in 1990, then-President George H.W. Bush and his Defense Secretary, Dick Cheney, had backed a Tutsi guerilla group, the

Rwanda Patriotic Front (RPF), to launch an insurgency from neighboring Uganda to seize control of Rwanda and topple its French-backed President Habyarimana.

Fresh from his training at Fort Leavenworth, Kagame was sent to take up the role of number two of the RPF, becoming Commander on the convenient death of the head. Kagame, developed close ties to the Pentagon, CIA and US State Department; Secretary of State Madeleine Albright referred to Kagame at one point as "a beacon of hope."[39] She neglected to say for whom.

Since the end of the 1994 genocide, Kagame had covertly backed the repeated military incursions by General Nkunda into the mineral-rich Kivu region on the pretext it was to defend a small Tutsi minority. Kagame repeatedly rejected attempts to repatriate those Tutsi refugees back to Rwanda, however, obviously fearing he might lose the pretext for his occupation of the mineral rich region of Kivu.

According to Canadian researcher Chossudovsky, the 1994 massacre of civilians between Tutsi and Hutu was "an undeclared war between France and America." As he saw it:

> *By supporting the build up of Ugandan and Rwandan forces and by directly intervening in the Congolese civil war, Washington also bears a direct responsibility for the ethnic massacres committed in the Eastern Congo including several hundred thousand people who died in refugee camps.*
>
> *Major General Paul Kagame was an instrument of Washington. The loss of African lives did not matter. The civil war in Rwanda and the ethnic massacres were an integral part of US foreign policy, carefully staged in accordance with precise strategic and economic objectives.*[40]

Kagame's former intelligence officer Nkunda led well-equipped forces to take Goma in the eastern Congo, as part of an apparent scheme to break the richest minerals region away from Kinshasha. With the US military beefing up its presence across Africa under AFRICOM since 2007, the stage was set for yet another resources grab, this one by the US-backed Kagame and his former officer, Nkunda.

Gorilla Preservation Or Guerillas?

Evidence from on-site interviews and Freedom of Information filings confirmed that the US Pentagon, working covertly through the USAID under the Department of State, had been diverting millions of dollars of USAID funds earmarked for 'gorilla conservation' in the Virunga National-al Park in eastern Democratic Republic of Congo and using it instead to explore the vast oil and mineral riches located in the same area. It was no confusion of the animal gorilla with the military guerilla, but a quite deliberate deception.

When skeptics investigated, they found that USAID money officially paid to the Dian Fossey Gorilla Fund International and Conservation International, were being misused. The two organizations had not filed required audit reports on almost $5 million spent during the previous two years. The USAID was apparently covering up for the diversion of US taxpayer dollars from gorilla conservation to minerals exploration and providing arms to various organizations in Congo's Kivu.[41] One serious researcher of US and Western covert warfare in Africa over its raw materials, Keith Harmon Snow alleged that "The white agents working for Western 'conservation' NGOs—and we know their names—are directly responsible for extortion, racketeering, land theft, human rights atrocities and for ripping apart the social fabric." [42] There was reason to believe that the USAID funds were being merely laundered via the conservation NGOs to create a massive arms buildup in the region.

Uganda and Rwanda were two of the Pentagon's premier military partners in Africa in recent years. In 2007 some 150 US Special Forces were added to the Pentagon's Uganda arsenal, while American and British military advisers had been training Uganda's UPDF troops.[43] AFRICOM would presumably upgrade those operations to counter Chinese presence in the Democratic Republic of Congo, using a variety of techniques such as diverting USAID gorilla conservation funds to arms purchases.

USAID was an official partner in Africom, making Africom unlike other US military commands that remained strictly military.

A key actor in the region was former US State Department and National Security Council senior official, Walter Kansteiner III. According to Snow:

> *[Kansteiner was] one of the shadiest architects of Congo's troubles. The son of a coltan trader in Chicago, Kansteiner was Assistant Secretary of State for Africa under G.W. Bush and former "National Security" insider and member of the Department of Defense Task Force on Strategic Minerals under Bill Clinton. Kansteiner's speech at The Forum for International Policy in October of 1996 advocated partitioning the Congo (Zaire) into smaller states based on ethnic lineage.* [44]

A former US Defense Department consultant, Kansteiner was also a trustee of the Africa Wildlife Foundation—another profit-based "conservation" entity tied to Conservation International, the Dian Fossey Gorilla Fund and the Jane Goodall Institute.[45]

The balkanization of Congo appeared to be a major objective behind the organized chaos in the Great Lakes region.

According to interviews with local people in the Kivu and adjacent war zones, the MONUC mercenary troops under UN command in the region delivered weapons back to militias to justify MONUC's one billion dollar a year occupation of Congo. "MONUC was giving weapons to the militias," claimed one Congolese official:

> *MONUC had their own ambitions. It was about gold. The peace that was achieved in Orientale around 2006 was not achieved by MONUC; the National Police Force from Kinshasa and the integrated FARDC brigades achieved it. MONUC was frustrating the peace.* [46]

During the eight-year Bush Administration, the Pentagon signed base agreements with the governments of numerous African countries, including Botswana, Gabon, Ghana, Kenya, Mali, Morocco, Namibia, Sao Tome and Principe, Senegal, Sierra Leone, Tunisia, Uganda, and Zambia. In addition, Dick Cheney's old firm, Halliburton and its KBR subsidiary, made a joint venture, Brown and Root-Condor, that brought together Halliburton and Algeria's state-owned oil company, Sonatrach, to enlarge the military air bases at Tamanrasset and at Bou Saada.[47] AFRICOM was to weld all that into a coherent US military presence across the African Continent to meet a new challenge.

The Target: China

If France had been the covert target of US 'surrogate warfare' in central Africa in the early 1990's, by 2008 it was clearly China that had become a real and growing threat to US control of Central Africa's vast mineral riches. China's rapid industrialization had made secure supplies of every mineral commodity imaginable a national state priority for China.[48]

Speaking to the International Peace Operations Association in Washington, D.C. on Oct. 27, 2008 General Kip Ward, Commander of AFRICOM, defined the command's mission:

> [I]n concert with other US government agencies and international partners, [to conduct] sustained security engagements through military-to-military programs, military-sponsored activities, and other military operations as directed to promote a stable and secure African environment in support of US foreign policy. [49]

General Ward was speaking to a gathering of the vast private mercenary military industry that had blossomed under the Bush Administration, including notably DynCorp and Blackwater. The latter had renamed itself the more anonymous "Xe" after Blackwater personnel had been linked to numerous deadly incidents in Iraq and elsewhere.[50]

AFRICOM was clearly organized to combine all such resources from hard military power to mercenaries to food aid and so-called 'soft power' to keep Africa's resource-rich countries under its sway and out of the control of rivals such as China.

AFRICOM's "military operations as directed to promote a stable and secure African environment in support of US foreign policy" were clearly aimed at blocking China's growing economic presence on the continent.

Africa at the Boiling Point

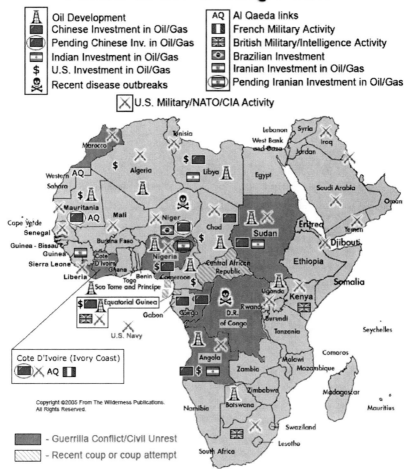

*Africa's vast raw materials riches have made the Continent
a strategic priority for the future of the Chinese economy*

Various Washington sources stated openly that AFRICOM was created to counter the growing presence of China in Africa, including most emphatically in the Democratic Republic of Congo, and to secure long-term economic agreements for raw materials from Africa in exchange for Chinese aid and production sharing agreements and royalties.

J. Peter Pham, a leading Washington insider who was an advisor to the US State and Defense Departments, stated that one of the objectives of the new AFRICOM was:

> ...protecting access to hydrocarbons and other strategic re-sources which Africa has in abundance, ... a task which in-cludes ensuring against the vulnerability of those natural riches and ensuring that no other interested third parties, such as China, India, Japan, or Russia, obtain monopolies or preferential treatment.[51]

In testimony before the US Congress supporting creation of AFRICOM in 2007, Pham, who was closely associated with the neo-conservative Foundation for Defense of Democracies, stated:

> This natural wealth makes Africa an inviting target for the at-tentions of the People's Republic of China, whose dynamic economy, averaging 9 percent growth per annum over the last two decades, has an almost insatiable thirst for oil as well as a need for other natural resources to sustain it. China is cur-rently importing approximately 2.6 million barrels of crude per day, about half of its consumption; more than 765,000 of those barrels—roughly a third of its imports—come from Afri-can sources, especially Sudan, Angola, and Congo (Brazza-ville). Is it any wonder, then, that...perhaps no other foreign region rivals Africa as the object of Beijing's sustained strate-gic interest in recent years. Last year the Chinese regime pub-lished the first-ever official white paper elaborating the bases of its policy toward Africa.

> This year, ahead of his twelve-day, eight-nation tour of Af-rica—the third such journey since he took office in 2003—Chinese President Hu Jintao announced a three-year, $3 bil-lion program in preferential loans and expanded aid for Af-rica. These funds come on top of the $3 billion in loans and $2 billion in export credits that Hu announced in October 2006 at the opening of the historic Beijing summit of the Forum on China-Africa Cooperation (FOCAC) which brought nearly fifty African heads of state and ministers to the Chinese capi-tal.

Intentionally or not, many analysts expect that Africa—especially the states along its oil-rich western coastline—will increasingly becoming a theatre for strategic competition between the United States and its only real near-peer competitor on the global stage, China, as both countries seek to expand their influence and secure access to resources.[52]

That was the framework for the events of late October 2008 when Nkunda's well-armed troops surrounded Goma in North Kivu and demanded that Congo President Joseph Kabila negotiate with him.

General Nkunda demanded, among other things, that President Kabila cancel a $9 billion joint Congo-China venture in which China would obtain rights to the vast copper and cobalt resources of the region in exchange for providing $6 billion worth of infrastructure: road construction; two hydroelectric dams; hospitals; schools; and railway links to southern Africa, to Katanga, and to the Congo Atlantic port at Matadi. The remaining $3 billion was to be invested by China in developing new mining areas.

This was, up to that point, the biggest single contract by China in Africa. In exchange for the infrastructure and mining development, China would get a share of Congo's precious natural resources for its industries – 10 million tons of copper and 400,000 tons of cobalt for use in manufacturing batteries, propeller blades, magnets and chemicals. It was a barter deal—what the Chinese called 'win-win'—not aid with strings attached, like Western powers had given DR Congo over the years.[53]

The Obama National Security Agenda

Within the first months of his Presidency, Barack Obama had begun to make clear that, whatever his personal inclinations, he was not about to challenge the fundamental strategic agenda of powerful US institutions, least of all their military and foreign policy agenda.

That was the real significance of Obama's asking George Bush's Secretary of Defense, Robert Gates, to stay on as Defense Secretary. Soon after his re-appointment, Gates made clear in public remarks that he continued to back the provocative US missile shield in Poland and the Czech Republic. In March 2009 Gates told an interviewer that the US missile program was in part to 'defend Russia' from possible Iranian missile attacks, a claim stretching the bounds even of Pentagon credibility.[54]

Obama Defense Secretary was a decades-long Bush Family
ally since George H.W. Bush's days at CIA

Additionally, Obama appointed an extremely senior military man, four-star Marine General James L. Jones, to become his National Security Advisor. Jones, former NATO Supreme Commander in Europe until December 2006, had played a central role in the creation of AFRICOM. After leaving NATO, Jones became a member of the Board of Directors of major defense contractor, Boeing, as well as of Chevron Oil Corporation. He was well connected within the same military industry-oil complex that Bush and Cheney had represented.[55]

Adding to his national security cabinet and advisors, Obama nominated Dennis C. Blair, a Four Star Admiral, to become his Director of National Intelligence, the so-called 'Intelligence Czar.' Blair, former Commander of the US Pacific Fleet, was a specialist on Asia and especially China.

In 1999 Blair, as Commander of US forces in the Pacific, explicitly violated a Clinton Administration order to instruct the Indonesian Army

General Wiranto to cease terror killings directed at civilians in East Timor. A large number of the Indonesian officers later indicted by Indonesia's national human rights commission for "crimes against humanity" committed in East Timor in 1999 were US-trained. Wiranto was also indicted. Blair spent much of his remaining time as Pacific commander fighting to restore the military ties to his allies in Jakarta, finally succeeding in 2002.[56]

Obama And Afghanistan: The 'Main Geopolitical Prize'

In one of his first acts as President in February 2009 Barack Obama ordered that an additional 17,500 more US troops be deployed into Afghanistan by the spring. It was part of what was being called the Afghan-Pakistan "surge," a reference to the controversial increase in US troops in Iraq. This puzzled most Americans, who were not even clear why US troops remained in Afghanistan at all after the 'War on Terror' had turned its attention away from Osama bin Laden to Iraq. President Obama justified his decision with the claim that:

This increase is necessary to stabilize a deteriorating situation in Afghanistan, which has not received the strategic attention, direction and resources it urgently requires....The Taliban is resurgent in Afghanistan, and al Qaeda supports the insurgency and threatens America from its safe haven along the Pakistani border.[57]

The President neglected to tell the American people the entire truth about his Afghan policy. The "resurgent Taliban" was in fact a mix of several distinct groups with quite different interests. One group were the so-called 'Black Taliban,' foreign mercenaries brought in and paid to incite terror incidents and killings. Who paid them remained a closely guarded secret, but rumors had it that the same financiers who earlier had financed Osama bin Laden to wage war against the Russians in Afghanistan in 1979 might be involved.[58]

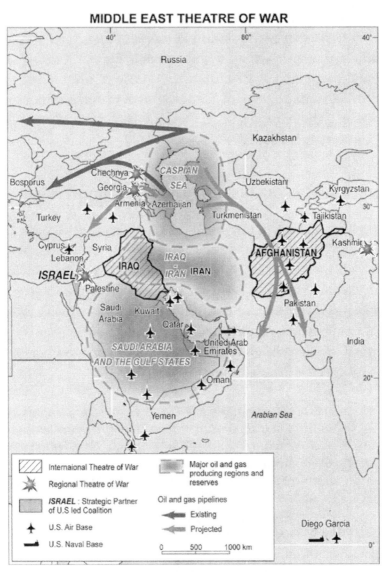

MIDDLE EAST THEATRE OF WAR

*The US Militarization of Central Asia since 2001
has made possible deep strikes into China and Russia*

A second group consisted of actual Afghans who, after thirty years of continual wars in their country, had taken up weapons against all foreign occupiers whether American or German or whomever. A third group was comprised simply of desperate Afghans who from time to time took up weapons in order to feed their starving families and relatives. In Pentagon propaganda, all of these groups were lumped together as 'Taliban' and all were tied somehow to the mysterious Al Qaeda.[59]

The US presence in Afghanistan was not really about routing the elusive Osama bin Laden out of some cave in Tora Bora. The Bush Administration had long since declared they were no longer interested in him. It was about geopolitics and the geopolitical encirclement of both China and Russia.

Zbigniew Brzezinski, a foreign policy adviser to candidate Obama during his campaign, had stated as far back as 1997 that for the United States, control of Central Eurasia—the region encompassing Afghanistan and Pakistan and their neighbors in the states of the former Soviet Union—was a prime goal of post-Cold War US military and foreign policy. He stated, "whoever either controls or dominates access to the region is the one most likely to win the geopolitical and economic prize." Naturally Brzezinski thought that prize should go to Washington.[60]

In contrast to the US occupation in Iraq, little US media attention had been given to Afghanistan, which some called the 'forgotten war.' Few knew that since the onset of US occupation at the end of 2001, the US military, with the help of Dick Cheney's Halliburton-KBR, had built no fewer than nineteen new military bases in Central East Asia and Middle Asia. These included fourteen air bases, large and small, in Afghanistan. The largest, Bagram and Shindand Air Bases, had been turned into multipurpose military bases with air and space surveillance systems to monitor air traffic throughout all of Eurasia, from China to Russia. As one defense analyst put it, Afghanistan had become one "huge land-based aircraft carrier."[61]

A Russian analyst, describing what the United States had established after 2001 in Afghanistan under the cover of the War on Terror, said the US and NATO had "established their own military, geostrategic, geopolitical and geo-economic bridgehead in the heart of Eurasia, deploying a powerful network of military bases in Afghanistan and the Central East and Middle Asia as a whole" Moreover, the Russian analyst charged:

*The war on terror is being used as a pretext and excuse for
building up the US and NATO military and organizational
machine in the region and maintaining its open-ended presence there.* [62]

It was little wonder that Russia was becoming increasingly alarmed
at the US decision to add more troops in Afghanistan. Since the US
toppled the Taliban in early 2002, and established a *de facto* occupation
force across its network of bases in the country, the opium trade—which
had been all but eradicated under the strict Taliban rule—now flourished
like never before.

US military officials, when questioned about the drug trade, usually
replied that it was not their 'mandate.' Notably, most of the opium found
its way into Russia where opium addiction had become a major social
problem after 2002. In Moscow, the US occupation of Afghanistan, and
the booming opium business under their noses, must have appeared like
a new version of the 1840's Opium Wars, or of the role of the CIA in
protecting the drug routes of Meo Tribesmen in Laos. [63]

Militarizing The Homeland

The overwhelming weight of the military industrial establishment
evident in Obama's intelligence and foreign policy Cabinet appointments, was matched by alarming signs that the United States itself was in
the process of domestic militarization. Bush had used the events of 9/11
to ram through a paralyzed Congress several pieces of legislation,
particularly the Patriot Act and the Homeland Security Act, which had all
but destroyed Constitutional checks and balances, as well as the Bill of
Rights.

The US Pentagon ordered 20,000 uniformed troops deployed inside
the United States by 2011. They would be trained to "help state and local
officials respond to a nuclear terrorist attack or other domestic catastrophe," according to Pentagon officials.[64]

This dramatic shift in the Defense Department's role in homeland
security was backed with troop commitments and funded by Congress. It

was a direct violation of the Posse Comitatus Act, a law dating from the post-Civil War era which explicitly limits the role of the Pentagon to defense of the United States from foreign attack, and forbids the use of combat troops for domestic law enforcement situations. The initial redeployment to the US in October 2008—at a time when the US military was already severely over-extended in Iraq and now Afghanistan—raised the spectre of police state control over expected domestic protests as the economic crisis worsened.

The Pentagon's plan called for three rapid-reaction forces to be ready for emergency response by September 2011. The first, a 4700-person unit, was based at Fort Stewart, Georgia, and was operational in October 2008. It was built around the Army's 3rd Infantry Division's 1st Brigade Combat Team that had just returned from 15 months in Iraq, hardly an ideal training ground for domestic US deployment.

Plans called for two additional US combat teams to join nearly 80 National Guard and reserve units comprising about 6,000 troops, to deploy with local and state officials nationwide. The troops would be trained to respond to a domestic chemical, biological, radiological, nuclear, or high-yield explosive attack, or a "CBRNE event," as the military called it. [65]

According to the Federal Government's official *Federal Register*, new rules would allow certain civilians to call American soldiers into action within the US in order to prevent "environmental damage" or respond to "special events" and "other domestic activities." [66] It was an alarmingly broad and intentionally vague mandate whose true justification was not made clear to the public.

It was the vague reference to "other domestic activities" that particularly alarmed many civil liberties organizations, and Americans in general. Such a wide open mandate could be used, they argued, to arrest protesting workers, such as the suddenly unemployed factory workers in Chicago who staged a peaceful occupation of their former factory. They were protesting the order by Bank of America to cut credit to their company while the bank enjoyed billions of dollars of US taxpayer bailout for its sub-prime real estate loans.

These new rules were contained in the Department of Defense's recently publicized plan for "Defense Support of Civil Authorities." According to the DSCA Plan, a specially designated Department of Defense official is given authority to recommend "the use of resources and DoD personnel needed to prevent or respond to a potential or actual domestic crisis."[67]

Use of the words 'potential or actual' leaves virtually unlimited discretion to the DoD to define the applicable "crisis." Moreover, while the DSCA Plan states that deployment of DoD "resources" and "personnel" would be "in response to requests for assistance from civil authorities," careful reading reveals that the designation of the "crisis" rests with the "judgment of a military commander or responsible DoD civilian official.[68]" In other words, one person.

Also troubling is the complete absence of the usual requirement for "notice" and "process" prior to government infringement on civil liberties, particularly considering the draconian powers authorized here. The key provision states that once a "crisis" has been declared, this one person may decide that it is "imminently serious."

> *Under these conditions, <u>timely prior authority</u> from higher headquarters to provide DSCA <u>may not be possible</u> before action is necessary for effective response.*[69]

In other words, apparently it is considered unnecessary even to check with the Secretary of Defense, or the President.

Under the US Constitution, soldiers inside the country essentially are given responsibility for quelling "insurrections" and repelling invasions as well as making sure each State has access to the republican form of government. The new rules went far beyond that, essentially establishing a plan to activate the US military inside the country to deal with social issues under provisions that appear to be devoid of any connection to the Constitution.

The decision to deploy US military forces domestically was more alarming in the context of proposals by candidate Obama—and later his White House Chief of Staff, Rahm Emanuel—calling for a National Civilian Security Force that would be "at least as powerful and well-funded as the US military."[70]

In November 2008 the US Army Strategic Studies Institute issued a document, *"Known Unknowns: Unconventional 'Strategic Shocks'* in Defense Strategy Development." The document, which received almost no notice, explicitly referred to possible domestic economic and social 'shocks' as being "both the least understood and the most dangerous." It warned, "it would be prudent to add catastrophic dislocation inside the United States or home-grown domestic civil disorder and or violence to this category." It then went on to state, "shock would result" if widespread civil disobedience were to occur inside the United States, "to such an extent that they forced the Department of Defense to radically re-role (sic) for domestic security, population control." [71]

By 2009, three months into the 'presidency of change' in the United States, it was becoming alarmingly clear to many that the only change was in presentation. The Full Spectrum Dominance of the world by America as the sole Superpower seemed clearly the only item on the Washington agenda. What remained unclear was the extent to which the most devastating economic crisis since the Great Depression would affect the ability of Washington policymakers to project that power.

For both Washington and for the rest of the world, the situation had reached a stage of strategic choice whose consequences could spell the end of the American Century from the rot of its own internal policy since the Vietnam War. An end to the obsessive military agenda of the warfare state would not be an easy process, but a necessary one for the survival not only of the world, but also of the United States as a functioning democracy.

Endnotes:

[1] Zbigniew Brzezinski, *The Grand Chessboard: America's Primacy and its Geostrategic Imperatives*, New York, Basic Books, 1997, p. 55.

[2] Travis Sharp, *US Defense Spending*, 2001-2009, Center for Arms Control and Non-Proliferation, Washington D.C., accessed in http://www.armscontrolcenter.org/policy/securityspending/articles/defense_spending_since_2001/.

[3] Ibid, *Global Military Spending*.

[4] Robert Wielaard, *Kosovo recognition irritates Russia and China*, The Associated Press, February 19, 2008.

[5] Wayne Madsen, *Clinton secretary of state had her own secretive trysts*, Online Journal, July 16, 2008, accessed in http://onlinejournal.com/artman/publish/printer_3497.shtml.

[6] Chris Hedges, "Leaders of Kosovo Rebels Tied to Deadly Power Play," *The New York Times*, June 25, 1999.

[7] Jerry Seper, "KLA finances fight with heroin sales Terror group is linked to crime network," *The Washington Times*, Washington, D.C., May 3, 1999.

[8] *The Scotsman*, Glasgow, 29 August 1999. Canadian researcher, Michel Chossudovsky, reported, 'Confirmed by British military sources, the task of arming and training of the KLA had been entrusted in 1998 to the US Defence Intelligence Agency (DIA) and Britain's Secret Intelligence Services MI6, together with "former and serving members of 22 SAS [Britain's 22nd Special Air Services Regiment], as well as three British and American private security companies." (Michel Chossudovsky, 'Osamagate,' October 9, 2001, accessed in http://www.globalresearch.ca/articles/CHO110A.html.

[9] Guenther Lachmann, *BND Kosovo affair: German spy affair might have been revenge*, Die Welt Online, November 30, 2008, accessed in http://www.welt.de/english-news/article2806537/German-spy-affair-might-have-been-revenge.html. In their February 22, 2005 report then marked 'Top Secret,' the German BND, its equivalent to the CIA, described the band around Thaci as follows: 'Über die Key-Player (wie z.B. Haliti, Thaci, Haradinaj) bestehen engste Verflechtungen zwischen Politik, Wirtschaft und international operierenden OK-Strukturen im Kosovo. Die dahinter stehenden kriminellen Netzwerke fördern dort die politische Instabilität. Sie haben kein Interesse am Aufbau einer funktionierenden staatlichen Ordnung, durch die ihre florierenden Geschäfte beeinträchtigt werden können.« (OK = Organisierte Kriminalität or Organized Crime): [*'In regard to the key players (for example Haliti, Thaci, Haradinaj) there exists the closest of links between political life, the economy and international organized crime structures in Kosovo. The criminal network behind them produces political instability. They have no interest whatsoever in building a functioning orderly state which might possibly threaten their booming business.'*]

[10] Jeremy Scahill, "*American Hypocrisy*," p. 7, accessed in http://coldtype.net.

[11] Owen Matthews, *Georgia's president is a man after the Republican nominee's heart. That's what worries some advisers*, September 20, 2008.

[12] Yalta European Strategy (YES), *5th Yalta Annual Meeting*, Yalta, Ukraine, 10 – 13 July 2008, accessed in http://www.yes-ukraine.org/en/programyes5.html. Helene Cooper and Thom Shanker, *After Mixed US Messages, a War Erupted in Georgia*, The New York Times, August 12, 2008.

[13] Peter Hirschberg, *Georgia: Israeli Arms Sales Raise New Concerns*, IPS, August 12, 2008, accessed in http://ipsnews.net/news.asp?idnews=43524.

[14] Ibid.

[15] Brian Harring, *Israel and the Teheran Attack*, August 21, 2008, accessed in http://www.tbrnews.org/Archives/a2868.htm#001.

[16] _____The Georgian Disaster, September 12, 2008, accessed in http://www.tbrnews.org/Archives/a2874.htm#001.

[17] Debka File, *Israel backs Georgia in Caspian Oil Pipeline Battle with Russia*, August 8, 2008, accessed in http://www.prisonplanet.com/israel-backs-georgia-in-caspian-oil-pipeline-battle-with-russia.html.

[18] Peter Hirschberg, Op. Cit.

[19] ZIK, *Ukraine continued supplies of arms to Georgia even after the conflict erupted – Valery Konovaliuk,* October 8, 2008, accessed in http://zik.com.ua/en/news/2008/10/08/152825.

[20] Ibid.

[21] Daniel Volman, *Africom: From Bush to Obama*, December 3, 2008, accessed in http://pambazuka.org/en/category/comment/52409.

[22] Anthony Smith, *The Great Rift: Africa's Changing Valley*, New York, Sterling Publishing, 1988.

[23] ___, *The Minerals of the Democratic Republic of Congo*, accessed in http://euromin.w3sites.net/Nouveau_site/gisements/congo/GISCONe.htm.

[24] William Reno, Warlord Politics and African States, Boulder, Lynne Rienner Publishers, 1998, p. 174.

[25] ____, *President Jiang Zemin Met with DRC President Joseph Kabila*, Ministry of Foreign Affairs of the Peoples' Republic of China, March 25, 2002, accessed in http://www.fmprc.gov.cn/eng/wjb/zzjg/fzs/gjlb/2959/2961/t16485.htm.

[26] The Democratic Republic of Congo is the former Zaire. It is often referred to as DRC or DR Congo. The name was changed to DRC in 1997 after the overthrow of the Mobutu dictatorship. It was formerly a colony of Belgium known as the Belgian Congo, and its capital is Kinshasa. The Republic of Congo, formerly a French colony, is a far smaller territory on the west coast of Africa adjacent also to Angola and Gabon whose capital is Brazzaville, hence also called Congo-Brazzaville to distinguish it from DRC.

[27] Simon Robertson, *The Deadliest War in the World*, Time, May 28, 2006.

[28] Congo News Agency, *War Crimes in the Congo by Laurent Nkunda and Paul Kagame*, Congo News Agency, October 30, 2008, accessed in www.congoplanet.com.

[29] Ibid.

[30] Díaz de Villegas, *My only option was to resign. It was my duty*, February 8, 2009, accessed in http://stopthewarinnorthkivu.wordpress.com/2009/02/08/diaz-villegas-resigns/.

[31] IRIN News Network, DRC: *Save eastern peace process from collapse*, UN OCHA, October 3, 2008, accessed in http://www.globalsecurity.org/military/library/news/2008/10/mil-081003-irin03.htm.

[32] The irony of a Belgian government attacking a Congolese government's human rights record was not lost on Kabila. Belgium's colonial history in the Congo is one of the most genocidal and brutal of the European colonial powers in the period before the Second World War. Belgian King Leopold actually carried out systematic torture and murder of Congolese on his rubber plantations until his death in 1909. See *Genocide Studies Program*, Yale University, Belgian Congo, accessed in http://www.yale.edu/gsp/colonial/belgian_congo/index.html.

[33] ____, *Belgian paper: Kabila says China is now key trade partner for Congo at expense of EU*, The International Herald Tribune, April 24, 2008, accessed in http://www.iht.com/articles/ap/2008/04/24/europe/EU-GEN-Belgium.

[34] George H. Wittmann, *Another Congo Crisis*, November 21, 2008, American Spectator, accessed in http://spectator.org/archives/2008/11/21/another-congo-crisis.

[35] Congo News Agency, Op. Cit.

[36] DanChurchAid, *Is there blood on your mobile phone?*, Copenhagen, September 22, 2006, accessed in http://www.danchurchaid.org/sider_paa_hjemmesiden/where_we_work/africa/congo_drc/read_more/is_there_blood_on_your_mobile_phone.

[37] Second Lt Aloys Ruyenzi, *Major General Paul Kagame Behind the Shooting Down of Late President Habyarimana's Plane: An Eye Witness Testimony*, Norway, July 5, 2004, cited in Keith Harmon Snow, Hollywood and the Holocaust in Central Africa, Global Research, October 16. 2005, http://www.globalresearch.ca/index.php?context=va&aid=1096.

[38] Robert E. Gribbin, *In the Aftermath of Genocide: The US Role in Rwanda*, iUniverse, 2005, p. 78. Also see, Memorandum from Deputy Assistant Secretary of Defense for Middle East/Africa, through Assistant Secretary of Defense for International Security Affairs, to Under Secretary of Defense for Policy, "Talking Points On Rwanda/Burundi", April 11, 1994. Confidential, Source: Freedom of Information Act release by the Office of the Secretary of Defense. Accessed in http://www.gwu.edu/~nsarchiv/NSAEBB/NSAEBB53/index.html.

[39] Wayne Madsen, *Jaded Tasks: Blood Politics of George Bush & Co.*, Oregon, Trine Day Publishing, 2006, pp. 25-27.

[40] Michel Chossudovsky, *The US was behind the Rwandan Genocide: Rwanda: Installing a US Protectorate in Central Africa*, Global Research, May 8, 2003, accessed in http://www.globalresearch.ca/articles/CHO305A.html.

[41] Georgianne Nienaber and Keith Harmon Snow, *Are USAID Gorilla Conservation Funds Being Used To support Covert Operations in Central Africa*, Global Research, September 20, 2007, accessed in http://www.globalresearch.ca/index.php?context=va&aid=6828.

[42] Keith Harmon Snow, *Merchants of Death: Exposing Corporate Financed Holocaust in Africa*, Global Research, December 7, 2008, accessed in http://www.globalresearch.ca/index.php?context=viewArticle&code=SNO20081206&articleId=11311.

[43] Ibid.

[44] Ibid.

[45] Ibid.

[46] Ibid.

[47] Daniel Volman, Op. Cit.

[48] Daniel Volman, *The Security Implications of Africa's New Status in Global Geopolitics*, African Security Research Project, Washington, DC, accessed in http://74.125.77.132/search?q=cache:kH8I2Gk5KC4J:ruafrica.rutgers.edu/events/media/0809_media/volman_nai.doc+Vice+Admiral+Robert+Moeller,+United+States+Africa+Command:+Partnership,+Security,+and+Stability,+Keynote+Address+at+the+Conference+on+Transforming+National+Security:+Africom.

[49] General William E. 'Kip' Ward, *Ward Speaks at International Peace Operations Association Annual Summit*, Washington, D.C., Oct 27, 2008, accessed in http://www.africom.

[50] Bruce Falconer and Daniel Schulman, *Blackwater's New Frontier: Their Own Private Africa*, Mother Jones, March 11, 2009.

[51] J. Peter Pham, *Africom Stands Up*, World Defense Review, October 2, 2008, accessed in http://worlddefensereview.com/pham100208.shtml.

[52] J. Peter Pham, *Testimony of Dr. J. Peter Pham - US House of Representatives Africom Hearing*, Washington, DC, August 3, 2007, accessed in http://www.gbmnews.com/articles/1097/1/Testimony-of-Dr-J-Peter-Pham—-US-House-Africom-Hearing/Page1.html.

[53] Tim Whewell, China to seal $9bn DR Congo deal, BBC News, April 14, 2008, accessed in http://news.bbc.co.uk/2/hi/programmes/newsnight/7343060.stm. For details of Nkunda"s demands on this, see *Agence France Press, DR Congo's Nkunda attacks China to boost political kudos*, November 19, 2008, accessed in http://www.google.com/hostednews/afp/article/ALeqM5g46hr8I4livXoIREvisopoJiyNkA .

[54] Robert Gates, *Gates on Missile Defense*, accessed in http://www.dodvclips.mil/?fr_story=FRdamp343479&rf=sitemap.

[55] ___, *Boeing Director Gen. James Jones Resigns Board Seat*, Boeing Corp., accessed in http://www.boeing.com/news/releases/2008/q4/081215b_nr.html. *Enrique Hernandez Jr. Elected to Chevron Board of Directors; Gen. James L. Jones Resigns Following National Security Adviser Appointment, Chevron*, December 2008, accessed in http://www.chevron.com/news/press/release/?id=2008-12-10. Retrieved on December 10, 2008.

[56] Bradley Simpson, *The Skeletons in Dennis Blair's Closet*, Counterpunch, December 26-28, 2008, accessed in http://www.counterpunch.org/simpson12262008.html.

[57] Barbara Starr, *Obama approves Afghanistan troop increase*, CNN News, February 18, 2009, accessed in http://edition.cnn.com/2009/POLITICS/02/17/obama.troops/.

[58] Yuri Kroupnov, *The Path to Peace and Concord in Afghanistan: The Problem of Afghanistan for Russia and the World, Russian Institute for Demography, Migration and Regional Development*, Moscow, March 10, 2008, accessed in afg-han.idmrr.ru/afghan.idmrr.ru_eng.pdf.

[59] Ibid.

[60] Zbigniew Brzezinski, Op. Cit., p. 140.

[61] Yuri Kroupnov, Op. Cit., pp. 15-16.

[62] Ibid.

[63] Ibid., p.6. For a detailed description of the CIA role in Vietnam and Laos drug operations, see Alfred W. McCoy, The *Politics of Heroin in Southeast Asia*, New York, Harper Colophon, 1972.

[64] Spencer S. Hsu and Ann Scott Tyson, *Pentagon to Detail Troops to Bolster Domestic Security*, Washington Post, December 1, 2008, p. Ao1.

[65] Ibid.

[66] Office of the Secretary, Department of *Defense, Defense Support of Civil Authorities (DSCA)*, Federal Register: December 4, 2008 (Volume 73, Number 234).

[67] Ibid

[68] Ibid.

[69] Ibid.

[70] Nathan P. Freier, *Known Unknowns: Unconventional "Strategic Shocks" in Defense Strategy Development*, Strategic Studies Institute United States Army War College, November 4, 2008.

[71] Ibid.

Index

Breinigsville, PA USA
03 December 2010
250636BV00002B/21/P